Ambition, a History

Ambition,
a History
from Vice
to Virtue

WILLIAM CASEY KING

Yale UNIVERSITY PRESS

New Haven and London

Published with assistance from the Kingsley Trust Association Publication Fund established by the Scroll and Key Society of Yale College.

Yale University Press books may be purchased in quantity for educational, business, or promotional use. For information, please e-mail sales.press@yale.edu (US office) or sales@yaleup.co.uk (UK office).

Designed by Sonia Shannon.
Set in Electra type by Integrated Publishing Solutions, Grand Rapids, Michigan.
Printed in the United States of America.

Library of Congress Cataloging-in-Publication Data

King, Casey (William Casey)
    Ambition, a history : from vice to virtue / William Casey King.
        pages   cm
    Includes bibliographical references and index.
    ISBN 978-0-300-18280-4 (clothbound : alkaline paper)
    1. United States—Civilization—To 1783.   2. Ambition—Political aspects—United States—History.   3. Ambition—Social aspects—United States—History.   4. National characteristics, American—History.   5. Christianity and culture—United States—History.   6. Social values—United States—History.   7. Social change—United States—History.   8. England—Civilization.   9. Ambition—Social aspects—England—History.   10. Christianity and culture—England—History.   I. Title.
    E162.K59 2013
    973—dc23   2012034912

A catalogue record for this book is available from the British Library.

This paper meets the requirements of ANSI/NISO Z39.48–1992 (Permanence of Paper).

10 9 8 7 6 5 4 3 2 1

To David Brion Davis

This book is the product of the last dissertation David Brion Davis will have directed, and it is dedicated to him. It is as much homage as argument. When I arrived at Yale it was already known that David was no longer taking on doctoral students. One day, over lunch, David invited me to be his final, taking me into retirement with him by special arrangement. He often placed demands on me that exceeded those I wished to comfortably place on myself. He made me want to listen, rather than speak, to recognize graduate school as an opportunity not merely to earn a PhD but, more profoundly, to mature intellectually and personally toward the elusive goal of saying something worth saying. I could not have done this without him: his work, his kindness, his patient belief, always more sure than I that I could somehow think my way out of ambition's labyrinth, his support even as I considered giving up. He never gave up on me. It is a gift that I cannot possibly ever repay.

On the day I delivered my dissertation, we sat in his living room. My two children, my wife, and his wife talked and shared coffee cake while David and I talked about the work. As we were leaving, he pointed to a long shelf of books. "These are the books from the dissertations I have directed. Yours will go here." The enormity of his career, the profundity of his influence, cannot be measured. It extends far beyond the sixty or so dissertations he has directed. But seeing that shelf of books, I thought of the line from *Henry V,* "We few, we happy few, we band of brothers." I realized how lucky I have been to have had the gift of his company and the inestimable generosity of his mentorship, in the company of so many others, touched by his life and inspired by his example.

Contents

Introduction

The plunge of ambition, like that of life
itself, as the animal soul takes it, is always
a plunge in the dark, into the infinite, into
the all-engulfing yet fertile bosom of chaos.
—George Santayana, "Philosophic
  Sanction of Ambition"

God detesteth ambition.
—Proverbs 39:6, Geneva Bible, marginal
  note

WHere does one begin a book on ambition in America? I started where one might expect—with Benjamin Franklin, the "First American," America's "first well-publicized success and premier go-getter."[1] And why not? With his exemplary life and pithy maxims, he seems to embody the essence of ambition in early America. Consider "Early to bed, early to rise / Makes a man healthy, wealthy and wise." It was the bon mot of the new nation, the phrase and Franklin disparaged by the ironic (by Mark Twain and D. H. Lawrence, most notably) and embraced as a "how to" in the early Republic, where self-making seemed self-evident.[2]

I was shocked, while on a Beinecke Fellowship at Yale University, when I stumbled across Franklin's famous slogan of Americanness in a commonplace book from the 1670s, some thirty years before his birth.[3] This is not to disparage Franklin. Despite the books of quotations and authors who for centuries have attributed the saying to Franklin, he never claimed that his aphorisms were original. It is we who imbue him and America with all that was new, exceptional, distinct. This was my first hint that Franklin might not be the place to begin my study of ambition in early America.

But a greater revelation came while researching Franklin's own references to ambition. Though modern readers may see Franklin as "ambitious," it is unlikely that Franklin would have seen himself in those terms. Certainly in 1750 he did not. In his "Last Will and Testament," a document devoid of characteristic Franklinian irony, he thanks God for giving him "such a Mind, with moderate Passions," freed early from "Ambition."[4]

I came to realize that ambition is more complicated, and perhaps less American, than is generally supposed. Today, ambition is widely considered to be a strong component of the American national character and intrinsic to the American mythos. It is defined as "an ardent desire for rank, fame or power; desire to achieve a particular end; . . . desire for activity or exertion."[5] But dictionary definitions fall short of capturing its import. From rags to riches, enslaved to liberator, log house to White House, ghetto to CEO, ambition drives the American dream.[6]

I have always wondered at the ambition that has driven me, and writing about it has helped me better come to terms with it. At twenty-three, a bond trader at Salomon Brothers in the 1980s, early to rise and liquored to bed, I was a servant of ambition's push and prod. I arrived at work before 5:00 a.m. and often returned to my apartment no earlier than 10:00 p.m. I was in a world where the "f" word was a noun, adjective, adverb, and, most often, personal pronoun for me, the new guy. I was drawn neither by greed—money is not my passion—nor by an inherent interest in buying and selling used debt instruments. I wanted it because it was what everyone else seemed to want and could not have. I wanted to prove myself better against those who were imagined to be the very best and was willing to torture myself for just that. When Oliver Stone rendered that time in his movie *Wall Street*, he portrayed his villain, Gordon Gekko, as a man driven by greed. But it was not greed that drove me, nor the others with whom I worked. Tom Wolfe, who spent some time at the government bond desk at Salomon Brothers while researching *Bonfire of the Vanities*, got closer to capturing the ambition that drove me, drove us, when he coined the term that described our motivation—we aspired to be no less than "masters of the universe." Or what's a heaven for?

Perhaps ambition is just compensatory longing, and I needed, still need, to fill some void with accolades and aspiration. Or, if we are delving into the psychological, perhaps it's as psychologist Heinz Kohut would have it: my ambition is a sign of my good mental health; the converse, a lack of ambition, might be a sign of arrested development.[7] Or are the external cultural cues too ubiquitous to tease from any individual? After all, American culture is a purgatory of longing. Ambition's measures are immeasurable. Our ardent desire for rank or power is continually quantified by titles, prizes, promotions, evaluations, hours billed, grades on papers, firsts, longests, mosts, bylines, batting averages, bank accounts, books published.

America has historically been and continues to be a nation driven principally by ambition. We promulgate ambition internationally through our cultural exports, celebrate it in self-help business books, market it in "motivational" seminars, chant its promise in pithy maxims like prayers. It is the "giant within," that which "makes us *go*," "the fuel of all achievement," greed's more comely cousin, the hope to each endeavor, the carrot and the stick; and if we fall short, it is attributable only to our lack of will or determination.[8] We are told that our reach should exceed our grasp. But, like Icarus, only after we have fallen from the sky are we retrospectively seen as having flown too close to the sun.

This was not always so. In the eighteenth century, as our independence was contemplated and finally declared, during Franklin's life, ambition was replete with associations of sin and vice rooted deeply in Western and Anglo-American culture. In Robert Burton's *Anatomy of Melancholy*, a proto-psychological text written in the seventeenth century but popular in the eighteenth (Franklin owned a copy), ambition is described as "a canker of the soul, an hidden plague . . . a secret poison, the father of livor [envy], and mother of hypocrisy, the moth of holiness, and cause of madness, crucifying and disquieting all that it takes hold of."[9] *An Homilie against Disobedience and Wylfull Rebellion*, required reading from English pulpits as well as Anglican churches in the colonies, identifies Satan as the chief embodiment and champion of ambition. It also identifies ambition as one of the major causes of human rebellion. In the Genevan translation of the Bible, the translation that accompanied John Winthrop to Massachusetts and the first company of settlers to Jamestown, there are some seventy-seven admonitions against ambition. It is associated with "crueltie of the wicked," "malice," and "all kind of vice." In the Geneva Bible, Adam was not fallen by pride but "fallen by ambition."

The central preoccupation of this book is answering this question: How is it that a quality that was so vicious at the moment of North American English colonization became a celebrated virtue, a facet of American national character?

Surprisingly, there are no book-length studies that detail ambition's transformation, and few books at all on the subject. Glen Pettigrove summarizes this peculiar lacuna in scholarship as follows: "Ambition is a curiously neglected topic. . . . Plato, Aristotle, Seneca, Aquinas, Machiavelli, Harrington, Locke, Rousseau, Smith, Santayana and a number of others have discussed ambition. But it has seldom received more than a few paragraphs worth of analysis, in spite of the fact that ambition plays a central role in Western politics . . . and in spite of the fact that Machiavelli, Harrington, Locke and Rousseau each considered it to be among the greatest threats to political security."[10] The few books that engage ambition either read what we imagine ambition to be today back into the historical record or discuss ambition in the nineteenth century with a cursory consideration of historical antecedents.[11] But this begs the question. If ambition is so central, why have scholars overlooked it?

Edmund Burke once wrote that "men are qualified for civil liberty in exact proportion to their disposition to put moral chains upon their own appetites."[12] American historians have spent considerable energy untangling the chains of political thought throughout the origins and evolution of the Republic. Notions like virtue, honor, and fame have been teased from the sources, proffered as the essential correctives to the appetites inherent in human nature and as fundamental to the American national character.[13] The maladies, however, the evils against which they were directed, receive considerably less attention. In the service of our national myths, we may be guilty of overlooking the appetites that may or may not have been sated.

Or maybe it is simply that what was once a sin to have is now a sin to lack. We take ambition for granted, like a dear, daily, companion or long-endured friend, we stop seeing it, and therefore it hides in plain sight in the historical record. Lewis Namier wrote that between the present day and the eighteenth century, "there is more resemblance in outer forms and denominations than in underlying realities; so that misconception is very easy."[14] The word *ambition* bears that outer resemblance. We think we know what it is, and so we ignore what it once was. So perhaps it is not nationalism or solipsism or shifting cultural significance. It might simply be an issue of language, of an inherited vocabulary that, in the words of philosopher Alasdair Macintyre, "misleads us by linguistic resemblance long after conceptual identity and similarity have failed."[15]

Is the project, then, inevitably doomed? I think not. I have proceeded cautiously, keeping in mind the words of Namier, who further wrote that one must "steep oneself in the political language of a period," before one can safely speak or be sure of understanding the language of a different time.[16] And part of this steeping demands an understanding of meanings often contested, rarely static, inevitably deeply rooted in cultural antecedents.[17]

But these contested meanings are inevitable in the history of ideas, rarely a story with punctual beginnings, neat transitions, or prompt arrivals and departures. A new idea rarely breaks out like a war or assumes a throne or emancipates a people. New meanings emerge as old meanings persist. Academic journals are filled with evidence that challenge the determinate dominant feature of epoch, signs of the Protestant ethic in the Middle Ages, evidence of modernity before the Machiavellian moment, revolutions before the Revolution.

Tracking a change in ambition has required a flexible approach, reflecting the fluidity of culture, and demanding that the term be continuously defined and redefined. Reconciling this need was more easily accomplished with the help of Raymond Williams. To describe changes in ideas through time, Williams suggests the use of the terms *dominant, residual,* and *emergent.*[18] This framework allows a certain flexibility that better reflects cultural shifts and guards against the assumption of absolutes that quickly crumble in the face of historical exceptions. Williams's framework allows for variation, complexity, and seemingly contradictory impulses at the same historical moment. Ideas often manifest themselves in a less linear, more baroque form, replete with point and counterpoint, overlap, progression and regression. The story of ambition's transformation from vice to virtuous vice is one such story.

But ultimately the exploration of ambition's miraculous redemption led me to transformations that occurred well before Benjamin Franklin and the cult of his autobiography. As Christian, national, and individual interests harmonized in New World settlement, ambition became not only a necessary evil but also a Christian good. Ambition suddenly saved souls of pagan Indians and Africans, planted flags, and won riches for kings. As men rose, so, too, did God and country.

But it is crucial to recognize three things: first, ambition was purged of some of its ties to sin at a significant cost—the degradation of Native Americans and Africans. In this case, as in other cases throughout human history, superiority required inferiority to substantiate it—the *Übermensch* cannot proclaim itself *über* without the presence of an *Untermensch*. Ambition, while "American," has often been realized at the expense of a degraded other.

The second is that ambition never fully lost its ties to vice. It emerged from the early modern period Janus-like, a two-faced passion, a virtuous vice, a vitiating merit. Well into the eighteenth century, the negative and sinful connotations of ambition persisted. The dual nature of ambition is evident even in the twenty-first century, unquestioned in times of prosperity, castigated in times of uncertainty. Even in times that do not try men's souls, ambition retains some of its negative aspect. It is a relative rather than an absolute trait, and whether it is deemed positive or negative depends on the ends, the means, and the individual who is expressing ambition.

The third is to emphasize the crucial importance of adopting a broader Western cultural perspective on early American history.[19] In so doing, new perspectives on American history are revealed, vistas once obscured by the restrictive confines of geography and period. In the final chapter, I illustrate how understanding ambition within a broader cultural and historical context even affords new insights on "American Scripture," our Declaration of Independence.

But even in the baroque there is a first note. Chapter 1 of this book begins with ancient Greece and Rome. The Founders' views on human nature, vice and virtue, ambition and self-abnegation were rooted in a classical tradition. The founding generation was preoccupied with Plato, Aristotle, Livy, Seneca and Cicero, Cato and Cataline, and they invoked these sources as models of Republican virtue or anti-models of ambitious self-promotion. The chapter traces ambition from antiquity through the Middle Ages and Renaissance with a specific eye toward the sources that would have preoccupied the Founders themselves. A fundamental question answered in this exploration is: If ambition was so sinful, why was it not identified as among the "deadly sins"? A close reading of the patristic texts reveals that, in fact, it was. Both Gregory and Augustine defined *avaritia*, "avarice," with terms that would include what we know today as both avarice and ambition. The chapter traces ambition as vice through the medieval allegories, Dante, and Machiavelli before moving finally to England, where ambition and sin are fundamentally linked. At the historical moment when England begins its colonization efforts, the marginal notes included within the dominant biblical translation proclaim, "God detesteth ambition."[20] The chapter illuminates the deep Western cultural associations of ambition, rebellion, and sin.

In chapter 2 I consider how ambition as sin, as conveyed in theology, became absorbed within broader English culture. Sources drawn from both "high" and "low" culture demonstrate ambition was widely held to be a pernicious and dangerous vice. These sources include histories, poetry, Elizabethan and Jacobean tragedy, character books modeled on Theophrastus that were popular in the early seventeenth century and even a popular ballad, sung in pubs, of a seventeenth-century self-made man. This chapter underscores ambition's cultural centrality but in so doing strives for a social history of ideas.

By the seventeenth century, as chronicled in chapter 3, there was a growing acceptance of the inevitability of ambition and the utter futility of appeals to the virtuous in man to quell its hunger. In response to the inadequacy of repression and cognizant still of ambition's destructive potential, new strategies for mitigating the dangers of ambition emerged. One of the most significant of these strategies is what we might colloquially term "fighting fire with fire," what would later be known as countervailing, or pitting one powerful passion against another.[21] The strategy of countervailing passions later finds its essential place in American history at the roots of the American system of government. It is succinctly and significantly articulated in Federalist No. 51 when James Madison writes, "Ambition must be made to counteract ambition."[22] In this chapter I unearth the specific origins of countervailing passions in the plague tracts and scientific writings of the seventeenth century and recognize a watershed in the trajectory of ambition. Whereas sin can only be repressed, ambition, once reimagined as illness, can be treated.

Chapter 4 captures another watershed in ambition's trajectory from Christian sin to problematic virtue. The chapter illustrates how ambition was harnessed and transformed. Roughly a hundred years before Bernard Mandeville wrote of transforming private vices into public benefits, and more than two hundred years before G. W. F. Hegel's doctrine of the cunning of reason, ambition implicitly spurred New World settlement and was explicitly harnessed by the state. This chapter adopts an Atlantic world perspective on colonization. Many historians mistakenly assume that Spain was exclusively an anti-model for English colonization, yet in fact Spain served as a spur to English ambition and was a model for successful colonization. England, citing Spain's example, created a new noble title for the purposes of harnessing ambition.

But regardless of titles conferred by the crown, America was often imagined as a place where ambition could be safely realized, as fundamentally ennobling, as a place where individuals could become nobility, no matter their birth. This was due not only to perceived availability of wealth, land and opportunity but to the presence of an indigenous population that was imagined to reinforce an innate superiority. This chapter turns from titular nobility to the more unofficial sort, focusing on the ways in which a Native American population complicated and reinforced European ambition. The Spanish and English were "superior" by virtue of their comparative excellence, as judged by their own cultural criteria.

In the Epilogue I consider ambition and rebellion at the time of the American Revolution. An understanding of ambition's legacy of sin can reveal new insights on documents that historians have studied and pondered for centuries. What we have come to know as our Declaration of Independence went through substantive rewrites. Why the first paragraph of the Declaration was altered from Jefferson's original remains a mystery. Some scholars argue that the final version "sounds" better, but I argue that it was rewritten to mitigate charges of the colonists' proclaiming ambition rather than independence.

Wresting ambition from the panoply of vice and reconstituting it as a virtue was a necessary ideological precondition to the American Republic. Although the Revolution is often portrayed as a secular war over the meaning of good government, in understanding ambition's legacy of sin and vice, we can view the Revolution as a battle over what constituted sin itself.

"Early to bed, early to rise," may have later become the credo of the new nation. The expression "self-made man" was coined in the early nineteenth century.[23] In early national America Benjamin Franklin became recognized through his aphorisms and autobiography as American ambition's prophet. But to begin with Franklin is to miss most of the story. Ambition, long associated with vice and sin through antiquity and the Middle Ages, escaped its Pandoran restriction the moment that Amerigo Vespucci and all of Europe realized that Christopher Columbus discovered not a new route to a place previously known but, in fact, a *Mundus Novus*, a New World. And in understanding the origins and evolution of ambition from pernicious vice to American necessity, we gain a more complex understanding of our founding and of ourselves.

1

From Vice to
Christian Sin

The story is told of an exchange between
the legendary economic historian Jack
Fisher and an importunate pupil who was
pressing him for a reading list on sixteenth-
and seventeenth-century English
economic history. [Fisher] said, "If you
really want to understand the period, go
away and read the Bible."
—Christopher Hill, *The English Bible and
the Seventeenth-Century Revolution*

[God] reprocheth Adam's miserie,
whereinto he was fallen by ambition.
—Genesis 3:22, Geneva Bible, marginal
note

The word *ambition* reaches English directly through Latin or sometimes by Latin through Old French. *Ambition* is derived from the Latin compound verb *ambire*, "go round." Does this mean that the concept that we attach to the word *ambition* did not exist before the Latin word emerged as its etymological root? Of course not. Scholars have recognized ambition as present throughout history. In the *Epic of Gilgamesh*, perhaps the oldest written story, from the ancient tablets of Sumeria, we learn of the king of Uruk, Gilgamesh. Gilgamesh is driven by the "spur on the . . . ambition to leave an enduring name" and enters the Cedar Forest guarded by Humbaba the terrible.[1] For eminent archaeologist and historian Nancy Sandars, Gilgamesh embodies our modern conception of ambition. But reading modern notions of ambition into ancient endeavors is a risky business and should be resisted to avoid the pitfalls of reifying the concept.

The ground in ancient Greece might seem steadier, as many sources on ambition in this period were those read and studied in Anglo-America.[2] Thucydides, popular among the Founders and listed in the libraries of Thomas Jefferson and John Adams, among others, wrote of the Athenians with a word translated into English as "ambition": "From motives of private ambition and private interest they adopted a policy which had disastrous effects in respect both of themselves and of their allies; their measures, had they been successful, would only have brought honor and profit to individuals, and, when unsuccessful, crippled the city in the conduct of war."[3]

Robert Faulkner, in his work on noble ambition, considers Alcibiades as a Greek example of "unbounded ambition."[4] John Dryden, too, in his English translation of Plutarch's Alcibiades, writes: "His conduct displayed many great inconsistencies and variations, not unnaturally, in accordance with the many and wonderful vicissitudes of his fortunes; but among the many strong passions of his real character, the one most prevailing of all was his ambition and his desire of superiority."[5]

The problem is that there is no one Greek word for *ambition*. Rather, three Greek words have been translated into our English word *ambition*. Just as historians must accept the change in the meanings of words through time, so they must not fall prey to assuming a stasis in translations of ancient concepts into contemporary parlance.

The three Greek words that have been translated into the English word *ambition* are: *philotimia* (alternatively *philotimeomai*), literally "the love of honor"; *eritheia*, "rivalry" or "strife"; and *philodoxia*, "love of acclaim."

Philotimia, love of honor, was a central theme in Greek life and culture. It was widely considered to be among the driving forces of Greek achievement, and therefore conveys much of the contemporary sense of ambition.[6] But *philotimia* was not as invariably positive, as many scholars assume. The word was originally imagined to be a negative personal attribute, "ambition for a person's own profit and private prestige."[7] But by the mid-fourth century, it began to be understood as "private contribution for the benefit of the polis, for which the contributor was rewarded with public gratitude, *charis*."[8] One wonders if part of *ambition*'s later duality might have been informed by a similar change through time in ancient Greece. Or, perhaps, as Greek culture became more fluid, a demos (the "people") spurred by *philotimia* likewise became more accepted.

The second word often translated into *ambition* is *philodoxia*, love of acclaim. In Plutarch, Alcibiades is characterized by both *philotimia* and *philodoxia*.[9] But *philodoxia*, like *philotimia*, can have a negative aspect. In addition to stating that love of acclaim can drive an individual to recognition aligned with the public good, Plutarch also calls *philodoxia* a "malady of the soul."[10]

The third word, *eritheia*, "rivalry or strife," is also translated into English as *ambition* or *selfish ambition*. The New International Version of the Bible, for example, defines *eritheia* as "selfish ambition." Strong's concordance defines *eritheia* as "rivalry, hence ambition," and the "seeking of followers and adherents by means of gifts, the seeking of followers, hence ambition, rivalry, self-seeking; a feud, faction."[11]

In Aristotle, *eritheia* denotes "a self-seeking pursuit of political office by unfair means."[12] The origin of the word is debated. Some scholars argue that it derives from *eris*, "strife," the name of the Greek goddess of discord, who possesses a golden apple that she throws to engender enmity among friends and war among enemies, notably the Trojan War.[13] Others argue that the word finds its roots not in *eris* but in *erithos*, "common laborer." They explain that the Greeks used the word to mean working in one's self-interest for a wage.[14] Yet perhaps a third possibility, not ventured in the literature, is the source.

We know that there had been a momentous change in ancient Greece during the eighth, seventh, and sixth centuries. During this period a "popular movement" of *demiourgoi* ("craftsmen") and *thetes* (literally, "doers") arose to form a new order and garner political power. These "democrats" demanded political recognition and reform, challenging the aristocrats. As people of humble origins vied for political power, upheaval, rivalry, and strife ensued.[15] I would argue that *eritheia* has its origins not in *eris* (rivalry, strife) or *erithos* (common laborer) but in *both*. The confusion over its origins is resolved if we look at this period of extraordinarily violent and tumultuous internal struggle, an era of the assertion of prerogative by the craftsmen and doers.[16] The rise of the common laborer was seen as the origin of rivalry and strife.

The Latin origins of the English word are decidedly less mysterious. *Ambitio* was originally used to describe Roman candidates for office who would canvass or solicit votes. There were no dictionaries of Latin usage per se during the Roman Empire. Modern Latin dictionaries look back and attempt to reconstitute meaning based on usage. For our purposes, this is extremely helpful in mitigating the risk of confusing linguistic similarity with conceptual similarity. It is not just the word. It is a concept reflected by the word.

Ambitio is used by the Romans almost exclusively for those with a public life.[17] While the first use of *ambition* was rather neutral, *canvassing* soon became "insistence in seeking favors, importunity," which soon became "corrupt practices in seeking honors, verdicts, graft and intrigue." It is worth listing all the Latin uses because the multiple meanings provide insight into the complexity of the notion both in antiquity and in later periods. In addition, because early Anglo-American culture was preoccupied with the Romans, Latin usage is informative. At any rate *ambitio* is defined as in *The Oxford Latin Dictionary* as: "1. Canvassing votes; 2. A standing for public office, candidature; 3. Rivalry for honors, competition; 4. Striving after popularity, currying favor; 5. Desire for advancement; 6. Interested motives, self-interest; 7. Partiality, favoritism; 8. Vain display, ostentation, show."

The Roman historian Titus Livius, known to us as Livy, uses *ambitio* in a neutral sense to mean "electioneering," although the negative connotations dominate his history of Rome.[18] *Ambitio* is found throughout Livy's work in his description of political evils. Livy considered *ambitio* an inescapable danger to *concordia* and *libertas*, a threat that when joined by the pernicious *avaritia luxuriaque* (avarice beyond bounds, luxurious avarice or greed), would destroy the Republic.[19] Livy also identifies laws in Roman history (*leges de ambitu*) enacted to mitigate the destructive potential of *ambitio*, the first of which was the Lex Poetelia, enacted in 358 BCE.[20] The law was specifically a restriction on the places where a candidate could canvass for votes, but it is generally agreed to have been passed to prevent the new men, the plebeians, from gaining political power.[21]

Not only Livy recognized the dangerous potential of *ambitio*. Of particular interest to late sixteenth- and early seventeenth-century Anglo-American culture are the works of the Stoics, much-studied ancient antecedents of early modern thought. Sallust (Gaius Sallustius Crispus), a Roman historian (86–35/34 BCE), takes up ambition in his *War with Catiline*, written around 40 BCE. In it, he portrays the struggle between civic virtue as embodied by Caesar and Cato and ambition and corruption as represented by the Roman patrician Catiline. Sallust warns that "ambition drove many men to become false; to have one thought locked in the breast, another ready on the tongue."[22] He explicitly condemns ambition as a vice (*vitium*), though not quite as evil as the sin of avarice (*avaritia*).[23]

For Cicero, ambition is a "malady," but it is a malady that seems to draw "the greatest souls" and "most brilliant geniuses."[24] It is, therefore, both a blessing and a curse, a deluding self-absorption that can cause its victims to "lose sight of their claims to justice." In his *De officiis* (On duties on obligations), Cicero writes an essay in the form of a letter to his son in which he elaborates on this virtuous vice:

> The great majority of people, however, when they fall a prey to ambition for either military or civil authority, are carried away by it so completely that they quite lose sight of the claims of justice. . . . We saw this proved but now in the effrontery of Gaius Caesar, who, to gain that sovereign power which by a depraved imagination he had conceived in his fancy, trod underfoot all laws of gods and men. But the trouble about this matter is that it is in the greatest souls and in the most brilliant geniuses that we usually find ambitions for civil and military authority, for power, and for glory, springing; and therefore we must be the more heedful not to go wrong in that direction.[25]

Seneca, like Cicero, considers ambition one of the evils of the mind, a "mala mentis humanae."[26] He also alludes to the deceptive, seductive nature of ambition. While it appears to be a source of greatness, it is in fact a trap leading to misery.[27]

Quintilian, however, suggests an interesting departure from the dominant view and recognizes ambition's positive potential. He wrote, "Though ambition may be a fault in itself, it is often the mother of virtues."[28] But in Quintilian's time, though he and Sallust both recognized ambition's duality, the dominant notion of ambition was still firmly *vitium*, "vice." One can trace this emergent strain, ambition's dual nature, in Quintilian, later realized in Machiavelli, the seventeenth-century Puritan divine Bishop Manton, and as I illustrate in later chapters, in colonization and Republican revolution.

The next question is how this secular vice becomes Christian sin. The patristic texts provide answers and clues for our later understanding of ambition in Anglo-American thought. It has been noted that a feature of later English Protestantism is the weight of patristic writing, especially that of the first five centuries. This tendency has been noted both before and after the English Revolution of 1640.[29]

Augustine uses the word *ambition* in *Confessions* when he speaks of *ambitio saeculi*, "worldly ambition," as the chief enemy of the good life. But it would be exceedingly narrow to exclude certain phrases that he uses synonymously with "worldly ambition." In *On True Religion*, he expresses the similar idea of *dominationis temporalis faustus*, "haughtiness of temporal domination"; in *The City of God*, he writes of *libido dominandi*, "lust for power"; and in *Confessions*, he uses *libido principandi*, "the lust for being first."[30] Significantly, however, in *ambition*, we witness Augustine as the Western cultural "Christianizer" of antiquity. In Augustine we see one path that *ambitio* makes from Roman vice to Christian sin.

In the *Contra Julianum*, written late in his life, Augustine directly links ambition and sin. Augustine imagines sin as "three-headed," using the word *capita*, "head," which leads one to speculate whether Augustine is evoking some monstrous beast of the sort found in medieval illuminations. One wonders, too, at his choice of three heads of sin. Augustine was a key figure in the Trinitarian debates, and it is tempting to speculate that "three" answers the need for balance between distinct elements of the Trinity with their evil counterpart, but this is pure speculation.[31] What is important is that the three sources are the lust for carnal experience, the lust for being first, and the lust for looking. This last one I have translated literally, but Michael Foley translates it "pernicious knowledge." He makes the intriguing case that Augustine does not condemn these traits per se, only the ends to which they aspire, writing that Augustine tries to emphasize the "importance of directing these desires towards their true fulfillment."[32]

If by this Foley is arguing that the notion of somehow "harnessing" or "channeling" sin toward God or goodness was present in Augustinian thought, I do not agree. For Augustine, the repression of sin and the habituation of cardinal virtue is one way toward a natural telos, or proper ordering of the soul. For example, when Augustine interprets the Sermon on the Mount:

For there are three things which go to complete sin: the suggestion of, the taking pleasure in, and the consenting to. Suggestion takes place either by means of memory, or by means
of the bodily senses, when we see, or hear, or smell, or taste,
or touch anything. And if it give us pleasure to enjoy this, this
pleasure, if illicit, must be restrained. Just as when we are fast-
ing, and on seeing food the appetite of the palate is stirred up,
this does not happen without pleasure; but we do not consent
to this liking, and *we repress it by the right of reason,* which has
the supremacy.[33]

Despite Foley's interesting argument, the paradigm does not shift
here. It is repression of sin, not channeling; restraint, and the habituation of virtue, not redirection. Redirection is in fact a feature of later
philosophers of the passions.[34] To Augustine, repression followed by
grace is the only hope for the fallen. And grace does not require individuals to redirect their passions toward Godly ends. The direction is
already determined by the inscription of God made on the heart.[35]

Augustine is arguing that sin is seeking satisfaction in man-made
diversions or inventions rather than in God. Consider Ecclesiastes 7,
"for they sought many inventions." Fallen man, led by the Devil, in-
vents many ways to happiness that are fundamentally false and against
God; these inventions are man's many sins. Only in God, the passage
suggests, can true happiness be realized. This is what Augustine is suggesting in his considerations of these three man-made inventions.

Consider Augustine's own inventions that resulted in his path away
from God: "In this I sinned, in that I sought pleasure, lofty things, and
truths, not in God but in his creatures, myself and others, and thus I
rushed into sorrows, confusions and errors."[36] In pursuing "pleasures,
lofty things, and truths, not in God," but in himself and others, Augustine suggests that one should pursue truth and pleasure in God, not in
man and his creations.

It is important to note that Augustine also urges a broad interpretation of avarice, explaining that Paul had intended avarice to include

not just the love of money but also an ardent or immoderate desire for anything.[37] In man's fall, for example, Augustine recognizes "avarice." This might come as a surprise, as we tend to associate it with monetary greed. But Augustine explains that Adam "hungered for more than should have sufficed for him."[38] An ardent or immoderate desire to be first or a lust for power would be considered by Augustine as both avarice *and* ambition.

Gregory the Great, echoing Augustine, also attributes Adam's fall to *avaritia*. To Gregory, the Devil lured Adam "with the advancement of avarice when he said 'knowing good and evil.' For avarice is not only a matter of money, but of high standing as well. For it is correctly called avarice when someone strives for loftiness beyond measure."[39] Like Augustine, Gregory considers avarice not "just a matter of money." The patristic texts do not treat avarice and ambition as the distinct passions they would become in the early modern period. Gregory defines avarice as a desire for money and high position. What the Romans called *ambitio*, Gregory includes in his definition of avarice: "Avarice has to do not only with money but high position; it is rightly called avarice when prestige is sought beyond measure. If grasping for honor does not pertain to avarice then did Paul say in vain concerning the only begotten Son, 'He thought it not robbery to be equal with God' [Phil 2:6]. Thus did the devil lure our parent into pride, exciting avarice of high position."[40]

The broad Augustinian and Gregorian interpretation of avarice might further explain why ambition eludes the consideration of some historians of religion in early America. In searching through texts they see avarice but miss the many vices that are included in the patristic conceptualization of it. Morton W. Bloomfield's *Seven Deadly Sins*, a comprehensive study of vices from their pagan and Jewish background through medieval Christianity, does not recognize ambition per se in any significant way.[41] Much of medieval allegory is based on Prudentius's *Psychomachia* and the list of Cassian and Gregorian sins.[42] But when Gregory names his Capital Vices, or Seven Deadly Sins, among which is avarice, scholars fail to recognize that in naming avarice he

likewise condemns ambition. Ambition is among the Seven Deadly
Sins by Gregory's own definition!

In what ways, then, if any, do theological treatments of ambition
change in the Middle Ages? And in what ways do these changes, if any,
impact ambition as sin? In the thirteenth century, we turn to Thomas
Aquinas and the *Summa Theologica*, the most influential and comprehensive theological doctrine of the Middle Ages.[43]

The *Summa Theologica* has a three-part structure. In part 2, Thomas
discusses the virtues and vices. These discussions are framed by questions and answers. Question 131 is "Is ambition a sin?" This may not
seem odd or surprising without appropriate context, but consider the
other questions regarding vice. Of pride, for example, begins, "Is pride
a special sin?" Of idolatry, "Is idolatry rightly set down as a species of
superstition?" Of prodigality, "Is prodigality the opposite of covetousness?" These questions are posed to provide answers that deepen the
reader's understanding of the vice, to add nuance and subtlety.

In the case of ambition, however, the question is not what sort of
sin is this but whether it is a sin at all. Who poses these questions? Are
they intended as a personal or radical interpretation of Scripture? Not
at all. The questions are posed and answers offered "partly because
frequent repetition has bred boredom and confusion in the minds of
the hearers." Thomas intends the work to "instruct not only the advanced but the beginner as well." Thomas is hoping, as any good
teacher does, to pose questions that reflect the thoughts and opinions
of his students.

The form of *Summa Theologica* can seem confusing to modern
readers. Thomas Aquinas poses a series of questions and then answers
them in two ways. First, in a section called *videtur*, or objections, he
poses a series of plausible false answers and the basis for these false
answers. He then follows these objections with the *responsio*. In the
responsio section he refutes the objections and provides the correct answer. Invariably, throughout the *Summa Theologica* we know that if
Thomas poses something as an "objection," it is not what he believes,
although it may be a reflection of a plausible contemporary incorrect

assumption. It is only in the *responsio* that we learn what he believes to be true.

That said, Thomas poses the following question: "Is ambition a sin?" The "wrong" answer is based on the following incorrect assumptions or "objections":

> Objection 1. It seems that ambition is not a sin. For ambition denotes the desire of honour. Now honour is in itself a good thing, and the greatest of external goods: wherefore those who care not for honour are reproved. Therefore, ambition is not a sin; rather is it something deserving of praise, in so far as a good is laudably desired.
>
> Objection 2. Further, Anyone may, without sin, desire what is due to him as a reward. Now honour is the reward of virtue, as the Philosopher states (Ethic. i, 12; iv, 3; viii, 14). Therefore ambition of honour is not a sin.
>
> Objection 3. Further, That which heartens a man to do good and disheartens him from doing evil, is not a sin. Now honour heartens men to do good and to avoid evil; thus the Philosopher says (Ethic., iii. 8) that *with the bravest men, cowards are held in dishonour, and the brave in honour*: and Tully says (De Tusc. Quaest.i.) that *honour fosters the arts.* Therefore ambition is not a sin.[44]

These are interesting objections because they reflect not only an interrogation but a desire to disprove that ambition is a sin in a way that seems unimaginable in Augustine or Gregory. But it is also fascinating that in this passage Thomas considers the topic of what we might call "good ambition," "honorable ambition," or "noble ambition." As ambition is a desire for honor and honor is a good thing, how could ambition be a sin? As honor is the reward for virtue, and ambition is the desire for honor, is it not logical to assume that ambition is the desire for virtue as well? Further, honor "heartens men to do good . . . and to avoid evil"; honor even "fosters the arts." Therefore, whatever sparks this desire cannot be sin. This seems to be a convincing argument, one supported by quotations from Aristotle and Tully.[45] These clearly are serious objections, although we know, given Thomas's form, that they are all false answers.

Thomas in his response refutes this possibility, writing, "Honour denotes reverence shown to a person in witness of his excellence." Because man excels not "from himself" but due to "something Divine in him," all honor is due "not to him, but to God." That is, "[T]he thing in which man excels is given to him by God, that he may profit others thereby." In other words, individual excellence from which honor is won is God given.[46]

He continues by enumerating three ways in which desire for honor can be "inordinate." First, when a man "desires recognition of an excellence which he has not: this is to desire more than his share of honour." The second way is "when a man desires honour for himself without referring it to God." And the third is "when a man's appetite rests in honour itself, without referring it to the profit of others." He concludes by defining ambition as "inordinate desire of honour." The last three objections, therefore, are implicit in this definition. In case any of his "students" missed it, he states unequivocally: *It is evident that it (ambition) is always a sin.*"[47] Thomas then reflects the Gregorian and Augustinian sense of "immoderate desire" as essential to understanding sin and conveyed by the word *avaritia* in the patristic texts. Ambition is the *immoderate* or *inordinate* desire for honor. This is an essential point to understanding ambition. It is not, as earlier suggested, the quality itself, but the excess of it.[48] For Thomas, according to one scholar, virtue is "found as a rational principle as a mean between two vicious extremes, one of deficiency and the other of excess."[49]

Thomas also rejects the possibility of what we later come to call "noble ambition" or "honorable ambition." Ambition is sin and cannot be anything else. That said, the mere fact that Thomas is questioning whether ambition is sinful is reason for pause, a suggestion of why it may have been downplayed in medieval allegories.

That is not to say that ambition is absent. When it is considered, it reflects the broad definition of ambition as connected to avarice, as one of the manifestations of immoderate desire.

The *Hortus Deliciarum* is one such medieval allegory. As it both serves as a bridge between the medieval and renaissance in chronology and provides visual evidence for the broad Augustinian and Gregorian concept of avarice, one that would include ambition, it is worth considering in some detail.

In twelfth-century Alsace, in the small abbey of Mont Sainte-Odile, the abbess Herrad of Landsberg, "like a bee" and "under the inspiration of God," composed this book "out of the honey and many flowers drawn from the Holy Scripture and works of philosophy."[50] The book, consisting of more than three hundred leaves, is a marvelous synthesis of medieval allegory, classical philosophy, and scriptural interpretation. Many of the ideas expressed in its pages are made concrete and palpable through illustrations drawn from a rich corpus of symbols and images from the culture of her time. Herrad of Landsberg was not unique in this regard. For a largely illiterate populace, medieval allegorical images were powerful tools for conveying theological abstractions.[51] The medieval peasant knew the Devil by the horns, a demon by a human face displayed on the creature's buttocks, original sin by a man and a woman hiding their nakedness, sanctity by the small gold circle levitating above a figure.[52] From the time of the early church, most likely among the Christians of Alexandria, animal or bestiary images were also used to interpret the Bible.[53] Herrad of Landsberg, too, uses animal imagery. In the *Hortus Deliciarum* animals represent virtues and vices.

One folio of the *Hortus Deliciarum* focuses exclusively on the vices.[54] Illustrated on this page is a circular, symmetrical design in the center of which is the Devil, labeled Avarice, "avaricia, id est, diabolus," represented by a woman in a cart or chariot. Why Herrad of Landsberg chose to make Avarice a woman is unclear. It may be that abstract nouns in Latin are feminine, but she uses animals to represent other abstractions, so this answer alone may be insufficient. At any rate, Avarice holds a trident or three-pronged hook in one hand and coins in the other hand. The inscription tells us that "Avarice lives evilly in soiled garments and holds a trident in her hand because of her rapacity."

But what makes this chariot of Avarice go? Two animals are yoked for the purpose: one a fox, the other a lion. In their teeth, the animals hold either end of a scroll that proclaims: "Avarice says: 'I lie with the fraud and cunning as it were of a fox, or pursuing wealth by force I gnaw like the cruel lion.'" The image of the fox in Christian art is universally negative, associated with guile, cunning and the Devil.[55]

The lion, in contrast, is a rich and contradictory symbol throughout medieval art and Christianity in general. It has been used to symbolize Christ, Saint Mark, Saint Jerome, magnanimity, strength, majesty, and fortitude.[56] But it has also been used, in rarer instances, to symbolize the Devil. The lion as satanic or evil is supported by Psalm 91:13 (KJV), in which Christ triumphs over the Devil "Thou shalt tread upon the lion and the adder," and in Peter 5:8 (KJV and D-R), "Your adversary the devil, as a roaring lion, walketh about, seeking whom he may devour."

In Dante, the lion in *The Inferno* is often interpreted to symbolize ambition and pride.[57] Herrad of Landsberg conveys a similar meaning in her work. As if to resolve any ambiguity, she includes inscriptions on the outer circle of the image. This is an image of vice. The chariot of Avarice is driven by the symbols of fraud (the fox) and ambition (the lion). If we focus on the lion as ambition, we see another message. Although a lion (ambition) is powerful and capable of pulling a chariot, he who yokes a lion yokes his own destruction.

Some two hundred years later, in 1449, *ambition* finally makes its appearance in an extant English text. Reginald Pecock writes of "vices [such] as pride, ambition, vainglory."[58] But of greater importance and impact on later Western thought in general and English thought in particular, published roughly fifty years later, was the work of Niccolò Machiavelli.

Machiavelli's influence on Western culture has been extensively considered. His work is considered as among the most important in modernity's Renaissance origins.[59] In England, from the sixteenth cen-

60. Hortus fol. 203ᵛ
Char d'Avarice

The twelfth-century nun Herrad de Landsberg's chariot of virtues and vices. Here
ambition is depicted as a lion yoked to the chariot. Collections of Bastard d'Estang,
fol. 203, Bibliothèque Nationale, Paris.

tury onward, Machiavelli was read, initially with some enthusiasm,
later with considerable disdain. Francis Bacon embraced him in the
seventeenth century, and many of Bacon's arguments for colonization
echo Machiavelli.[60] For the most part, in Elizabethan and early Stuart
England, to be Machiavellian was to be impious, crafty, manipulative,
and amoral, "an enemy of mankind and a confederate of Satan."[61] His
works, or rather the perception of their content, were nonetheless significant, reflected on the Elizabethan stage in the plays of Marlowe and

Shakespeare.[62] His philosophy was "answered" in the writings of Hugo
Grotius. In America, we know that John Adams was quite familiar with
Machiavelli and even wrote that he was "a student of Machiavelli,"
claiming that his "writings contain a good deal of wisdom," though he
qualified it as "mixed with too much wickedness."[63] Other scholars
trace Machiavelli's influence on the thinking of James Madison.[64]

Machiavelli does give ambition considerable attention. The use of
ambizione, along with the variants *ambizioso* and *ambiziosamente*, oc-
curs 204 times in his works: 13 times in *Il principe* (The prince), 80
in the *Discorsi* (Discourses on the first ten books of Titus Livy), 72 in
Le istorie fioretine (The history of Florence), and 3 in *Dell'arte della
guerra* (Art of war).[65] Given the characterizations of Machiavelli's philosophy as devoid of any moral component, it may be surprising that he
thoroughly condemns ambition in most of his work.[66] In his writings
Machiavelli characterizes *ambizione* as *scoretti*, "wrong." *Ambizione*
is often grouped with other negative qualities among which are envy,
idleness, violence, rancor, and corruption.[67]

In a lesser known work, *I capitoli*, Machiavelli writes a poem on
the subject, "Dell'ambizione" (Tercets on ambition). Machiavelli's poetry has received comparatively little attention from literary scholars.[68]
It is rarely included in collections of his work and eludes comprehensive collections of Renaissance poetry. Critic and translator Joseph Tusiani suggests that one reason may be that "Machiavelli was capable of
observing the world as it was and then filtering it through the beauty of
the world as he himself saw it. Crudity, therefore, remained just crudity, and observation was not redeemed by exaltation of dream."[69] But
this assessment seems unfair, suffering from the solipsism of the contemporary expectation in measuring Machiavelli's worth by modern
aesthetics rather than by Aristotelian standards. What poetry is to us is
not the same as what it would have been to Machiavelli, who would
have looked to Aristotle. Aristotle wrote, "Poetry is something more philosophical and serious than history, because it tends to give the universal, whereas history gives the particular facts."[70] Leonard Tennenhouse
rightly suggests that during the Renaissance, "literature and political

discourse had not yet been differentiated in the manner of a modern critical discourse."[71] Machiavelli's poetry is a casualty of shifting aesthetic expectations. By an Aristotelian standard, Machiavelli achieves both a poetic and historical excellence, capturing in "Dell'ambizione" both the universal and the particular.

Machiavelli wrote "Dell'ambizione," in 1509, before *The Prince* and the *Discourses*. The poem is dedicated to Luigi Guicciardini and begins as an address to him. Machiavelli is surprised by Guicciardini's shock at the situation in Siena, chastising him for not taking "this world of ours for what it is" and urging him to "reflect more" on the depravity of human nature (lines 1–3).[72] He is referring here to Siena's ruler Pandolfo Petrucci, whom Machiavelli in the *Discourses* labels a tyrant. An assassination plot was hatched to rid Siena of Petrucci but was uncovered, after which he ruled Siena with brutality, though the intrigues continued. Machiavelli uses this historical particular as a springboard from which to discuss certain human "universals"—ambition and avarice.

Machiavelli recognizes the ubiquity of these ills, reminding Guicciardini that his situation argues no fault in Siena; the fault is in mankind, fundamental to his condition, from the moment of his creation:

> What province or what city escapes it? What village, what
> hovel? Everywhere Ambition and Avarice penetrate
> When man was born into the world, they were born too;
>   and if
> they had no existence, happy enough would be our condition
> (lines 10–15)

He calls ambition and avarice "Furies," intended to "deprive us of peace and to set us at war" (lines 28, 29). These furies are never sated, and Machiavelli illustrates this with the image of a bottomless urn, a vessel that can never be filled: "These drive Concord to the depths. To show their limitless / desire, they bear in their hands a bottomless urn" (lines 40–42). Ambition is responsible for "arming Cain," the "first violent death."

Oh human spirit insatiable, arrogant, crafty, and shifting, and
above all else malignant, iniquitous, violent, and savage,
because through your longing so ambitious, the first violent
    death
was seen in the world, and the first grass red with blood!
(lines 55–60)

In describing the "first murder" caused by ambition, Machiavelli uses
the evocative image of the earth itself blushing, the grass bleeding. By
anthropomorphizing the earth and its suffering and outrage, Machiavelli conveys the sense of the unnaturalness of the act and the revulsion
of the ambitious wish. He seems to imply that Cain's act is more than
just an act against his brother. It is not just Abel who bleeds but the
grass, the very earth itself.

From this single act, there spawned an "evil . . . multiplied." Machiavelli extends individual ambition to the rise and fall of "states." He
regards it as indefatigable but argues that it can be controlled—not,
however, by one's will or self-restraint, and not by God's grace, as Augustine surmises, but by laws and the order and power of the state. "To
this our natural instinct draws us, by our own motion and / our own
feeling, if laws or greater forces do not restrain us" (lines 79–81). This
passage suggests that the role of government or princes and states is to
curtail, repress, and order human nature, "Since man with his sole
strength cannot discard her" (line 85).

But Machiavelli suggests that ambition may be used "produc-
tively" if it is ordered and then given a channel for expression against
"external foes."

When through her own nature a country lives unbridled, and
then, by accident, is organized and established under good laws,
Ambition uses against foreign peoples that violence which
neither the law nor the king permits her to use at home
(wherefore home-born tourble almost always ceases); yet
    she is

sure to keep disturbing the sheepfolds of others, wherever that
violence of hers has planted its banner.
(lines 94–102)

Some scholars have interpreted Machiavelli's "ambition" as having
a dual nature, "internal" and "external" ambition. Although he never
explicitly defines *ambizione*, Machiavelli considers *ambizione* in terms
closely related to its Roman antecedent.[73] *Ambizione* is the use of public office or power for the attainment of private ends that are at odds
with public good.[74] Some scholars contrast this meaning with "external
ambition"—that is, when the individual finds an outlet for his ambition that aligns itself with the public good, in this case the "gloria" of
the state. Machiavelli recognizes that even "external ambition," that
which might benefit the state, does so at the expense of another state.
If Machiavelli's recognition of ambition and humanity's depravity is
without morality, it is certainly not devoid of a certain sympathetic consideration. While Machiavelli might recognize the alleviation of one's
own painful struggle with ambition, he does not glory in it. Instead, he
seems to lament those "outsiders" who suffer when ambition "disturbs
their sheepfold" wherever "that violence of hers" plants its "banner."
It is tempting to read this in the context of the early sixteenth century,
when the Spanish banner is planted throughout the Caribbean at the
expense of the native inhabitants. But regardless of any explicit New
World connection, Machiavelli anticipates American conquest and colonization, when national, Christian, and individual ambition conflate
in violence and glory (a subject I address in depth in chapter 4).

In this poem and in other writings, Machiavelli suggests that ambition is a passion, a vice, with the sinful and unnatural associations
associated with Cain in his act of fratricide. In England, by the sixteenth
century, this association grows stronger, and ambition and sin become
more fundamentally linked. This point is made in the definitive prescriptive source on European behavior, the Bible.

Earlier in the chapter I proposed two possible reasons why ambition
might have been ignored despite its central place in Anglo-American

and early American thought. A third and final reason is the "problem" of the source itself. The Bible often receives cursory attention as a cultural historical source. Christopher Hill tells the story of "an exchange between the legendary economic historian Jack Fisher and an importunate pupil who was pressing him for a reading list on sixteenth- and seventeenth-century English economic history. [Fisher] said, 'if you really want to understand the period, go away and read the Bible.'"[75] Though we ignore the Bible at our peril, some historians of early America are more than willing to take that risk.

Further, those who do discuss the Bible sometimes fail to differentiate specific biblical translations used during the period of study. The Bible is often treated as if it is, in fact, the word of God, not the multiple interpretations and translations of human beings. Religious historian Harry Stout speaks to this error when he writes, "With all of the attention to Puritan Biblicism, the actual translation used . . . has not come under very close scrutiny. Entire histories of Puritanism in Old and New England have been written which do not even consider the possibility that a crucial element may have been the particular translation employed."[76] This critical point may well be the most salient explanation of why ambition has been overlooked. The current King James translation of the Bible contains no specific reference to ambition.

The Geneva Bible, however, contains seventy-six such references, and one particular feature of this Bible explains this discrepancy. The Geneva Bible may, in fact, be regarded as two distinct works. The first is the actual English translation of 1560. The second is the commentary of some three hundred thousand words, integrated throughout chapter and verse and incorporated with the first printing. As such, the Geneva marginalia may be viewed as a separate political text, the most widely read and extensively distributed political treatise of the early modern era.[77]

In the second century CE, Christians reordered the Hebrew Scriptures, "converting" them into what became known as the Old Testament. The New Testament shunned Gnostic texts. The Book of Revelation and the Epistle of James did not become part of the official

A comparison of references to *ambition* or *ambitious* in three biblical translations

	Geneva Bible	King James, 1611	King James, 21st c.
Genesis	4	—	—
Exodus	1	—	—
Judges	1	—	—
2 Samuel	2	—	—
2 Kings	2	—	—
1 Chronicles	2	—	—
2 Chronicles	3	—	—
Esther	3	—	—
Job	2	—	—
Psalms	4	—	—
Proverbs	2	—	—
Ecclesiasticus	0	1	—
Isaiah	3	—	—
Jeremiah	4	—	—
Daniel	4	—	—
Hosea	1	—	—
Wisdom of Solomon	1	—	—
Matthew	6	3	—
Mark	1	2	—
Luke	3	2	—
John	1	1	—
Acts	1	—	—
Romans	1	—	—
1 Corinthians	13	—	—
2 Corinthians	4	—	—
Galatians	2	—	—
Philippians	2	—	—
1 Timothy	1	—	—
3 John	1	1	—
Jude	1	—	—
Total	76	10	0

"Bible" until much later.[78] But marginal notes added an explicit English-language political text made "sacred" by its inclusion with the translation.[79] Most common men and women did not differentiate between text and marginalia. The Bible, those words included between the front and back cover, were God's words.

It is in these marginal notes that one unearths the more than seventy references to ambition. Though notes, the references are extremely significant. As Stout correctly avers, the Genevan commentary was "the only literary product all people shared in common and it exerted far more direct influence on the popular religious imagination than the less widely circulated sermons, devotionals and spiritual autobiographies."[80]

For our purposes the Geneva Bible is a rich and relatively "overlooked" source, reflecting the attitude not just of elites but of common folk. Historians of ideas are sometimes criticized for privileging the words or documents of elites at the expense of the vox populi. It is essential to listen for the public voice, though at times more difficult to hear through the traditional sources. A vernacular Bible in a largely literate, profoundly biblical culture affords us a unique opportunity.[81]

The Bible was the *basso ostinato* of everyday life: present at every significant ritual from birth until death, supplying everything from the reasons for a good harvest to the language of mourning. In the prologue to the 1540 Great Bible, Thomas Cranmer wrote:

> Herein may princes learn how to govern their subjects; subjects obedience, love and dread to their princes: husbands, how they should behave them unto their wives; how to educate their children and servants: and contrary the wives, children and servants may know their duty to their husbands, parents and masters. Here may all manner of persons, . . . of what estate or condition soever they be may in this book learn all things what they ought to believe, what they ought to do, & what they should not do, as well concerning Almighty God, as also concerning themselves and all other.[82]

In 1635 the Puritan minister Thomas Shepherd proclaimed that "the [biblical] word descends to the most petty occasions of our lives; it teacheth men how to look, (Ps. cxxxi. 16;) how to speak, (Matt. xii.36;) it descends to the plaiting of the hair, (I Pet. iii.5,) [and the] moving of the feet, (Is. iii.16;)."[83] When John Winthrop considered the validity of the English right to purchase Indian lands, he mused on Abraham's purchase of land from Ephron the Hittite.

It was the "biblical word" that Shepherd emphasized. It was thought to be the word of God. William Hunt, in his discussion of Puritanism in Essex County, England, emphasizes the importance of the words that represented "The Word" in Anglo-American culture in this period. The Judeo-Christian tradition conceives "of God himself linguistically," Hunt writes. "God does not merely speak. God *is* language: 'the Word was with God and the Word *was* God.'"[84] In Anglo-American culture, God was primarily known through the vernacular translation of the Bible. That is, God's word had become English words, sanctified or vilified by their treatment in biblical texts.

This is why Stout underscores the importance of identifying the specific biblical translation used during a given time. Many scholars look exclusively at the King James Bible, but to do so is a grave oversight. The Geneva Bible remained the dominant biblical translation from the mid-sixteenth century to the mid- and perhaps late seventeenth century, both in England and in the American colonies. The Geneva represented a revolution in vernacular Bibles. Stout calls it the "first popular reformation document." Other vernacular Bibles preceded the Geneva, but the Geneva was smaller in size and moderately priced. It quickly became the "family Bible" in England and Scotland. Although its use was discouraged by ecclesiastical authorities after the publication of the King James Bible in 1611, the Geneva Bible continued to be the "people's choice" for three-quarters of a century, published in no fewer than 160 editions. The Geneva Bible was the Bible of Shakespeare and Milton and of John Cotton and John Winthrop as well. Early inventories show two copies brought over on the *Mayflower*. Governor William Bradford of Massachusetts owned a copy printed in

London in 1592. This was the copy he drew on for his *History of Plymouth Plantation, 1620–1647*. It was used exclusively in the Plymouth Colony and extensively throughout New England. Sermons from early Virginia demonstrate its pervasiveness. Even into the late seventeenth century the Geneva retained its popularity. When Oliver Cromwell's men went into battle, they carried pages from the Geneva Bible in their boots.[85]

Many early Americanists have overlooked the Geneva Bible in part because the secondary literature on the Geneva, beginning around the mid-nineteenth century, either ignores the translation or inaccurately minimizes its significance. Biblical scholar David Daniell writes:

> In histories written since the mid-nineteenth century, with some rare exceptions, the Geneva Bible has generally been treated briefly, if mentioned at all, and condemned. A complete list of such dismissals and omissions would be a long, sad, and depressing revelation of ignorance or bias. . . . Readers in later ages need not feel smug, however. Hostility towards the Geneva Bible persists. It is possible to accumulate pages of references to books (and broadcasts) in which what has become the standard negative description is stated, or in which the Geneva Bible and its massive popularity have been omitted.[86]

Further, scholars who emphasize the importance of the King James, or "Authorized," Version fail to note that between 1642 and 1715 eight editions of the King James Bible were published with the Genevan notes.[87]

Marginal notes are not unique to the Geneva. Both Martin Luther's German translation and John Calvin's French biblical translation employ notes. Such commentary was an attempt to help readers interpret scripture, but it also had a political and social aim. The central question of the post-Reformation era was how to maintain social order after men like Luther and Calvin proclaimed that it is one's duty to God to rise up against "ungodly ministers." Biblical justifications became readily available after the Bible was translated from Latin. Just what constituted "ungodly" could for the first time be ascertained by a populace who could read for themselves what "God says" and interpret what constituted godly and ungodly behavior.

The Geneva Bible's admonitions against ambition, seventy-six in all, made sacred by their incorporation into a translation, were an attempt to ensure that the Reformation did not generate anarchy, a failed effort at putting some of the "genie back into the bottle," at mitigating the revolutionary potential of the Protestant Reformation. The Reformation encouraged ordinary people to read and make use of the Bible. It challenged traditional papal authority. By singling out and identifying ambition as a vice and evil, the Geneva's authors found a way to redraw boundaries and check individual self-making.

Ambition first appears in the Book of Genesis as sin slithers its way into the Divine Order. Chapter 3, verse 6, captures the moment when Eve and Adam first sample the fruit of knowledge. Adam's motivation for this usurpation of divine prerogative is discussed in the second note. He ate the fruit, "Not so much to please his wife, as moued by ambition at her persuasion." The note makes clear that it is not out of Adam's "uxuriousness" (as Milton would later claim) or "pride," as some earlier interpretations assert. Eve pricked in Adam something that was already within him, even in Eden: ambition. By this account, therefore, even before man knew good or evil, the Divine Being had endowed him with the capacity to express ambition.

Ambition, therefore, is at the core of original sin. This point is reiterated in chapter 3, verse 22, as God reproaches Adam before casting him from paradise. The verse reads, "And the Lord God said, Beholde, the man is become as one of vs, to knowe good and euill." God derides Adam for his ambition, ascribing his fall to the vice, as made clear by the marginal note that accompanies this passage: "By this derision he reprocheth Adams miserie, whereinto he was fallen by ambition."

The Geneva Bible also makes clear that pride and ambition are closely related. In Genesis 11:4 human beings boast a proud self-sufficiency, symbolically attempting to elevate themselves to the level of God by their construction of a tower that can reach "vnto the heauen." The explicit motivation for the Tower of Babel is explained in the margin note: "They were mooued with pride and ambition, thinking to preferre their owne glorie to Gods honour." Here ambition is coupled with pride in an impious union, making clear that the two are distinct. It also begins a rhetorical pattern repeated throughout the marginal notes, in which ambition is conjoined by an "and" with some other generally recognized unsavoriness. Ambition is associated with "crueltie of the wicked," "malice," "vaine glorie," "superfluitie," "wicked desires," "rage," "greedy desire to reigne," and the catchall "crueltie and all kinds of vice."

As in Adam's fall, the expression of ambition has dire consequences. The last reference to ambition in the notes to Genesis describes the war among various kings and princes. The "chiefe cause of warres among princes" is "ambition" (14:3). As the first account of war in the Bible, its purported cause assumes additional significance. This was likely magnified in the seventeenth century. The first waves of the great exodus of English colonists reached American soil between 1630 and 1635, as the Thirty Years' War consumed Europe. In addition, from 1625 to 1630 England engaged in a number of frustrating military campaigns against the Spanish, French, and Germans, all of which accomplished little and were generally regarded with disdain.

Ambition, then, can apply to kings, original man, and even the common man. In Exodus the reference to ambition is included in the "front matter," which, like the marginal notes, serves an interpretive function. The front matter is an explanatory table of contents at the beginning of each book that summarizes "the argument." In the front matter of Exodus the recently emancipated children of Israel expressed their ingratitude when they forgot "Gods wonderfull benefits" and "fell to distrust, and tempted God with sundrie murmurings and grudgings against him and his ministers: sometime moued with ambition, sometime for lacke of drinke or meate to content their lustes, sometime by idolatrie, or such like."

God answers ambition and the other evils attendant with "sharp roddes and plagues, that by his corrections they might seeke to him for remedie against his scourges, and earnestly repent them for their rebellions and wickednesse."

Ambition continues to plague man throughout the Geneva Bible. God's attitude is again made explicit in Isaiah 39:6, when the notes proclaim, "God detesteth ambition," and in 1 Corinthians 3:16, where it is written that "ambition is not only vaine, but also sacrilegious."

The biblical commentary in the Geneva Bible does not simply inveigh against ambition. As mentioned, it is prescriptive; it suggests correct behavior. Whereas modern readers may assume that humility is the antipode of ambition, the Geneva Bible asserts that the antipode is, in fact, "mediocritie." This might surprise the modern reader, for whom *mediocrity* is a dirty word. But the marginalia on Jeremiah 22:15 extols the virtues of a mediocre life. The passage addresses "A Kings prosperitie," contrasting it with Isaiah's contentment. The note explains: "Meaning Iosiah, who was not giuen to ambition and superfluitie, but was content with mediocritie and did onely delite in setting foorth Gods glory and to doe iustice to all." Of course, God's approval is won not by mediocrity alone. But it is certainly a component and one that is contrasted by ambition. "Mediocritie" is defined by Henry Cockeram's 1624 *English Dictionarie* as "a meane, or measure." In other words, God wants us, according to the framers of the Geneva Bible, to be content with our averageness, our "meane." Even the later definition of *ambition,* one associated with achievement, excellence, the aspiration for self-transformation, and accomplishment through industry and endeavor, contradicts this sentiment. There is an echo of the Augustinian denunciation *libido pricipandi* (the desire to be first) in this God-sanctioned virtuous mediocrity, this Thomistic virtuous mean.

This contentment in the "meane" is further developed in Romans, chapter 12. In Romans, Paul considers the application of God's precepts to daily life. Chapter 12 addresses the notion of vocation, an idea closely related to ambition.

Adhering to one's occupational vocation, like renunciations of ambition, is a theme that runs throughout the Geneva. In Proverbs 11:2,

Numbers 16:40, 1 Corinthians 7:21, and Psalm 131:1 the notes warn men to stay within their vocations and not seek to be exalted above them. The marginal notes do not condemn the choice of a vocation, provided that there is no aspiration to a higher status.

Romans 12 addresses the fact that every member of the church has different abilities and talents, emphasizing the recognition and respect for our individual limitations. The note contained within Romans 12:3 states, "hee admonisheth vs very earnestly, that euery man keepe him-selfe within the boundes of his vocation, and that euery man bee wise according to the measure of grace that God hath giuen him." In Ro-mans 12:4, the marginal note makes an analogy to a body that has many parts and that no man should "passeth the bounds of his voca-tion."[88] All men, according to the Geneva Bible, may be created equally but are quickly differentiated, "because God hath not committed euery thing to be done of euery man: and therefore, he doeth backewardly, and not only vnprofitably, but also to the great disprofite of others, wea-rieth himself and others, which passeth the bounds of his vocation." Further, it is inequality, not equality, that binds a community, "for that this diuersitie & inequalitie of vocations and giftes, redoundeth to our commoditie: seeing that the same is therefore instituted and appointed, that we should be bound one to another." Those who are, unfortunately, less "gifted" should make no attempt to rectify the situation because the communal body needs both the high and the low: "no man ought to be grieued thereat, seeing that the vse of euery priuate gift is comon." The reward for maintaining one's vocation is clear, as, according to a note in Luke 9:46, "the ende of ambition is ignominie: but the ende of modest obedience is glory."

But if piety is observing the bounds of one's vocation, what about the carpenter who sets out to vanquish death? The annotators make it clear that Christ's seeming renunciation of his vocation is not a course to be emulated. The margin note in John 8:54 explains that "there is nothing farther off from all ambition then Christ, but his Father hath set him aboue all things." Christ did not aspire to be the Son of God; his elevation was predestined and God given. This justification extends, too, to Christ's miracles. After Jesus cures the leper, the note in Mark 1:44 explains, "He was not mooued with ambition, but with the onely desire of his Fathers glory, and loue towardes the poore sinners."

Christ may be "far off" from ambition, but he was certainly close enough to recognize the danger it posed to his project. In Matthew 21:23 to 23:39, the opposition to Jesus from religious leaders continues to grow toward a crescendo. As Jesus' popularity increases, so does the tension until the imminent confrontation crests when the chief priests and elders fall to silence, muted by their inability to truly understand Christ, who pronounces seven woes against the scribes and Pharisees. Their chief sins, as labeled by a marginal note, are "ambition, couetousness, and hypocricie." According to a note in Matthew 23:8, "Modestie is a singular ornament of Gods ministers."

Christ's own disciples are not immune from similar danger. In Matthew 6:1, "Take heede," Jesus warns, "that ye giue not your almes before men, to be seene of them, or els ye haue no reward of your Father which is in heaue." The notes explain that "Ambition maketh almes vaine," and "This worde, Rewarde, is always taken in the Scriptures for a free recompence & therefore the schoolmen doe fondly set it to be answerable to a deseruing, which they call, merite." In other words, Christ warns of the pitfalls of practicing piety to sate the craving for human approbation. Jesus recognizes the possibility of ambition in even his most devout followers. Even piety can be corrupted by ambition.

When God made heaven and earth, he also made ambition. By all references in the Geneva Bible, it is a most dangerous evil: capable of driving men to war, polluting man's relationship with God, corrupting Jesus's disciples, and even disrupting the Divine Order in Eden. On no occasion is there any sense of "lofty ambition." Aspirations to goodness are never associated with the word *ambition*. These were tumultuous times. The marginal notes set boundaries, reestablishing an order at a time of fundamental disorder.

In reformation were the seeds of rebellion. This leads to a final, and especially relevant, point regarding ambition and its relationship to sin in late sixteenth- and seventeenth-century Anglo-American culture: the relationship between ambition and rebellion as suggested in the Tudor *Homilie against Disobedience and Wylfull Rebellion* (1570).

Tudor homilies, required reading from the pulpits of sixteenth- and seventeenth-century England, were simple set-pieces written to help parish priests disseminate liturgical and doctrinal reformation and interpretation. Homilies were intended for the common and middling sort, usually devoid of scholastic and "high" pretension, composed of simple language and clear directives. These were to be propagated throughout the realm, and, as such, are interesting sources. They are clearly an elite source but one targeted at the common folk. Literacy rates in the sixteenth century are important, but here the people are being read to, in "their" language, each week.[89]

Tudor homilies are traditionally seen as a primarily Elizabethan source, yet this is simply not the case. According to Millar MacLure, the homilies continued to exert "the single greatest influence" on Jacobean and Caroline divines. In 1708 Bishop George Bull urged the clergy to rely on the homilies, "not to trust at first to their own compositions, but to furnish themselves with a provision of the best sermons, which the learned divines of our church have published . . . use the Homilies of the church."[90]

Although *An Homilie against Disobedience and Wylfull Rebellion* was written in 1570, there is evidence that as late as the eighteenth century candidates for the Anglican clergy were compelled to read this homily on the anniversary of the death of Charles I.[91] It is here, in the fifth of seven parts of the homily, that we find an explicit definition of *ambition:* "the unlawful and restles desire in men to be of higher estate then God hath geven or appoynted unto them."[92] This definition seems to place ambition within the realm of status hierarchy, of not knowing one's place and aspiring to a role above one's "station." It condemns those men and women "clymyng up of theyr owne accorde to dominion."[93] Note, too, that in this passage women as well as men are capable of ambition.[94] One wonders who these ambitious women were. What does this statement indicate about the role of women in Elizabethan and Jacobean society? Why was it necessary for the homily to include women in its most dire warnings?

Women in this era were private figures, subordinated within the social hierarchy. Women could not attend university. They could not be heirs to title, could not enter the public sphere, could not act in the theaters. As the Scottish Protestant John Knox wrote, "Woman in her greatest perfection was made to serve and obey man, not to rule and command him."[95] These gender expectations would suggest that "ambition" was largely unavailable to women.[96]

Curiously, these restrictive stipulations were in place when the dread sovereign was, in fact, a woman. It seems hard to imagine that the place Elizabeth played in the English cultural imagination did not in some ways challenge the traditional role that women were expected to play. There are suggestions that regardless of the doctrinal restrictions, women challenged and assailed limits, or were perceived by male authority so to do.

For example, cultural ideas and rules of law prohibited women from seeking legal redress in courts of law.[97] Yet in his book *Women Waging Law in Elizabethan England*, Tim Stretton documents that women did just that.[98] Stretton examines records from the Court of Requests, a court with a more flexible procedure than other English courts. Due to its broad jurisdiction and accessibility to the middling and poorer plaintiffs, it was sometimes called the "poor man's court." Laurel Thatcher Ulrich, in her study on women in colonial America, suggests that on the frontier, traditional roles of women often broke down by necessity.[99] In some ways, life in poverty or relative want can be conceptualized in similar terms, a situation in which traditional roles are a luxury. Even the "poor man's court" catered to people of some means, however. And again, the homilies provide evidence of a mainstream fear of ambition in women that would not require a frontier or other extraordinary condition to challenge conventional roles.

At any rate, the Court of Requests was a place where property and debt were litigated. Stretton finds that despite the cultural bias against women bringing suit, not to mention legal restrictions, women were in fact litigants in the Court of Requests. Granted, they represented a small proportion of suitors. Stretton also observes that women employed a strategy of rhetorical self-abasement, a desperate proclamation of their complete and utter helplessness. Men, by contrast, typically couched their debt in terms of a momentary setback. But this would suggest that if women were ambitious, they needed to carefully obscure or deny the appearance of ambition. That said, Stratton's study suggests a more complex view than the stereotypic portrayal of Elizabethan women.[100]

Sumptuary legislation, however, suggests a certain performative, a self-fashioned costumed "climbing" both of men and women. In apparel, men and women could say nothing yet speak in tomes. They could climb into another dominion without entering into the masculine world of merchant activity or politics. With clothing, women could claim a higher station publicly but quietly simply by choosing a certain garment. Sumptuary laws stipulated what a person could or could not wear based on his or her station. And these laws were regularly flouted, much to the considerable consternation of those who wished to create visual markers between themselves and others. Later in America, race came to function in a similar way, as a garment that could not be shed. In England a more malleable and ultimately less effective means was attempted. One 1577 indictment for sumptuary offense, for example, reads: "Item, we present that concerning the statute of apparell we fynde walter earle to ware gardes of velvat on his hosse, John delylls wyffe a peticot gardid with vellat . . . John goddardes wyffe a hatt of taffitie lynid with vellat, John mylls wyffe a cape of vellat and gardes in her gowne, John hoptons wyffe a taffytie hatt, Roger mylls wyffe a hatt of vellat."[101]

But sumptuary legislation, while dramatizing the aspirations of ordinary people, does not quite convey the serious consequences of ambition. In *An Homilie against Disobedience and Wylfull Rebellion*, ambition, the climbing to dominion, is inveighed against because it is at the root of serious rebellion and its resultant damnation. The homily tells us that though "many causes of rebellion may be reckened . . . almost as many as there be vices in men and women . . . *the principall*

and most usuall causes [are] ambition and ignoraunce." Rebellion is
"an abominable sin against God and man," and "horrible plagues, pun-
ishementes and deathes, with death everlasting finally, doth hang over
the heades of all rebels."[102] The chief embodiment and "first aucthour
of which rebellion, the roote of all vices and mother of all mischiefes,
was Lucifer, first Gods most excellent creature and most bounden subject, who by rebelling against the majestie of God, of the brightest and
most glorious angell is become the blackest and most foulest feende
and devill, and from the height of heaven is fallen into the pit and
bottome of hell."[103] This, one would think, would not be where one
would find Mistress Mylls in her hat of velvet. There was another
realm, though, one in which both men and women shared an equality
of damnation: witchcraft.

Witchcraft is explicitly mentioned in the Geneva Bible, 1 Samuel
15:23: "For rebellion is as the sin of witchcraft." This association of
witchcraft with rebellion links ambition and witchcraft. Witches could
be male or female; witchcraft was another frontier of sorts, outside the
established social order, the realm of the supernatural. It is difficult to
know whether the homily had witchcraft in mind when it spoke to the
rebellion and ambition of women, but it does seem to be the only place
where women could express both these damning qualities, regardless
of the restrictive legal and cultural stipulations. One did not need to be
elected, have property or wealth, or desire kingship to rebel. One
needed only to have the ambition to power through pledging an allegiance to the Devil or to be perceived to have done so.[104]

Ambition and rebellion are intimately linked and further explored
in *An Homilie against Disobedience and Wylfull Rebellion,* but women
are dropped from this particular consideration. According to the homily there are "men in whom these vices [ambition and ignorance] do
raigne." These men are the "restles ambitious" who cannot "by peaceable meanes clime so high as they do desire, they attempt to the same
by force and violence." These "restless ambitious . . . when they can not
prevayle agaynst the ordinarie authoritie and power of lawfull princes
and governours them selves alone, they do seeke the ayde and helpe of

the ignoraunt multitude, abusing them to their wicked purpose."[105] This public expression of ambition, one fraught by violence and realized within a public sphere, seems to be reserved exclusively for men.

I do not wish to imply that "ambition as sin" was a singular, uncontested narrative or a constellation of ideas manifested in the culture without challenge or competing cultural expressions. In fact, ambition as sin was constantly challenged both by the fact of upward mobility and by its concomitant expressions by individuals. Still, elite authorities were remarkably successful over many centuries in maintaining their power, suppressing peasant unrest, and using Christian culture in a hegemonic way.

2

Ambition as Sin in Early Modern English Culture

Perilous Acts of Self-Elevation, Subversive Acts of Self-Negation

Oh blind Ambition and desire of Raigne
How camst thou by this rule in mortall breasts?
Who gave thee this dominion ore the braine?
Thou murdrest more, then plagues or fatall pests.
—Thomas Heywood, 1609

I have no spur
To prick the sides of my intent, but only
Vaulting ambition, which o'erleaps itself,
And falls on th' other.
—*Macbeth* 1.7.25–28

Tracking an "idea" like ambition requires a flexible approach. Culture is fluid. Ideas do not conform neatly to historic periodization. There are inevitable overlaps. One can find suggestions that ambition is good when the dominant ideology proclaims it sin, just as one can find evidence that ambition is sin, or vice, at a time when it is celebrated.

Literary critic Raymond Williams proves invaluable to this study. To describe the changes in ideas through time, he suggests the use of the terms *dominant, residual,* and *emergent.*[1] This framework permits a certain elasticity that better reflects cultural shifts and guards against assumptions of absolutes that crumble in the face of historical exceptions. Williams's approach allows for variation, complexity, and seemingly contradictory impulses all present at the same historical moment.

In the last chapter I provided evidence that in early modern England "ambition as sin" was more than simply theological doctrine. It was state policy. Ambition was inveighed against in official Elizabethan homilies read by order of the state in pulpits throughout England; defined as "the unlawful and restles desire in men to be of higher estate then God hath geven or appoynted unto them"; identified as one of the major causes of rebellion; and associated with Satan, madness, damnation, and sin.[2] Concomitantly, a political text, in the form of marginal notes, was made sacred by its inclusion in the dominant biblical translation, a text that warns more than seventy times against the evils of ambition. Borrowing from Williams, then, we can identify ambition as sin as the dominant ideology of the sixteenth and early seventeenth centuries.[3]

The political benefit of this ideology for the Elizabethan nobility is clear. It helped sustain a political system, a status hierarchy built on hereditary entitlements. But, less obviously perhaps, the dominant ideology also helped build support among individuals or groups of individuals (what in later time might be termed subordinate classes) even though their support might be to their own detriment.

I think the concept of hegemony is helpful in order to understand this dynamic. The work on hegemony is extensive, and a specific definition remains contested ground. That said, resolving the distinctions is not the concern of this chapter. Rather, I define the concept in a broad sense and use it to illuminate ambition's cultural centrality, the willingness of both prince and pauper not only to adhere to but also, at times, to celebrate its strictures.[4]

It was Antonio Gramsci who was the first, in the words of critic Todd Gitlin, "to specify the concept [of hegemony] in the modern Marxist context."[5] As Gitlin rightly notes, Gramsci, writing from prison, fails to define the concept of hegemony; rather, "it is a leitmotif throughout his entire work."[6] Assembling aspects of hegemony throughout Gramsci's notebooks, Gitlin offers a working definition that is well suited to my analysis of ambition: "Hegemony is a ruling class's (or alliance's) domination of subordinate classes and groups through the elaboration and penetration of ideology (ideas and assumptions) into their common sense and everyday practice; it is the systematic (but not necessarily or even usually deliberate) engineering of mass consent to the established order."[7] Gramsci might have recognized his broad sense of ideology in sixteenth- and late seventeenth-century England. As David McClellan writes, "Gramsci's paradigm for his broad sense of ideology was religion, which he saw, like ideology, as producing a 'unity of faith between a conception of the world and a corresponding norm of conduct.'"[8]

But as Gitlin's distillation of Gramsci suggests, for an idea to be truly hegemonic, there must be a certain penetration of the ideology into the broader culture; it must extend beyond a single site, in this case religion. Stuart Hall identifies this penetration as one of the essential aspects of hegemony. He writes of its "multi-dimensional, multi-arena character." He further elaborates:

> It cannot be constructed or sustained on *one* front of struggle alone (for example, the economic). It represents a degree of mastery over a whole series of different "positions" at once. Mastery is not simply imposed or dominative in character. Effectively, it results from winning a substantial degree of popular consent. It thus represents the installation of a profound

measure of social and moral authority, not simply over its immediate supporters but across society as a whole. It is this "authority" and the range and the diversity of sites on which "leadership" is exercised, which makes possible the "propagation," for a time, of an intellectual, moral, political and economic collective will throughout society.[9]

In the case of ambition, the efforts to influence ideas and assumptions through religion were discussed extensively in the last chapter. The question remains, to what extent were these efforts successful? In other words, to what extent were they "hegemonic," or realized within culture?

The short answer is that culture, across a "broad range and diversity of sites," in many ways was effectively influenced by ideology. The long answer is the central preoccupation of this chapter. Whereas "ideology has the precise function of hiding the real contradictions and reconstituting on an imaginary level a relatively coherent discourse," culture, on the other hand, is fluid.[10] While I identify expressions of the dominant ideology, I do not suggest that this period was without emergent challenges to the ideological hegemony of ambition as sin.[11] Even within the "imaginary discourse" as reflected in literary texts, there are at times significant contradictions. As Michel Foucault writes, "A culture, imperceptibly deviating from the empirical orders prescribed for it by its primary codes . . . frees itself sufficiently to discover that these orders are perhaps not the only possible ones or the best ones."[12] At times these deviations, these challenges, can even be masked as explicit support of the dominant doctrine. This chapter considers the cultural expressions of ambition as sin present even in emergent challenges.

In poems, plays, pamphlets, sermons, and political tracts there is a clear and nearly ubiquitous influence of the dominant ideology—that is, ambition as sin. This was present, too, in histories of the time. Consider, for example, the 1609 history of the Spanish king *Morindos*.[13] When describing the Spanish witch Miracola, whom Morindos married, the anonymous author writes, "Her garments were of the finest Medean silkes, weav'd upon silver loomes by *Arabian* queens: Thus pomp and pride elevating her minde, as it were beyond the ambition of *Lucifer,* who sought to pull God out of heaven and esteemed no man of that royall birth, worthy to match with her in miriage."[14]

In Henry Roberts's *Defiance to Fortune; the Miseries of Andrugio, Duke of Saxonie* of 1590, the author breaks from his history for a brief disquisition on ambition consistent with the theological imperatives: "Ambition . . . is nothing but a desire to injoy honours, estates and great places. Further, it is a device of excesse, and contrary to modestie. . . . Oh that men would consider the fruits of ambition? . . . pawning their soules, to an eternall and moste miserable thraldome. Thus let us detest ambition whiche is an infinite evill, and companion of pride, so much hated of God and men."[15]

In poetry, too, ambition as sin, as evil, was a recurring theme in the late sixteenth and early seventeenth centuries. For example, Thomas Heywood, best known for his dramatic works, in his 1609 epic poem *Troia Brittanica* personifies ambition as a demon, one that feeds on human blood and flesh:

Oh blind Ambition and desire of Raigne
How camst thou by this rule in mortall breasts?
Who gave thee this dominion ore the braine?
Thou murdrest more, then plagues or fatall pests;
Thy drinke Mans bloud, thy food dead bodies slaine,
Treason and *Murder* are thy nightly guests:
Ambition knowes no lawe, he that aspires,
Climbes by the lives of brothers, sonnes, and Syres.[16]

Condemnation of ambition is most virulent among those most invested in mitigating its potentially challenging nature. Consider, for example, William Herbert (alternatively "Harbart"), Third Earl of Pembroke. Herbert was chancellor of the University of Oxford and later one of the founders of Pembroke College, Oxford. He was also a patron of

Shakespeare. He also wrote poetry, and in his *England's Sorrow* of 1606 he describes ambition as an

> Inhumane monster, borne of *Adam's* pride,
> *Eves* wish, sinnes scourge, God's wrath, heavens just ire,
> Earths shame, hells sonne, bloods river, envies pride,
> Natures defect, Deaths Queene, intestine fire,
> Men's grave, Kings feare, worlds woe, mans first desire;
> Ambition is th' essentiall cause of warre,
> Heavens bad prophet, murther blazing starre.
>
> State rending hooke, ambition is a fire,
> Which though it smothered lie deepe of breast,
> Still lively breaths, (how boundless is desire)
> And scornes prowd barre, albee that wisdome wrest
> Natures worst gift, yet nature cannot rest,
> But doth unmaske her blame, blame worthy all
> Who raise their fortunes by a kingdome's fall.
>
> Ambition is selfe-praising envies childe,
> Who doth beget of wrath, disdaine and rage,
> Cities sad spoiles, where many worthies pilde,
> In heapes consume, and she in every age,
> Workes strange effects upon this lower stage:
> Shee's deare to all, but most to them on hie,
> "Ambition seldome lives with miserie."
>
> Ambition is the roote of every ill,
> Whence discord (civil monster) doth arise
> Like Snake from dung: so springs inhumane will
> From heape of clay, sedition is all eyes,
> Which as a States-man to each secret pries:
> The ladder to ascend the breach of wall,
> "Intestine tumult works a Kingdomes fall.[17]

But these are what one might expect from the literary production of poets, the refined literary voices, or the passionate and eloquent exhortations of the elite.[18] If ambition as sin is truly a hegemonic concept, then one should find similar expression among the middling sort and common folk. But where to listen for that voice?

Fortunately, in early modern England, we need not strain too much but may turn instead to John Taylor, "The Water Poet," a humble ferry operator who had the unbridled audacity to speak in verse.[19]

Taylor was an unlikely candidate to attempt poetry. Born in Gloucester in 1578, he received a grammar school education before traveling to London, where he became an apprentice waterman. Watermen were cross-Thames ferrymen, proto–taxi drivers of sorts, at a time when London Bridge was the sole alternative for crossing the river.[20] Eventually he rose in his trade, and in 1613 he became one of roughly forty or so watermen responsible for ferrying members of the king's family and court. He made his home on the South Bank, a well-known haven for all manner of debauchery, an early modern Las Vegas without the glitter, a playground for the dissolute.

Those with Taylor's background who wished to write turned their talents most often to ballads, drinking songs, and the like. Not John Taylor, who recognized the profound social and educative challenges in climbing to the rank of poet. In the early seventeenth century, poets were members of an elite profession, molded with the gravity of learning and forged with the magic of the Muses.[21] Historian Robert Zaller argues that the elite men of letters, including poets, helped, through language, define the legitimacy of Tudor and early Stuart England.[22] Certain poets, too, were aware, as John Dryden wrote later in the century, of "that great charge which nature did ordain."[23] In fact, later in the century, Dryden would equate the restoration of the English monarchy with the restoration of literature itself!

> At length the Muses stand, restored again
> To that great charge which nature did ordain;

And their loved Druids seem revived by fate,
While you dispense the laws and guide the state.
The nation's soul, our monarch, does dispense
Through you, to us his vital influence.[24]

It seems that, to Dryden, Muses, like angels, recognize the wellspring of monarchy.

Taylor, aware of the seeming contradiction of the heroic expectations and his profession as waterman, wrote of himself in caustically self-deprecating terms as "a worthless gnat," "in poesy an artless creature," and of his "weak laborious muse."[25] He understood that, no matter his talents, he would never be regarded as a serious poet because of his station, background, and vocation.

Saying, the fellow that the same hath made,
Is a mechanick waterman by trade;
And therefore it cannot worth reading be,
Being compiled by such an one as he.[26]

And yet he prospered and achieved celebrity in early Stuart England, counting among his acquaintances some of the best-known, most respected poets of the period.[27]

Unlike Ben Jonson, Thomas Dekker, or Heywood, who targeted the refined reader, Taylor targeted a broad and popular audience. Of one poem he wrote, "There is no degree of man or woman, whatsoever, from the court to the cottage, or from the palace to the plough, but may make good use of this poem, either for merry recreation, or vice's defamation."[28] Another poem, "A Common Whore," was dedicated to "Lord, Master, Goodman, Gaffer, or Knave; Lady, Mistress, Goodwife, Gammer, or Whore."[29] Given his efforts to reach a broad audience, in his poetry we might expect the reflection of a certain popular sentiment. If Taylor was successful in accurately gauging this sentiment, we might also expect his works to sell well.

And sell well they did. It is estimated that by 1636 Taylor had sold between three hundred thousand and four hundred thousand copies of his work.[30] He accomplished this feat largely through grandiose acts of self-promotion, pioneering sales through subscription, and publicizing his works through outrageous public spectacle, all involving risk, or the perception of deadly risk. Could John Taylor take to the water in a paper boat and survive? Thousands lined the banks of the river to find out. Could John Taylor walk to Scotland with no money and no food without starving to death? His return to London was triumphant.[31]

He has been described as a Renaissance everyman.[32] But his verse may have been largely overlooked by scholars of Renaissance literature as beneath serious consideration.[33] For the cultural historian, however, and especially for those listening for the popular voice, Taylor is illustrative.

He is even more illustrative for our purposes. What would Taylor, the autodidact, the self-fashioned Water Poet who reached a broad audience, say about the quality that seemed to spur him? We might expect him to celebrate ambition or at least question its sinful nature. But this was not the case. In his poetry, he damned the swelling from which he himself might seem to suffer, as not only vice but sin. In "Urania," Taylor identifies

> The greatest plague, that ever came from Hell,
> Is to be puft and stuft with self-conceit:
> When men too *Ill*, esteeme themselves to *well*,
> When over-valued worth proves to light in weight,
> When *Self-love* and *Ambition* makes us swell
> Above the limits of Discretions height.
> When the poore *lay* displays his borrowed *plumes*,
> And man (unfeeling sin) to sinne presumes.[34]

The irony in these lines is striking. If ambition is that ardent desire for a higher station, the waterman who aspires to be a poet certainly qualifies. Taylor endeavors to realize his ambition through verse that damns the ambition he himself expresses in the act of writing poetry. Taylor cleverly subverts the social order while loudly proclaiming his support of it.

Stephen Greenblatt, in his seminal essay "Invisible Bullets," proposes that much of Elizabethan and Jacobean drama helped exert social and political control through a process of acting out a cycle of "subversion" and "containment."[35] That is, threats to social order are acted out and neutralized on stage as object lessons to those who might dare such things outside the drama. Sin could be acted out, order could be disrupted, but by the end of the play, sinners are punished and order is restored. John Taylor, however, enacts what I would suggest is an inversion of Greenblatt's paradigm. Taylor's literary ambition is subversive as it implicitly endeavors to elevate a waterman to a higher station than God hath given, while explicitly damning those who would endeavor to climb to a higher station than God hath given. The Water Poet subverts hierarchy in verse that extols the virtues of containment. At least this is the case when Taylor discusses ambition, the "greatest plague that ever came from Hell."[36] Elsewhere he calls ambition a "quenchlesse thirst" and "infernall Hag accurst," as well as a "damned Necromanticke Spell," the spur "to aspire to rebel."[37]

This striking contradiction is part of what makes Taylor so fascinating. One isn't sure if he is winking at the reader, damning ambition while cleverly rising. I think not. I think, rather, that he is conflicted, his struggle emblematic of a time when the dominant ideology overlaps with an emergent challenge to ambition as sin. He is more zeitgeist than trickster, reflective of warring ideals. *Ambition* was a buzzword in early modern England, like *communist* or *red* in the United States in the mid-twentieth century, a dirty word, connoting sin and insalubrity. Ambition could provoke a theological hegemonic knee-jerk response— to wit, ambition is sin and must be denounced—without necessarily a thorough consideration of the personal implications.

Yet dominant notions do not dissipate suddenly. They erode slowly. Perhaps there was no other way a waterman poet could rise to such heights, unless he was willing to damn that very aspiration. Not surprisingly, Taylor was never afforded the respect he so desperately craved.

While he was popular, his literary ambitions were thwarted by a culture that deemed his work mere doggerel.[38]

These seeming contradictory impulses in Taylor were present, too, in a roughly contemporaneous myth, captured in a popular tavern song of the era. Ballads, like poems by watermen, are helpful in gauging a popular attitude toward ambition, in listening for the common voice, this time sung, not spoken. The verses of this ballad tell of a boy and his cat and the great wealth and power that he achieved in what we might call a rags-to-riches story from early modern England.

This may come as a shock to some Americans. As Americans, we tend to lay claim to the rags-to-riches mythos as integral to our national character, a source of domestic pride. We can witness this tendency in the novels of Horatio Alger and, earlier still, in Benjamin Franklin's writings. In his autobiography, Franklin published a letter addressed to him that suggested his own attitude toward ambition: "How little necessary all origin is to happiness, virtue or greatness."[39] Franklin is, of course, also famous for his maxims, among them, "Early to bed, early to rise, makes a man healthy, wealthy and wise," the bon mot of the new American, the credo of the spirit of capitalism.[40]

We associate this maxim today with Franklin, but in fact it was a common English proverb of the late seventeenth century, dating to at least sixty-five years before Franklin's birth.[41] In fairness to Franklin, he never claimed that his maxims were original. He stated unequivocally in the 1746 *Poor Richard's Almanac*, "I know as well as thee, that I am no poet born; and it is a trade I never learnt. . . . Why then should I give my readers bad lines of my own, when good ones of other people's are so plenty?"[42] Subsequent generations have endowed Franklin with the mantle of American exceptionalism, as if he and the notion of ambition originated without antecedent.[43] Franklin is neither the first American, nor is he the first modern man, and the culture of achievement did not begin with him.

At a time when ambition as sin trumpets its dominance, we find England's most celebrated rags-to-riches tale dated to roughly 1605, a hundred years before Franklin's birth. It was, and continues to be, a powerful national myth that has retained its significance in England for more than four centuries. The question is, to what extent is the tale of Dick Whittington and his cat a reflection of, or evidence of, an emergent celebration of ambition, an indication of a shift? A careful consideration of this subversive tale demonstrates that although it seems to celebrate ambition in the rise of a Whittington to wealth and power, Whittington's myth is carefully circumscribed in ways that in fact reinforce the strictures against ambition. It is a rags-to-riches story that celebrates passivity, the observance of one's vocation, and trust in God's will. It is a rags-to-riches tale that both celebrates and condemns ambition, a story of a spectacular rise in which the hero's birth and station impeded nothing.

If you visit London, take the Tube to Archway and walk north up Highgate Hill. It is a tawny borough, marked by red Victorian buildings and Georgian architecture. Highgate Hill formerly adjoined the bishop of London's hunting estate, and it is here that one finds the Chapel of St. Michael's, whose crypt holds the remains of Samuel Coleridge, among others. Karl Marx is buried in Highgate Cemetery, as are George Eliot and Michael Faraday. The singer Sting bought Yehudi Menuhin's home in this neighborhood. As you walk along gray-brown perpendicular brick streets and modern apartment buildings, you will come upon a curious wrought-iron cage along the sidewalk. The cage itself is more than six feet high, surmounted with a flourish of twisting iron like the tendrils of a plant seeking the sky. Though the cage looks as if it should hold a bird, the spaces between the upper portions are too wide, and as one nears the cage, one realizes that it is intended not to keep anything in but to keep others out, to protect the bronze cat that sits on a stone in the middle of the enclosure. The cat sits on four legs, his body leaning southward. His face is nondescript, almost generic, as if he might be just an average house cat, unremarkable. But his eyes tell a different story; they are like the Greek and Roman vacuities, blank, noble spaces most often found in the sculpture of gods and emperors, eyes that convey history and myth. Those eyes are cast backwards, as the cat's small, oblong head twists northward toward London. The little statue seems odd and slightly out of place unless you know its history. For it is on this spot that the pivotal moment in the plot of England's first rags-to-riches myth is said to have occurred.[44]

The tale is of a poor boy who comes to London and rises from obscure origins to become a wealthy merchant and lord mayor of London. The unlikely vehicle for his rising is a cat. This common pet is transported across the seas by Dick's merchant master and traded to a foreign king—in some accounts, the king of Barbary—who is plagued by rats and has never seen a cat. The king pays a small fortune for the creature, and Dick is the fortunate recipient of the king's uninformed beneficence. Whittington, after achieving his station and fortune, uses them to help both the poor, building at his own expense several public buildings, and the English king, funding wars against France, for which Whittington is knighted. The history on which the tale is based tells a different story. "Poor Dick" Whittington was modeled on Richard Whittington, the third son of Sir William Whittington of Gloucester, born in 1360 or 1379. Although his year of birth is disputed, there is no arguing that he was not a commoner but was born to a father who was a knight. It is not known how Whittington came to London; once there, however, he did serve as an apprentice, probably to his father-in-law. He rose to serve as a councilman in the Coleman Street Ward and later became an alderman and a sheriff. When the mayor of London died in 1397, King Richard II named Whittington lord mayor.[45]

There is no reference in the records to "a cat," and some historians have speculated that "a cat" was really *achat*, a word for "trade" in medieval English, from the French *acheter*, "to buy," indicating that Whittington's wealth came from mercantile activity.[46] Others speculate that the reference may be to a type of ship, called a *cat*, used for transporting coal.[47] Coal, used primarily for iron smelting and lime burning, was a profitable trade in the latter half of the fourteenth century, and Whittington's fortunes came in part from the coal trade.[48]

Richard Whittington is mentioned in Richard Grafton's *Chronicle* of 1569: "This yere (1406) a worthie citizen of London, named Rychard

Whittyngton, mercer and alderman, was elected maior of the sayde citie, and bare that office three tymes. This worshipfull man so bestowed his goodes and substaunce to the honor of God, to the reliefe of the pore, and to the benefite of the comon weale, that he hath right well deserved to be regestered in the boke of fame."[49] Whittington's "fame" was recognized in Grafton, then, as one due to his commitment of his "goodes" to the "honor of God, to the reliefe of the pore, and to the benefite of the common weale." These characteristics are present, too, in the later myth, a celebration more of Whittington's unlikely rise than of the public benefits of that rise in the early seventeenth century. At a time identified by economic historians as one of nascent capitalism and societal transformation, the culture created a myth of rising even as the dominant ideology inveighed against ambition as sin. To what extent was this myth of rising, a myth of ambition, realized?

Consider the first published reference to the Whittington myth. It is made in 1605 and is a reference in passing from the stage play *Eastward Hoe*.[50] But a more interesting and illustrative reference is from Thomas Heywood's 1606 *If You Know Not Me, You Know No Bodie*. This two-part play, written soon after Elizabeth's death, is a dramatic rendering of the monarch's life and reign.[51] The passage that concerns us is found in part 2, which details the construction of the Royal Exchange:

> *Dean Nowell.* This Sir Richard Whittington, three times
>   Mayor,
> Sonne to a knight and prentice to a mercer,
> Began the Library of Gray-Friars in London,
> And his executors after him did build
> Whittington Colledge, thirteene Alms-houses for poore men,
> Repair'd S. *Bartholomewes*, in Smithfield,
> Glased the Guildhall, and built Newgate.
> *Hobson.* Bones of me, then I have heard lies;
> For I have heard he was a Scullion,

And rais'd himself by venture of a Cat.
Nowell. They did the more wrong to the gentleman.[52]

It is not surprising that Whittington appeared in a play that has come to be regarded as evidence of nascent capitalism in seventeenth-century England. But this passage indicates a certain disconnect between the historical Whittington and the Whittington of popular imagination. This was not uncommon. Many "learned fictions" arose in a time when the lines between legends and scholarship were not yet distinctly drawn.[53] Historian Adam Fox notes, "One of the most important features of the oral culture of sixteenth- and seventeenth-century England was the repertoire of stories and songs which concerned the past."[54] Those things that everyday men and women chose to claim as historical, regardless of the inaccuracies, are illustrative of contemporary cultural concerns.

This is certainly the case with the learned fiction of Dick Whittington. The first full account of the story is found not in a play or prose work but in a ballad. In the words of Anglo-American folksong scholar Phillips Barry, "The ballad is, the world over, a tale of common things. Simple events in human experience are its subjects."[55]

Ballads were a widespread form of popular entertainment in early modern England. As Fox writes, "Rhyming and singing were a ubiquitous and natural accompaniment to almost every aspect of work and leisure."[56] Some of the ballads were sung, others published on broadside sheets sold for a penny and consumed even by those who could not read. Nicholas Bownd noted in the 1590s, "Though they cannot reade themselves, nor any of theirs, yet will have many ballades set up in their houses, that so they might learne them, as they shall have occasion."[57] Bownd observed that these ballads performed a decorative function as well. Bownd found printed ballad pages in "the shops of artificers, and cottages of poore husbandmen," and Francis North commented on chimneys "where ballads are pasted round, and the folk sit about it working or merrymaking."[58] Fox notes that by "the early seventeenth century, if not before, every country alehouse had its 'painted cloath, with a row of balletts pasted on it,' or its 'cleanly room' with 'twenty ballads stuck about the walls.'"[59] Surprisingly, most historians of ideas ignore these sources. Yet a look at how common folk constructed or reconstructed the past allows us a view into the cultural attitudes beyond the elite sources.

In the ballad of Dick Whittington we hear the vox populi, a reflection of their attitudes toward ambition, their "cultural lies" and "learned fictions." The ballad, by Richard Johnson, is titled, "A Song of Sir Richard Whittington, Who by Strange Fortunes Came to Bee Thrice Lord Maior of London; with His Bountifull Guifts and Liberallity Given to This Honourable Citty," and was published in 1612 in Johnson's compilation of popular ballads, the *Crowne Garland of Goulden Roses*. I offer the myth from this ballad before considering the history from which it is drawn. The story continues to be told and published even some four hundred years later, as evidenced by the bronze cat that was dedicated in 1964, a sculpture of Whittington and his cat that complements the loggia of the 1999 Guildhall Art Gallery in London, and the many contemporary accounts in children's literature.[60]

Turning to the song of 1612, the words might be "new," but they were intended to be set to the tune of "Dainty thou come to me," a popular folk song. It is set in D major, within a limited melodic range, intended for common expression and general consumption rather than for a trained musician and rarefied audience. It was a song to be sung widely rather than performed.[61]

The ballad is a historical fiction, but again, as the quotation from Heywood's play indicates, it was widely assumed to be fact. The song tells the story of a poor boy, bred in Lancashire, who sets out for London. Later versions explain that Dick heard rumors of streets paved with gold, but there is no such suggestion in the 1612 version. In fact, there is no explanation for his migration, and from this, one can surmise that no explanation was necessary. In the early seventeenth century, the majority of London's population originally lived outside the city. Even at the top of the civic hierarchy, three-fourths of aldermen

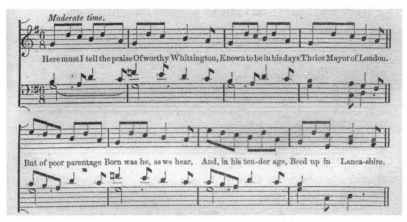

Self-made or God-made? The score to the popular ballad of Dick Whittington. William Chappell, *Popular Music of Olden Time: A Collection of Ancient Songs, Ballads, and Dance Tunes, Illustrative of the National Music of England* (1855–1859; reprint, New York: Dover, 1965), 517.

had been born outside London. This was a time of great internal migration, and London was a source of considerable pull.[62]

Dick Whittington finds a "dwelling" with a "marchant-man" who puts him to work in the kitchen as a "scullion."

> Poorely to London than
>   Came up this simple lad,
> Where, with a marchant-man,
>   Soone he a dwelling had;

Clearly, Dick is not content with his station. He accepts it, but grudgingly.

> And in a kitchen plast,
>   A scullion for to be,
> Whereas long time he past
>   In labour grudgingly.

The word *grudgingly* is significant because it indicates the seeds of a
rebellious soul, one who is ill-content with his vocation and station.

> His daily service was
>   Turning spits at the fire;
> And to scour pots of brasse,
>   For a poore scullions hire.
> Meat and drinke all his pay,
> Of coyne he had no store;
> Therefore to run away,
> In secret thought he bore.

Interestingly, the reason the ballad gives for Dick plotting to run away,
to break his bond to his master, is that his compensation is in room and
board, "meat and drinke," not "coyne." He is disappointed with the
lack of monetary compensation for his labor. There was a disparity in
modes of compensation for labor in seventeenth-century England. In
small agricultural economies, compensation was primarily from
household or agricultural production, "meat and drinke," as it were. In
London, however, workers received wages.[63] But the implication is that
he is a runaway; his plans are made "in secret." Dick is breaking an
implicit agreement of indenture and rebelling against his master. Quit
rates for premodern apprenticeship were quite high, despite the legal
disincentives to take that risk. It was an issue, however, especially
within the first two years of service, even within those guilds with an
expectation of an eventual mastery.[64]

Nonetheless, Dick decides to "purchase his liberty," though steal is
more apt, running away "towards his country," presumably back toward
Lincolnshire. But as he is running, he hears the church bells ring.
Though he had often heard them chime, on that day they sounded
somehow different.[65] As he listened more carefully, he could discern
actual words. The words were prophecy, a glimpse of his future, a promise that if he turned back, accepted his indenture and reassumed his
position, he would one day be rewarded.

But as he went along
    In a fair summer's morne,
Londons bells sweetly rung,
    "Whittington, back return!"

Evermore sounding so,
    "Turn againe, Whittington;
For thou in time shall grow
    Lord-Maior of London."
Whereupon back againe
    Whittington came with speed,
A prentise to remaine,
    As the Lord had decreed.

Dick returns to his apprenticeship as the Lord has decreed, but only after the religious prophecy and revelation encouraged him. This, while unusual, would not have been seen as outside the realm of possible, even given Dick's station. Keith Thomas writes, "One cannot disregard the fact that religious prophecy and inspiration were potentially open to everyone. Only the qualified could teach, remarked a mid-seventeenth-century writer, but anyone might be inspired to prophesy."[66]

What is unusual, however, is that this divine revelation is pre-occupied with the most seemingly irreligious of objectives: Dick's rise. The Lord seems to lure Dick back to his apprenticeship, to his vocation, not with a stern remonstrance against disobedience but with certain chiming enticements of wealth and status, of high station. Dick now turns quickly back resuming his life as a scullion before anyone is aware that he is gone. He suffers no punishment for his departure and thereafter works at his vocation with great contentment largely due to the fact that it is only temporary.

"Still blessed be the bells";
    (This was his daily song),
"They my good fortune tells,
    Most sweetly have they rung.

If God so favour me,
   I will not proove unkind;
London my love shall see,
   And my great bounties find."

Dick doesn't want to "prove unkind" to God. After all, God was kind enough to reveal to Dick his fantastic destiny, despite Dick's restlessness in his vocation and his grudging approach to his labor in it. If one accepted the ideology espoused by the homilies and Genevan sources as indicative of cultural attitudes, Dick Whittington would have been largely unimaginable. Ambition may be sinful, but aspiring to a high station may be acceptable if it is somehow indicated or encouraged by God. Yet this aspiration comes with a certain twist. Dick's ambition is a passive aspiration, a docile self-making. Unlike the witches in *Macbeth*, a play I discuss later in this chapter, whose satanic revelation pricks Macbeth to ambitious action, Dick Whittington's divine chimed revelation inspires him to do exactly nothing, a mediocre inaction. And for this he is ultimately rewarded.

Or is Dick Whittington's story a parable about ambition at all? Doesn't the acceptance of Divine Providence thoroughly preclude the possibility of luck, self-made? In the words of the Elizabethan bishop Thomas Cooper, "That which we call fortune, is nothing but the hand of God, working by causes and for causes that we know not."[67] Whittington is successful by remaining within his station, by working within his vocation, not by running off as Benjamin Franklin later would. Franklin's rags-to-riches story is one of actively disregarding certain constraints, legal, familial, and filial. In many ways, Dick Whittington's rags-to-riches story is a conservative parable, one that seems to celebrate ambition but in fact celebrates the opposite. Dick is not self-made but cat-made:

But see his happy chance!
   This scullion had a cat,
Which did his state advance.

Further evidence to this subversive parallel that suggests that it was intended to dissuade apprentices from quitting their masters is in a first verse added in 1649:

Brave London Prentices,
  Come listen to my song,
Tis for your glory all
  And to you both belong.
And you poor country lads,
  Though born of low degree,
See by God's providence
  What you in time may be.

Dick Whittington's ballad, while in some ways an emergent celebration of ambition, in others reflects the dominant strictures against it. It is meant to be sung, to encourage "prentices" to know their place and stay in it. It is a celebration of the possibility of great social mobility at a time when even a poor scullion could rise to become lord mayor of London, a myth in which one's birth need not determine one's destiny.

Two further aspects of the ballad are worth considering: how Dick makes his fortune and what he chooses to do with it once it is won. Dick makes his fortune through the almost alchemic magic of overseas investment and adventure, a merchant voyage in which lead is transmuted to gold or, in Dick's case, a common housecat is transmuted to gold. In the seventeenth century, the world outside England seemed to be the philosopher's stone, where both men and merchandise might be transformed from base metal to gold. Dick's cat is sold for "heapes of gold" to the king of the foreign land. And after the merchant ship returns, Dick gives up his life of scullion for the life of a merchant.

In this, Dick is extremely successful. After his success, he turns to public service. He becomes sheriff and later lord mayor of London. But according to the ballad, Dick Whittington further advanced his fame by conflating his individual ambition with national ambition. Whittington lends money to the king for England's wars.

More his fame to advance,
   Thousands he lent his king
To maintaine warres in France,
   Glory from thence to bring.

It is interesting to note that in Grafton's *Chronicles*, Whittington is acknowledged for forgiving loans and not given to suits, but there is no mention of loans to the king. We know that Henry VIII and Elizabeth both relied on merchants for loans, but James I was more dependent on loans than any of his successors.[68] This suggests the possibility of a historical loan made but is more likely reflective of an early seventeenth-century practice.

Nevertheless, service to the Crown in the ballad of Dick Whittington is consistent with the emergence in the late 1590s of the merchant hero figure in Elizabethan England. "It is no accident," writes scholar Laura Caroline Stevenson, "that the valiant principal citizen appeared in Elizabethan literature at the same time as the stereotype of the usurer was in decline; the authors who celebrated the virtues of merchants . . . [and] brought the exploits of famous and semi-legendary men of trade to the attention of the Elizabethan audience; . . . their works formed a popular history of merchants which showed that businessmen had a long tradition of service to the commonwealth and, more particularly, to the crown."[69]

Some of these merchant heroes found in the works of John Stow, Thomas Deloney, Thomas Dekker, William Haughton, and Thomas Heywood, among others, include characters with trajectories similar to Whittington's.[70] In the 1590s two plays and a poem appear about a fishmonger named William Walworth who rises to become mayor of London in 1381.[71] Like Whittington, Walworth demonstrates his allegiance to the king and exemplar service to the City. Other writers create fictional characters that show that tradesmen can exhibit a nobility that was thought to be a singular quality of the noble born.[72]

In the Whittington myth, however, Dick's nobility of spirit exceeds that of a merchant, as he transcends business concerns with a chivalric gesture.[73] Not only does he fund the foreign war, but he forgives all the loans to the king.

> And after, at a feast,
>   Which he the king did make,
> He burnt the bonds all in jeast,
>   And would no money take.
>
> Ten thousand pound he gave
>   To his prince willingly,
> And would not one penny have.
>   This in kind courtesie.

After using his good fortune to fund national military adventure and, as a "courtesie," refusing to be repaid, Whittington turns his attention to the poor.

Again, his ambition is not simply individual but indistinguishable from the public good.[74] But, avoiding the debates over what exactly constitutes English republicanism, perhaps it's best to simply summarize the constituent elements of the ambition as expressed in the Whittington myth, as this perhaps signals a shift toward an ambition that may be "acceptable." The salient features of this "new" form of ambition are as follows: a passive, patient waiting to rise within one's vocation; a belief in God's providence; foreign adventure, in this case mercantile; a merging of individual ambition with national ambition; and service to the people, which one could argue is also service to the king in that it ameliorates discontent and the potential for rebellion.

I qualify my recognition of an emergent form of ambition in the previous paragraph to allow for another interpretation. The other possibility is that the ballad of Dick Whittington, though a rags-to-riches tale, is not about ambition at all. If one believes in divine providence, then Whittington's rise was not self-made but God determined. Whittington remained in his vocation, was given a sign from God, and passively waited for fortune to find him. Unlike Benjamin Franklin, who broke his obligation to a brother to whom he was apprenticed, Whittington fulfilled his obligation to his master.

This more closely follows the Greenblatt subversion-containment paradigm, but in Whittington's case, the lesson is taught with sugar rather than vinegar. Whittington realizes the error of rejecting his station, of taking rebellion into his hands, before the act is done. Therefore, he is able to sneak home before the house awakes, and thus his act is undiscovered and can be undone. His reward for his self-containment is riches and power. God directs him. He listens and is rewarded. Can this, then, really be a tale of ambition? If ambition is "having a higher station than God have given or appointed unto us," certainly Dick Whittington achieves his station, duly appointed by God, as signaled by the speaking of the church bells.

The problem was that these subtleties might be lost on those "prentices" who would hear the song and aspire to a similar rise. In John Stephens's character book of 1615 we have some indication that these qualifications on aspiration were largely overshadowed by the myth of the rise itself.[75] Stephens's work was one of many character books that came into vogue as a literary genre in early seventeenth century. Character books updated a classical tradition associated with the Greek philosopher Theophrastus. Stephens's work followed Joseph Hall, the first English character writer.[76] Hall regarded the Theophrastan characters as "speaking pictures, or living images, whereby the ruder multitude might . . . learne to know vertue, and discerne what to detest."[77] He adopted the classical model but expanded on the Theophrastan characters to reflect a contemporary sensibility: "trod in their paths, but with an higher and wider step; and out of their Tablets [I] have drawn these larger portraitures." Yet Hall was a minister, a moralist, and later a bishop who was best known for his sermons.[78] His goal went beyond merely characterization. In his characters there was a moral objective: "If thou do but read or like these, I have done good hours ill; but if thou shalt hence abjure those vices, which before thou thoughtest not ill-favoured, or fall in love with any of these goodly faces of vertue; or shalt hence finde where thou hast anie little touch of these evils, to cleere theyselfe, or where any defect in these graces to supply it, neither of us shall need to repent of our labor."[79]

Hall's *Character of Vertues and Vices* was divided into two parts, the virtuous containing nine characters, and the vicious containing fifteen. Among his vicious characters was the "ambitious":

> Ambition is a proud covetousnes, a dry thirst of honor, the longing disease of reason, an aspiring and gallant madnesse. The ambitious climes up high and perillous staires, and never cares how to come downe; the desire of rising hath swallowed up his feare of a fall. . . . Finally, he is an importunate sutor, a corrupt client, a violent undertaker, a smooth factor, but untrusty, a restlesse master of his owne; a bladder puft up with the winde of hope, and selfe-love. Hee is the common body as a Mole in the earth, ever unquietly casting; and in one word, is nothing but a confused heape of envie, pride, covetousnesse.[80]

Hall's work inspired a spate of imitators, many of whom expanded their purview to satirical sketches of the world around them. One of those who followed Hall was John Stephens, not a minister but a member of Lincoln's Inn. Stephens did not include an ambitious man among his characters but did express his distaste for the quality itself.[81] This was most probably relevant to Stephens as by 1615 social mobility was a more common feature of life in England:

> Many aspiring fellowes you may see,
> Who after they and fortune doe agree,
> Come (by briefe windings) to be men elect;
> Through private means, heaven knows how indirect.
> To flourish quickly and advance their head,
> As if they tooke possessions from the dead.[82]

While the dominant ideology might proclaim ambition as sin, this passage reflects the anxiety over the social mobility that was rampant at the time. Lawrence Stone labels 1540–1640 in England as "the century of mobility."[83] He further discusses the "seismic upheaval of unprecedented magnitude" occasioned by the profound changes owing to this mobility.[84] Vertical mobility became common, and perhaps even more striking was the growth of the upper classes, which, according to Stone, "trebled at a period when the total population barely doubled. The number of peers rose from 60 to 160; of baronets and knights from 500 to 1,400; of squires perhaps 800 to 3000; of armigerous gentry from perhaps 500 to 15,000."[85] Ambition, like beauty, is in the eyes of the beholder. One man's aspiration is another's ambition. As God is mystery, it is difficult to determine the extent of God's gifts or appointments.

That said, Stephens expresses a common anxiety among the elite that the mobility smacked of the pernicious implications of ambition, as if the rise of many was unnatural or counterfeit, not at all what nature had intended:

> But now they flourish, and with honour swell,
> Whose poore beginnings every Groome can tel:
> As if a newfound Whittingtons rare Cat
> Come to extoll their birth-rights above that
> Which nature once intended.[86]

Here Dick Whittington is emblematic of the ambition of the poor, a group rising without any recognition that ambition must be qualified. Stephens calls Whittington's cat "rare," though it was well known from the tale that his cat was common. But Stephens is emphasizing that Whittington's trajectory and meteoric rise is meant to be a rarity, the exception rather than the rule. As Stephens indicates in his sketch, a man who endeavors to rise too high above his birth is attempting to "turne base copper into perfect gold: Counterfeit couzning wares." [87]

Stephens's emphasis on ambition as the spur to the creation of an unreal or artificial self was a common trope of Tudor and Stuart England, often found in tracts, pamphlets, poems, sermons, and, of course, in one of the most popular forms of entertainment, the theater.

In Elizabethan and Jacobean drama, ambition is firmly located, not surprisingly, in tragedy. I say not surprisingly because, as critic Irving Ribner astutely observes, myths of tragedy and myths of sin share common fundamental assumptions. Ribner writes:

> The experience of tragedy may bear a closer relation to that of religion than usually has been recognized. Different as the method of tragedy may be from that of religion, both pursue the same kind of knowledge. Tragedy and religion seek by different means the same affirmation of order. . . . Tragedy must impose upon the raw material of human experience a pattern in which the relation of human suffering to human joy becomes apparent, and out of this must come the feeling of reconciliation. . . . Like the Christian paradox of the fortunate fall, tragedy searches for order and purpose in apparent disaster, and in doing so it reinforces a system of belief which essentially is religious.[88]

This model for tragedy is consistent with Stephen Greenblatt's paradigm of subversion and containment discussed earlier. The Elizabethan and Jacobean model, however, is a departure from the classical theory of tragedy as articulated in Aristotle's *Poetics*. In the Aristotelian model, at the risk of oversimplification, a tragic hero, required to be "good," through some tragic flaw (*hamaritia*) brings about his own destruction and often simultaneously imperils the world that he inhabits, as his fate is often linked to that of the state or kingdom. By the end of the tragedy, the hero loses all but gains self-knowledge.[89] In Greenblatt's paradigm, the tragic hero is more complicated, sometimes evil. He exhibits a tragic flaw, yes, and his fate is often linked to the fate of the kingdom, but there is less emphasis on the self-knowing that Aristotle claimed as essential to tragedy. If one accepts the Greenblatt paradigm, essential to the ritual of subversion and containment in tragedy is the audience's recognition of the folly and ultimate demise of those who would attempt to subvert the natural order.[90]

This pattern is present in the works of the major tragedies of the period. When I speak of "the period" I include both Elizabethan and Jacobean drama under the general category of early modern drama, roughly the years 1574–1642. Considerable differences distinguish Elizabethan from the later Jacobean drama.[91] That said, as English colonies were being planted in the Americas, early modern tragedy conveys an attitude toward ambition consistent with the dominant ideology— that is, ambition as sin. Although the dominant ideology may be increasingly challenged during the first decades of the seventeenth century, ambition as sin retains its salience in the tragedies of Shakespeare, Ben Jonson, and George Chapman. In other words, challenges were clearly emerging, but the dominant ideology was still, well, dominant.

In Elizabethan and Jacobean drama, ambition is invariably rendered as incitation to vitiation, not only wrong but unnatural, frequently symbolized by shadow, artifice, monstrous birth, or hideous defects. These signs and symbols serve as both a reflection of the common understanding and a warning to those in the Elizabethan and Jacobean audience who would risk the destruction caused by ambition, rebellion, and other perilous acts of self-elevation. For example, Christopher Marlowe's *Tamburlaine the Great* and *The Tragical History of Doctor Faustus* have been seen as two distinct explorations of two distinct manifestations of ambition in man.[92] In *Tamburlaine*, the protagonist is ambitious for power through conquest, whereas in *Doctor Faustus*, the protagonist sells his soul to the Devil for the power of a Godlike knowledge. Leo Kirschbaum interprets *Doctor Faustus* as an orthodox text: "There is no more obvious Christian document in all Elizabethan drama than *Doctor Faustus*."[93] James T. F. Tanner reads *Faustus* as "an Orthodox Christian Sermon."[94] Marlowe begins the play following a pattern established by medieval morality plays, using a chorus to state the moral of the drama. The Chorus speaks of Faustus:

> Excelling all whose sweet delight disputes
> In heavenly matters of theology;
> Till, swoll'n with cunning of a self-conceit,

His waxen wings did mount above his reach,
And melting heavens conspired his overthrow.
For, falling to a devilish exercise,
And glutted now with learning's golden gifts,
He surfeits upon cursèd necromancy.
(Prologue.18–28)

By invoking the figure of Icarus, Marlowe, with great economy, employs a figure that in the sixteenth century was an emblem of ambition, of overreaching. Carlo Ginzburg, in his work on the image of Icarus, indicates that as the pursuit of scientific knowledge became more accepted in England, the figure of Icarus shifted from a warning to the emblem of a heroic, albeit not necessarily successful, aspiration.[95] But in the late sixteenth century, Icarus was still a figure that the English audience would have associated with the perils of ambition. An image from Whitney's *Emblemes* visually conveys the dominant conception of Icarus, principally informed by Ovid's *Metamorphoses* in late sixteenth-century England.[96]

This does not imply that an emblem of Icarus would have been necessary to convey the damning import of the pursuit of knowledge at the cost of one's soul. Historian of science Peter Harrison, in his work on curiosity, emphasizes the impact of the scriptural focus on discouraging the pursuit of "forbidden knowledge." He writes: "Protestant reformers came to emphasize the literal text of Scripture in an unprecedented way. This scriptural focus meant in turn that the Genesis narratives of the Creation and the Fall, including the crucial episode of the tree of knowledge, came to occupy a central position in early modern intellectual life. 'Forbidden fruit' was commonly associated with 'forbidden knowledge.'"[97] John Calvin wrote, "The desire for knowledge is naturally inherent in man and happiness is supposed to be placed in it." This was the temptation in Eden, and it continued to plague man, as "we all daily suffer under the same disease, because we desire to know more than is right, and more than God allows."[98] In terms that could have been applied to Marlowe's Dr. Faustus, the Calvinist theologian

Icarus falling. Geffrey Whitney, "On Astrologers," A *Choice of Emblemes* (Leiden, 1586), 28.

Lambert Daneau wrote of "the swelling and puffed Artes of Naturall Philosophie . . . a most stronge poison of humaine ambition."[99]

Though Marlowe rarely uses the word *ambition* in these plays, the edifying moral destruction that accompanies the unbounded pursuit of power or a Godlike knowledge serves as a dire warning. Like Adam, like Icarus, those who would fly too close to the sun fall. In their destruction and containment is the dramatic restoration of order. The Chorus in Marlowe's play concludes:

Faustus is gone. Regard his hellish fall,
Whose fiendful fortune may exhort the wise

> Only to wonder at unlawful things,
> Whose deepness doth entice such forward wits
> To practise more than heavenly power permits.
> (Epilogue.4–8)

In those lines one hears echoes of sixteenth-century interpretations of Ovid's Icarus:

> Wee also lerne by Icarus how good it is to bee
> In meane estate and not to clymb too hygh, but too agree
> Too wholsome counsell: for the hyre of disobedience is
> Repentance when it is too late forthinking things amisse.[100]

Often, in Elizabethan and Jacobean tragedy, the playwright identifies tragic villains by their association with ambition. The villains are those who would celebrate ambition or recognize it as either inspiration or an inevitability of human frailty, a temptation too tempting to resist. In *Tamburlaine*, Marlowe uses this device when Tamburlaine the conqueror expresses words that are as suitable for Dr. Faustus as for himself, in recognizing "aspiring minds" as fundamental to natural man:

> Nature, that framed us of four elements
> Warring within our breasts for regiment,
> Doth teach us all to have aspiring minds:
> Our souls, whose faculties can comprehend
> The wondrous architecture of the world
> And measure every wand'ring planet's course,
> Still climbing after knowledge infinite,
> And always moving as the restless spheres,
> Wills us to wear ourselves, and never rest.[101]
> (2.7.18–26)

It is not the temptation that distinguishes the hero from the villain. It is the acting upon it that damns a Faustus or a Tamburlaine.

Marlowe is not alone in using an attitude toward ambition to help an audience distinguish between a villain and a hero in tragedy. In George Chapman's *Tragedy of Chabot, Admiral of France*, the Chancellor Poyet, who is the embodiment of courtly corruption and the perversion of justice, posits a theory of man and ambition. He speaks of obedience as an "infection," warning the treasurer:

> Come, be not Sir infected with a spice
> Of that too servile equitie, that renders
> Men free borne slaves, and rid with bits like horses.[102]
> (1.181–183)

The Chancellor inverts the dominant religious teachings regarding submission and slavery. In the preceding passage, man is not a slave to sin, but a slave to obedience. He continues:

> When you must know my Lord; that even in nature
> A man is *Animall politicum*,
> So that when he informes his actions simply
> He does it both gainst policie and nature,
> And therefore our soule motion is affirm'd
> To be like heavenly nature circular,
> And circles being call'd ambitious lines
> We must like them become ambitious ever,
> And endles in our circumventions;
> No tough hides limiting our cheverill mindse.
> (1.184–193)

The notion that politics are the product not of fallen man but of natural man would signal villainous intent and, again, the inversion of the proper order. Ultimately, order is restored as the good king recognizes the Chancellor's villainy for which he is duly punished.

Ben Jonson, too, explores the destructive and damning potential of ambition in his tragedies. Jonson uses Roman history as the subject for his tragedies, notably *Sejanus His Fall* and *Catiline His Conspiracy*. *Catiline* was first performed in 1611. In chapter 1, I discussed the Stoics' treatments of Catiline as a figure of ambition. Recall that Sallust warned that "ambition drove many men to become false; to have one thought locked in the breast, another ready on the tongue."[103] Drawing on Sallust and Plutarch, Jonson reflects a similar attitude toward ambition. Both *Catiline* and *Sejanus* portray a Rome corrupted by plots, conspiracy, ambitious courtiers, and dark intrigue. The classical, stoic preoccupation with ambition as *vitium*, as I discussed in chapter 1, is now reinterpreted on the stage in early modern England. Sejanus is an ambitious, tragic villain who rises by the patronage of the emperor Tiberius and is destroyed by rising too high. Tiberius did "emboldeneth Sejanus to farther, and more insolent projects, even the ambition of the Empire."[104] Ironically, Sejanus comments while manipulating his co-conspirators, "Ambition makes more trusty slaves, then need" (1.2.106). In fact, Sejanus has been made untrustworthy by his ambition.

In *Catiline*, Jonson again turns to Rome and the threat that ambition poses to the stability of the state. In act1, scene 5, the state of Rome is bemoaned, its dissolution, the "excess is her disease" (line 20).[105] It is a place, once great, now corrupted:

And now, ambition doth invade
Her state, with eating avarice,
Riot, and every other vice.
(1.5.46–48)

But this play takes a more complex view of ambition. Certainly it has been a place invaded by ambition. But it is not only the villain Catiline who embodies that vice. Cicero, too, is the product of ambition. Catiline is from an old, established family, yet he seeks to destroy the Roman republic. Cicero is not a man of noble birth, and considered an upstart, a "popular man"(2.96). Yet he is called upon to save the Republic. Catiline shows a profound contempt for Cicero, remarking on his low birth:

Remember who I am, and of what place,
What petty fellow this is, that opposes;
One, that hath exercis'd his eloquence,
Still to the bane of the nobilitie:
A boasting, insolent tongue-man.
(4.157–161)

Cicero, for checking Catiline, is rewarded and celebrated by Rome, and in Jonson's neo-Stoic tragedy we witness the seeds of what later would be called a "republican virtue," an ambition tempered and in service of the public good.

But Jonson was fairly faithful to the original sources. Though called "tragedies," in many ways Jonson's plays are more in the vein of historical drama than the typical Elizabethan or Jacobean tragedy.[106] His resistance to the form may be one of the reasons why Jonson's plays were so poorly regarded in his time, a time largely dominated by the works of William Shakespeare.

Throughout Shakespeare's works, tragic heroes often exhibit a dangerous ambition, one that drives them upward beyond the prescribed limits of their birth. These tragic figures endeavor to manufacture selves of higher estate, but these, ultimately, cannot be sustained. Their heroic transformation is a paradox, one in which a tragic character is both made and unmade. In grasping at all, they often lose themselves, as their "unlawful and restles desire" to have "a higher estate then God hath geven or appoynted unto them" ultimately betrays them. There is an inevitable turmoil within the individual, a "madness" of sorts, a warring between selves, one substantive, one illusory, one God intended, the other man-made, one a mask, the other a face hidden and torn by what Stephen Greenblatt calls the "chaos of infinite desire."[107] In their desire, they endeavor to subvert the natural order. In their fall and destruction, the desire for subversion among the audience is thereby contained.

When Shakespeare speaks about ambition in the early seventeenth century, he speaks from a perspective formed by, and to an audience

generally familiar with, biblical and homiletic injunctions against ambition. Shakespeare's plays do not leave the world turned upside down.
Inevitably there is a restoration of order and a destruction of those who
would defy it. Shakespearean scholar Robert N. Watson writes of ambition in Shakespeare's plays as a "Sisyphean task . . . a perpetual quest
for elevation that is baffled by some moral equivalent of the law of gravity."[108] This "law of gravity" assumes a poetic justice in which these
tragic heroes, or villains in the case of Richard III, are destroyed by the
disorder they, in fact, create in their "unnatural" subversion of natural
order. The word *villainy* itself is derived from the word *villein*, or low-
born serf. It is no accident that the essence of villainy in Elizabethan
drama often assumes the dramatic action of intriguing to rise.

This interpretation of Shakespearean tragedy supports Stephen
Greenblatt's subversion-containment paradigm. That is, threats to the
social order are performed and then mitigated on stage, thereby reas-
serting the social norms and political order. But Greenblatt's assumptions are not uniformly accepted. Critic Jonathan Dollimore suggests
a challenge: "To contain a threat by rehearsing it one must first give it
a voice, a part, a presence — in the theater, as in culture."[109] Franco
Moretti suggests that tragedy is radically different than other forms of
literature. While he suggests that literature endeavors to "secure consent," for the dominant hegemonic ideology, Elizabethan and Jacobean
tragedy "more radically than any other cultural phenomenon of the
same period" endeavored to subvert "the values of absolute monarchy,
thereby paving the way, with wholly destructive means, for the English
revolution of the seventeenth century."[110] Moretti further suggests, "Tragedy disentitled the absolute monarch to all ethical and rational legitimation. Having deconsecrated the king, tragedy made it possible to
decapitate him."[111]

Let us consider both the radical and conservative perspectives
through a play preoccupied with both regicide and ambition, Shakespeare's *Macbeth*. *Macbeth* is the Shakespearian tragedy that most
closely suggests ambition as sin, with the homiletic and Genevan biblical implications, a drama that echoes the rebellions of both Lucifer

and Adam.[112] The play is a parable of the temptation and resultant damnation of a man who succumbs to ambition's seductive siren call. It may be that it serves a subversive function in that it imagines a regicide, and in that imagining the English people recognize its possibility. But this was not Shakespeare's intent. The play is a profoundly conservative dramatization of the hazards of ambition, in which self-making is fashioned with the blood of a king and motivated by "vaulting ambition."

The *Macbeth* that we know, the only substantive text, is from the 1623 folio, though it is generally agreed that Shakespeare originally wrote the play in 1606, a few years after James I took the throne. It was almost certainly performed on August 7, 1606, at Hampton Court before two kings, James I and King Christian of Denmark, who seemed, by all accounts, oblivious to any subversive intent gleaned by twentieth-century critics like Dollimore and Moretti.[113] *Macbeth* opens with a short scene, a mere thirteen lines long. Three witches enter amid thunder and lightning. They speak in juxtapositions, opposites, tensions, and unresolved ambiguities, suggesting a certain disruption in order, mirrored in the angry skies, linked rhetorically to a single name, Macbeth. It is a scene in which battles may be "lost and won" (1.1.4), in a time when "fair is foul, and foul is fair" (1.1.12). These mysteries set a tone for the play, and as such, the witches are more than mere prologue and might be considered an induction. Induction is a dramatic technique, according to scholar Muriel Clara Bradbrook, in which "the presenter introduced the character or expounded a moral . . . sometimes particular personages were used to cast a certain tone over the rest of the play."[114]

What, then, is the tone or moral they are expounding? *Macbeth* is a drama of sin, the sin of regicide and rebellion, spurred by the sin of ambition. Witches, as I discussed earlier, are more than just magical occult figures. The Bible couples witchcraft and rebellion in 1 Samuel 15:23: "For rebellion is as the sin of witchcraft." And, indeed, the very next scene helps clarify any ambiguity in what Shakespeare's use of witches intends. King Duncan, his son, Malcolm, and several Scottish thanes and attendants enter as alarms sound. King Duncan demands that a bloody captain report on the status of a revolt that is under way. The disorder that the witches suggest, as well as the rebellion, is confirmed by the state of affairs in Scotland. Duncan's kingdom is in revolt.

But much to his pleasure, it is reported that one of his thanes, "brave Macbeth," has fought valiantly to crush the rebellion.

> For brave Macbeth—well he deserves that name—
> Disdaining Fortune, with his brandished steel,
> Which smoked with bloody execution,
> Like Valour's minion carved out his passage
> Till he faced the slave,
> Which ne'er shook hands, nor bade farewell to him,
> Till he unseamed him from the nave to th'chaps
> And fixed his head upon our battlements.
> (1.2.16–23)

The rebel Macdonwald is referred to here as "the slave." Here Shakespeare uses "slave" in a religious rather than a literal sense. According to *An Homilie against Disobedience and Wylfull Rebellion*, rebellion is not simply one sin but "all sins against God and man heaped together," exemplified by Satan, "the grand captain and father of rebels."[115] Macdonwald, in committing the sin of rebellion, has become a slave to sin as expressed in John 8:34, "He who commits sin is a slave to sin."[116] Elsewhere in his oeuvre Shakespeare suggests this fundamental religious connection as in the *Rape of Lucrece*: "Eater of youth, false slave to false delight, / Base watch of woes, sin's pack-horse, virtue's snare!" (lines 927–928). Scholar Lily Campbell views the connection between sin and Shakespeare's tragic heroes: "The tragic hero sins under the influence of passion, his reason failing to check his passion. When . . . passion has taken possession of his will, has perverted his will, when in perfect accord with passion his reason directs evil through the will, then we have a villain, one who is dyed in sin."[117]

We cannot be sure what passion has moved Macdonwald to rebellion. But an early modern English audience would be familiar with
the "principall causes of rebellion" as identified from the pulpits
throughout England at the time: "Though many causes of rebellion
may be reckened, and almost as many as there be vices in men and
women . . . the principall and most usuall causes, as specially ambition
and ignoraunce. By ambition, I meane the unlawful and restles desire
in men to be of higher estate then God hath geven or appoynted unto
them. By ignoraunce, I meane no unskilfulnesse in artes or scienes,
but the lacke of knowledge of Gods blessed wil declared in his holy
word."[118]

But the play quickly turns away from Macdonwald to Macbeth,
who inherits Macdonwald's former titles, both thane and rebel. And
while Macdonwald's motivation might be obscure, suggested by the
Homily, but never explicitly stated, Macbeth's temptation will be soon
explicitly named—ambition.

Macbeth is first enticed by the witches in act 1, scene 3. They serve
like a foul fair wind on the smoldering coals of Macbeth's ambition
when he is hailed both by his current title and, potentially, his future
title, that of king. When Macbeth presses them for further information
of this "strange intelligence," they vanish. Banquo and Macbeth describe their departure as follows:

> *Banquo.* The earth hath bubbles, as the water has,
> And these are of them. Whither are they vanished?
> *Macbeth.* Into the air, and what seemed corporal
> Melted as breath into the wind.
> (1.3.77–80)

This description is remarkably close to the way in which Shakespeare in *Hamlet* describes the quality of ambition itself: "dreams indeed are ambition, for the very substance of the ambitious is merely
the shadow of a dream. . . . I hold ambition of so airy and light a quality that it is but a shadow's shadow" (2.2.245–246, 248–249).[119] Like

dreams, like shadows, the witches disappear. In *Julius Caesar*, ambition is described as the soldier's virtue. But initially Macbeth, the soldier, is unmoved by the promise of becoming king. He proclaims a policy of passivity. In an aside he remarks: "If chance will have me king, why, chance may crown me / Without my stir" (1.3.142–143).

Macbeth believes that he can resist the temptation of ambition. His wife, Lady Macbeth, recognizes Macbeth's ambition but not his corruption by it. In act 1, scene 5, Lady Macbeth comes on stage alone, holding a letter from her husband that recounts his strange moment with the witches and their prophetic promise. Lady Macbeth responds with fear, not at the witches or their sinful temptation, but:

> Yet do I fear thy nature,
> It is too full o'th'milk of human kindness
> To catch the nearest way.
> (1.5.14–16)

Lady Macbeth fears that her husband's humanity might stand in the way of his greatness. She speaks to him, in response to his letter, though still in soliloquy:

> Thou wouldst be great,
> Art not without ambition, but without
> The illness should attend it.
> (1.5.16–18)

It is not that Macbeth is without ambition. But he is, at this moment in the play, able to check his passion. His ambition has not yet perverted his will and he is not yet moved by the inordinate desire for kingship that would spur him to take it. Lady Macbeth, like Eve, will move her husband towards damnation:

> Hie thee hither,
> That I may pour my spirits in thine ear

And chastise with the valour of my tongue
All that impedes thee from the golden round.
(1.5.23–27)

But Lady Macbeth recognizes that all that makes her human mili-
tates against the act of regicide and rebellion. Shakespeare juxtaposes
humanity with these sinful acts, of which one is capable only if one
willingly relinquishes that which makes one human, kind, caring, loving and dutiful. Lady Macbeth must, as the Devil does in inciting rebellion, "blow the cole, to kindle [his] rebellious hearte to flame into
open deede."[120]

But she is not the devil and worries that she is all too human. She
calls on spirits to help her shed the impediments of her humanity, this
time rooted in her gender:

Come, you spirits
That tend on mortal thoughts, unsex me here
And fill me from crown to the toe topfull
Of direst cruelty; make thick my blood,
Stop up th' access and passage to remorse
That no compunctious visitings of nature
Shake my fell purpose nor keep peace between
Th'effect and it.
(1.5.38–45)

She even calls on hell to obscure the act, from heaven itself:

Come, thick night,
And pall thee in the dunnest smoke of hell,
That my keen knife see not the wound it makes,
Nor heaven peep through the blanket of the dark,
To cry, "Hold, hold."
(1.5.48–52)

The desire to hide from God, reminiscent of Genesis 3:9–10, is further echoed after the regicide.

Banquo suggests:

And when we have our naked frailties hid
That suffer in exposure, let us meet
And question this most bloody piece of work,
To know it further.
(2.3.1119–122)

Recall Genesis 3:9–10: "But the LORD God called to the man and said unto him, Where are thou / Who said, I heard thy voice in the garden, and was afraid, because I was naked, and therefore I hid myself." Holinshed, in his histories, from which Shakespeare drew, describes Lady Macbeth as the Eve-like spur to the act of regicide, pricked by ambition. Lady Macbeth "lay sore upon him to attempt the thing, as she was verie ambitious, burning in unquenchable desire to beare the name of queen."[121]

This is not the first time the killing of the king is linked to Adam's fall in Shakespeare. Consider, for example, in *Henry V*, when the conspiracy of Cambridge, Scrope, and Grey is exposed, King Henry condemns them thus,

I will weep for thee,
For this revolt of thine, methinks, is like
Another fall of man.
(2.2.138–140)

The Edenic allusions in *Macbeth* are suggested, too, in Lady Macbeth's urging that her husband obscure his true purpose, to "look like th'innocent flower, / But be the serpent under't" (1.5.64–65).

The Genevan notes explicitly recognize the cause of Adam's fall: "he was fallen by ambition." They also explicitly state that Adam ate the fruit "not so much to please his wife, but moued by ambition at her persuasion" (Gen. 3:6, marginal note).

In the moment before his act of regicide, Macbeth recognizes the motivation for his own fall and the injustice of it. He begins with the triple obligations, that of kin, subject, and host:

> First, as I am his kinsman and his subject,
> Strong both against the deed; then, as his host,
> Who should against his murderer shut the door,
> Not bear the knife himself.
> (1.7.13–16)

Then he extols Duncan's virtue as king and recognizes that his act of murder is not only wrong but will result in "deep damnation":

> Besides, this Duncan
> Hath borne his faculties so meek, hath been
> So clear in his great office, that his virtues
> Will plead like angels, trumpet-tongued against
> The deep damnation of his taking off.
> (1.7.16–20)

Further, the resultant impact of his death will cause such mourning and despair that the "tears shall drown the wind." In this evocative image, Shakespeare, with economy, conveys the absolute inversion of order, as kings die, and rather than the wind producing tears, angels produce tears that can quell even the wind:

> And pity, like a naked newborn babe
> Striding the blast, or heaven's cherubin horsed
> Upon the sightless couriers of the air,
> Shall blow the horrid deed in every eye,
> That tears shall drown the wind.
> (1.7.21–25)

Macbeth fails to adequately rationalize his barbaric act and recognizes his motivation finally:

> I have no spur
> To prick the sides of my intent, but only
> Vaulting ambition which o'erleaps itself
> And falls on th'other—
> (1.7.25–28)

Ambition in *Macbeth* is the spur to rebellion and regicide. But again, Shakespeare suggests that the act of regicide is an extreme perversion of the will. A passion, an ambition that can drive Macbeth, or anyone for that matter, to that pinnacle of damnation is unlike any other sin. *An Homilie against Disobedience and Wylfull Rebellion* places rebellion at the most extreme of sins:

> All sinnes that may be committed against man, who seeth not that they be all contayned in rebellion? For first, the rebels do not only dishonour their prince, the parent of their countrey, but also do dishonour and shame their naturall parentes, if they have any, do shame their kinred and freendes, do disher-ite and undo for ever their chyldren and heyres. Theftes, rob-beries and murthers, which of all sinnes are most lothed of most men, are in no men so much, nor so perniitiously and mischievously, as in rebels. For the most errant theeves and cruelest murtherers that ever were, so long as they refrayne from rebellion, as they are not many in number, so spreadeath their wickednesse and damantion unto a fewe: they spoyle but a fewe, they shead the blood but of few in comparison. But rebels are the cause of infinite robberies and murthers of great multitudes, and of those also whom they should defende from spoyle and violence of other; and as rebels are many in mum-ber, so doth their wickednesse and damnation spread it selfe unto many. . . . Thus you see that al Gods lawes are by rebels

violated and broken, and that all sinnes possible to be committed against God or man be contained in rebellion.[122]

In Shakespeare's play, Macbeth's crime is so terrible that the sin is one
that requires the abnegation of his humanity. Macbeth, like Lady Macbeth, recognizes that in order to kill Duncan he must be something
other than a man. When she urges him to the act he responds, "I dare
do all that may become a man; / Who dares do more is none" (1.7.46–
47). Maynard Mack observes a trajectory in Macbeth's character after
the act of regicide towards "an uneven and continuing retrogression
from the earlier awareness to a condition in which all faculties are at-
tenuated to a male and murderous courage, noble and admirable only
as a beast of prey is noble and admirable. Macbeth's tragedy . . . is of
decreasing internal awareness. . . . a diminished and gradually empty-
ing consciousness.[123]

His narrowing into a beast of prey is mirrored in the imagery of
Macbeth as a "bear" tied to a stake (5.4.1–2). By using animal imagery
and an increasingly narrowing perspective, Shakespeare illustrates the
hold of ambition, as Macbeth has become a slave to sin, a beast. David
Brion Davis has observed the crucial link between slavery and animalization.[124] In Macbeth, the protagonist becomes a slave to sin and bound
to his ambition, he becomes nothing better than a beast, a man of actions, not thoughts. Bound to ambition, Macbeth becomes an ignorant
brute, and his life a "tale / Told by an idiot, full of sound and fury /
Signifying nothing" (5.5.25–27).

Well, that's not entirely true. But at this point in the play, Macbeth's perspective is ironic, as his parable signifies the risks of ambition,
rebellion, and regicide to an audience not bound to sin and capable of
a humanity and perception that now eludes the beast Macbeth. It is a
life replete and imbued with echoes to the myth of Satan and Adam's
fall, original sin and damnation, told by a man damned by ignorance
and ambition.

This may be why Macbeth's death is staged without any expected
soliloquy or redemption that might accompany it. Macbeth's death is

sudden, curtailed, and anticlimactic. He is killed offstage. We learn of his death in act 5, scene 8, through a stage direction: *"Exeunt[,] fighting. Alarums. [Re] enter fighting[,] and Macbeth slain. [Exit Macduff, with Macbeth's body.]"* Furthermore, Macbeth's final words in the play are words of action, rather than reflection:

> Before my body,
> I throw my warlike shield. Lay on, Macduff,
> And damned be him that first cries, "Hold, enough!"
> (5.8.32–34)

Given that Macbeth dies, we can only suppose that it is he who first cried, "Hold, enough!" if not in words, in his ultimate physical submission. But we already know that Macbeth is damned, and Shakespeare alludes to this in Macbeth's final line, "And damned be him that first cries, 'Hold, enough!'" He is the one who submits. He is the one who is damned well before his death in battle, in his dark act of ambition.

But still, when Macduff reenters carrying Macbeth's body, it is surprisingly sudden, rather abrupt. One is left wanting the closure of some consideration. The 1623 text does not even offer a last elegiac anti-tribute to Macbeth, a reiteration of the perils of immorality and ambition. Macbeth's only consideration is offered by Malcolm, who refers to him as a "dead butcher," and Lady Macbeth as a "fiend-like queen," in the final speech of the play (5.9.36). The last words belong to the king, who will not dignify ambition with any lengthy or eloquent disquisition, nor is Macbeth dignified in the abstract as we are left finally with the concrete image of only his bloody head.

Restoration dramatists were troubled, too, and recognized this absence. Sir William Davenant, editing the play for audiences in the late seventeenth century, gives Macbeth a final line: "Farewell vain world, and whats most vain in it, ambition!"[125] This awkward line is later purged. But for most of the eighteenth century, it was the Davenant version that was performed both in England and the colonies. There is evidence that George Washington was in the audience at Williamsburg when

the Davenant version of *Macbeth* was there performed in 1759.[126] Theater was frowned on in much of colonial North America as an impious
diversion. Some early theater companies sought to assuage this criticism by billing their productions as "moral lessons in five acts."[127] One
can almost imagine Colonel Washington, in the eighteenth century,
sitting in the theater for a moral lesson against ambition and rebellion
in Shakespeare's *Macbeth*.

David Garrick, friend of Samuel Johnson and famous actor on the
English stage, inserted a speech in *Macbeth*, a final reflective soliloquy. In the eighteenth century Shakespeare's texts were not yet sacro-
sanct.[128] His plays were altered and "improved" by well-meaning editors who believed that such matters as poetic justice required that
Cordelia live.[129] It is not too much of a stretch to suppose that Garrick
may have found Shakespeare's original, one that eludes us some four
hundred years and a London fire or two later:

> 'Tis done! The scene of life will quickly close.
> Ambition's vain, delusive dreams are fled,
> And now I wake to darkness, guilt and horror;
> I cannot bear it! Let me shake it off—
> 'Twill not be; my soul is clogged with blood—
> I cannot rise! I dare not ask for mercy—
> It is too late, hell drags me down; I sink,
> I sink—Oh!—my soul is lost forever!
> Oh![130]

Well into the nineteenth century, *Macbeth* was performed with this edition, though it disappeared in the nineteenth and twentieth centuries.
It is tempting to read into this omission. Was an explicit denunciation
of "ambition" less attractive as ambition itself became more acceptable
in Anglo-American culture? That is, Macbeth can be condemned but
not so ambition.

Whether this can fully account for the omission is open to debate,
but what is interesting is that some later critics argue that the play is not

at all a condemnation of ambition but instead an affirmation of its attraction, the seductive allure of its destructive potential.[131] Nietzsche, adopting this position to the extreme, writes of Macbeth's ambition: "He who is really possessed by raging ambition beholds this its [sic] image [Macbeth] with *joy*; and if the hero perishes by his passion this precisely is the sharpest spice in the hot draught of this joy. Can the poet have felt otherwise? How royally, and not at all like a rogue, does [t]his ambitious man pursue his course from the moment of his great crime!"[132] Though Nietzsche argues that Shakespeare must have shared his view, there is little evidence in the play itself. The spice in the pot is Nietzsche's pinch, not Shakespeare's.

But I think Nietzsche hints at something here, though he overstates it, telling us more about his philosophy than Shakespeare's. *Macbeth* was written and first performed at a time when ambition was being realized to a greater extent than in any other time in English history. As I mentioned earlier, Lawrence Stone labels 1540–1640 in England as "the century of mobility."[133] *Macbeth* is a play about ambition's damning and destructive potential at a time when the men and women in the audience might have been shifting uncomfortably in their seats, aware of their own perilous passions.

Given the overwhelming rising in this period in *Macbeth*, unlike in *Richard III*, Shakespeare allows his audience a sympathetic avenue of understanding. Macbeth is a villain, but he is a complicated villain. Shakespeare intended his audience to identify with Macbeth to a certain extent, to experience a vicarious passion, and perhaps that is what Nietzsche was on the edge of when he spoke of the "joy." Robert Watson agrees: "We may view Richard [III] with a horrified admiration, but we identify with Macbeth from within. Shakespeare accomplishes this, makes Macbeth eligible for the fear and pity that permit catharsis, by encoding many of our repressed impulses, many of the rash wishes society has obliged us to abandon or conceal, within Macbeth's conventionally dramatic desire to replace the king."[134] Although I agree that we see Macbeth "from within," I would argue that during this period of "seismic upheaval" and the concomitant agonizing over it, Shakespeare in *Macbeth* is suggesting, rather, an absolute other against which the audience might favorably measure their own passions. Rather than relishing in the joy of ambition, or simply an audience's identification with a dramatic desire, Shakespeare suggests a line, a Lady Macbeth and Macbeth, behind which all the ambitious men and women of the audience might stand and find comfort. *Macbeth* warns but reassures, for while those who lived in that time may be ambitious, they are safely within the limits. They may burn with the passion of ambition, but they are not Macbeth, that Satanic other, the regicide, well, not yet.

3

The Plague and Countervailing Passions

We are much beholden to Machiavel and
others that write what men do and not what
they ought to do.
—Francis Bacon, "Of Ambition"

Ambition must be made to counteract
ambition.
—James Madison, Federalist No. 51

In the first two chapters I discussed that ambition as sin was the dominant ideology in early modern England. Recall that it became a form of official English state policy. This policy was effected through local clergy who were given written homilies. These homilies were read from the pulpits throughout England. These were dire homilies, packaged messages delivered from the pulpit to mitigate individual longings in an era when individuals, for the first time in history, might read the Bible in English. As I discussed, the marginal notes in the Geneva Bible were another political message, wrapped in a sacred text, that gave greater weight and sanctity to the seventy or more warnings against the evils of ambition. These biblical and homiletic warnings were reflected, too, in the literature of the period, as consistently negative portrayals of ambition and the ambitious were captured in poems, plays, ballads, and histories.

But by the seventeenth century, it was clear that even though ambition might be inveighed against as sin, defined as a truly destructive, vicious passion, and associated with rebellion, Satan, madness, and malcontent, it was a constant phenomenon of English life and culture.[1] In *The Passions and the Interests: Political Arguments for Capitalism before Its Triumph*, a seminal work on the rise of capitalism, Albert O. Hirschman notes the emerging recognition in this period of the impossibility of repressing the passions, among which he notes ambition. Hirschman describes the repression of the passions as a misguided effort "of assuming the problem away."[2]

By the 1600s, there was a growing recognition of the inevitability of ambition and the utter futility of appeals to the virtuous in man to quell its hunger. In response to the inadequacy of repression, and recognizing still ambition's destructive potential, new strategies for mitigating the dangers of ambition emerged. One of the most significant of these was what we might colloquially term "fighting fire with fire," what David Hume would later call countervailing or pitting one powerful passion against the other.[3] The idea of countervailing passions later finds its essential place in American history at the roots of the American system of government. It is succinctly and significantly articulated in Federalist No. 51 when James Madison wrote, "Ambition must be made to counteract ambition."[4]

Hirschman represents the scholarly consensus in attributing the emergence of pitting one passion against another to the early seventeenth century, particularly to Francis Bacon and the rise of new secular scientific empiricism. Hirschman considers the emergence of countervailing as "a consequence of [Bacon's] systematic attempt at shaking off the metaphysical and theological yokes that kept men from thinking inductively and experimentally."[5] In addition, he writes that "the idea of controlling the passions by playing one off against the other is, moreover, highly congruent with the irreverent and experimental bent of his thought." He further attributes the origins of Bacon's thought to his "intensive experience as a politician and statesman."[6] Yes, Bacon did seek to shake off the theological yokes, was a politician and statesman, and had an experimental bent to his thought. Yet these generalizations fail to recognize the specific context of Bacon's emergent thought and the precise ways in which science and medicine influenced his political strategies. As a matter of fact, no scholar who writes on the Federalist Papers and the significance of countervailing passions in American and English constitutional history, suggests anything other than vague generalities in explaining why or how Bacon makes this conceptual leap. While scholars attribute the origin of Bacon's theory of countervailing passions to a single source, *Advancement of Learning,* I look to the ways in which Bacon articulates the theory of countervailing passions, focusing on ambition, in texts that are invariably ignored by scholars. Bacon's importance and how he reimagines ambition signal a watershed in the trajectory of the idea. Bacon suggests new strategies for managing ambition, urging that we think of it in terms other than sin and Satan, and he even suggests the shocking proposition that ambition might be harnessed for noble purposes.

Francis Bacon was writing at a time when the plague periodically decimated London's population. Science and medicine in this era were largely preoccupied with understanding the causes and remedies for this devastating illness. This chapter places the origins of countervailing within this context with a specific eye to what Bacon calls "the secret virtue of sympathy and antipathy."[7] In the early seventeenth century, illness was evidence of God's anger for humankind's many sins. In many cases, plague victims themselves became the embodiment of sin. This occurred during the rise of science and the science of medicine, which included the belief that disease could be effectively treated. The logic follows that if sin and disease are synonymous, and disease can be treated, then sin, too, could be treated.

The plague, as described in the medical tracts of early modern England, was attributed primarily to three causes: sin, humoral imbalance, and corrupted air. The passions, like the plague, were linked or likened to humoral imbalance, corrupted air, and sin. Ambition, in fact, was called a "plague," a "choler," a "canker on the soul," like the cankers on the bodies that wasted with ubiquity.

In attempting to treat the plague, philosophers of medicine, including Bacon, formulated many hypotheses predicated on a fundamental concept: poison could be used to counteract poison. As poison could be used to counteract poison, passion could be pitted against passion, and ambition could be used to counteract ambition. Reimagining ambition as illness allows for a corresponding shift in strategies for managing it. Sin can only be repressed. Illness, however, can be treated. Ambition retained its insalubrious associations but shifted from the theological to the medical and scientific realm. And in these realms, one devastating illness preoccupied the best minds of the day: the plague.

But the plague was more than just a medical epidemic; it was a violent cultural rupture that shattered the social order and touched the lives of men, women, children, paupers and princes, bishops and magistrates. Although the plague was first noted in 1348, with the increasing urbanization of England's population in the late sixteenth and early seventeenth centuries, it revisited with a renewed devastation and epidemic desolation.[8]

The statistics tell one story; they quantify to some extent the destruction. The plague struck in 1563, 1578, 1593, 1603, 1625, 1636, and 1675, with mortality rates exceeding 20 percent in the peak years of 1563, 1603, and 1625. These, again, are just the mortality rates. They do not include the estimated 20 to 40 percent of the populace who managed to recover from the disease. Even when mortality from the plague was not at its peak, the threat was constant, with frequent, though less deadly, outbreaks through the years 1603–1611.[9]

Significantly, the statistics of mortality are not simply retrospective. In the early seventeenth century death was quantified and mortality rates intruded violently into the public consciousness. For the first time, the City of London took administrative measures to publish and distribute reliable statistical data in the form of readily available "bills of mortality" printed on broadsides. These were printed weekly, sold for a penny, and subsidized by the royal and municipal authority.[10] From 1603 onward, death became more than personal and anecdotal. It was public, official, printed news, not an elite source but a penny tract of quantifiable despair.

Although these statistics suggest the extent of the impact, individual accounts do better service in aiding our comprehension of the ubiquity of the illness, death's ghastly visage: "Death stares us continually in the face, in every infected person that passeth by us, in every coffin which is daily and hourly carried along the streets: the bells never cease to put us in mind of our mortality."[11] The images, the infected people, were a dreadful sight. Contemporary accounts depict and describe the suffering and the symptoms. These were attempts to comprehend the incomprehensible, leveling empirical observation toward a malady that took both the wicked and the innocent, the young and the old, the wealthy and the poor. As one author wrote, these forays into empirical observation were intended to "express the nature of the Plague . . . for we can scarce comprehend it in a proper definition."[12] The many tracts on the plague were intended to exert some measure of control over that which defied control, to make sense of the senseless. They describe the horrific symptoms in considerable detail, in quasi-medical language, the Galenic theories of humoral imbalance and early modern scientific certitude on the efficacy of leeching, cupping, vapors, and bad air, pressing to the surface of these descriptions, adding poignancy, underscoring the futility and inadequacy of the tools within their reach:

> They are molested with a desire to vomit, and oftentimes with much and painfull vomiting, wherein greene and blacke matter is seene . . . answering in proportion to the excrements of the lower parts, the Stomacke being drawne into a consent with the Heart, by reason of the vicinitie and communion of the Vessels; oftentimes Blood alone, and that pure, is excluded and cast up in vomiting; and it is not onely cast up by vomiting out of the Stomacke, but also verie often out of the Nosethrils, Fundament, and in Women out of the Wombe; the inward parts are often burned, and the outward parts are stiffe with cold, the whole heat of the Patient being drawne violently inward, after the manner of a Cupping-Glasse, by the strong burning of the inner parts; then the Eye-lids wax blew, as it were through some contusion, all the whole Face hath a haspect, and as it were the colour of Lead, the Eyes burning red, and, as it were, swolne and puffed up with Blood, or any other humour, shed teares; and to conclude, the whole habite of the Body is some-what changed and turned yellow.[13]

This condition was accompanied by a delirium, a fever-induced madness: "Many have a burning Feaver, which doth shew it selfe by the Pacients ulcerated Jawes, unquenchable thirst, drynesse and blacknesse of the Tongue, and it causeth such a Phrensie by inflaming the Braine, that the Pacients running naked out of their Beads, seeke to throw themselves out of Windowes into the Pits and Rivers that are at hand."[14] If the afflicted did not die from the fever, the illness advanced to produce visual signs of its visitations in the forms of "tumour[s] under the Armeholes or in [the] Groyne, or Spots (vulgarly called Tokens) appeare over all the Body, or Carbuncles arise."[15] Modern microbiologists identify the tumors as swelling in the lymph nodes called "buboes," from which bubonic plague derives its name.[16] Early modern accounts provide anecdotal evidence for determining the likelihood of death, based on observations of behavior (including a "loathing of meats"), a wide variety of physical manifestations and delirium, as well as a "reading" of the carbuncles themselves:

> If the Flesh of the Carbuncle be dry and blacke, as it were seared with a hot Iron, if the Flesh about be black and blew, If the matter doe flow backe, and turne in, if they have a laske, with greatly stinking, liquid, thin, clammy, blacke, greene, or blewsish ordure. . . . If the Eyes waxe often dimme, if the Nose thrils be contracted or drawne together, if they have a grievous crampe, the Mouth be drawne aside, the Muscles of the Face being drawn or contracted equally or unequally; If the Nailes be blacke; If they be often troubled with the Hickit, or have a Convulsion and revolution over all the Body, then you may certainly prognosticate that Death is at hand.[17]

There were generally thought to be three main causes of the plague: God, as punishment for sin; infected air; and an imbalance of humors in the individual. This formulation is consistent throughout pamphlets and tracts on the plague. The documents make little distinction between science and theology and often combine the two in identifying the sources of the plague. While acknowledging God's role in punishing sinners as a major cause of the epidemic, the tracts attempted to provide scientific (albeit to our standards pseudoscientific) causes for the pestilence. God may work in mysterious ways, but in the plague literature of early modern England, considerable ink was spilled to demystify these workings. God and science had not yet assumed a stark polarity. Explanations divine and otherwise comfortably occupy texts without any need to explain what modernity might demark contradictory realms. Some texts stipulate that God works through nature to effect his will.[18] Others list God among other causes of pestilence. This is part of what makes these texts so very interesting. It has been said that in the early seventeenth century the "English intellectual was more than half medieval and around 1660 he was more than half modern."[19] These texts are substantive examples of a world in transition.

More important, in discussing the transition of sin, by attributing the pestilence to sin, sin became imagined as illness. While medieval allegories of hell and vice might have imagined the vicissitudes of eternal damnation, in early modern England, with the horrific visual reminders of the wages of sin, man had made his own hell on earth. Sin was manifested and visited on man as epidemic illness, the reminders of which were inescapable, the causes of which were explicitly suggested in scripture. "The first cause, I say, is sinne," wrote the medical practitioner Thomas Thayre in 1603. Citing scripture, Thayre "proved" the divine origins of pestilence: "How long will this people provoke me," the Lord demands of Moses, "and how long will it be ere they beleeve me, for all the signes I have shewed among them? I will smite them with the pestilence." He posed the rhetorical question "why?" The answer was "because they have murmured against me, and have rebelled, not keeping nor observing my lawes."[20] Here, sin, rebellion, and the plague are linked. As we saw in chapter 2, any reference to rebellion, particularly rebellion against God, is by extension a reference to ambition. Recall that in the 1570 *Homilie against Disobedience and Wylfull Rebellion*, the principal and most usual causes of rebellion are ambition and ignorance.[21] In the plague tracts of the early seventeenth century, the scriptural sins of rebellion against God are tied to the contemporary plague that is evidence of his displeasure: "Manie and great plagues hath this our land tasted of in times past, and it is not yet tenne yeares since this Citie of London was visited and afflicted with this sicknes . . . cutting off and taking away a great multitude of people . . . and I doubt not but sin was a great cause thereof . . . we daily dishonour him by committing of sinne."[22] During the plague outbreak of 1625, one minister reminded his suffering flock that "the Devill watcheth all occasions to mutinie and rebellion."[23] Margaret Healy notes the increasing rhetorical link between the political sedition and plague in early modern London.[24]

In addition to the great suffering, these tracts impressed on the people a shame, a guilt, a certain national and personal responsibility for their affliction. England was suffering the pestilence because of the great sin of its people. "Our sins indeed testifie against us, that we are a rebellious & stifnecked people."[25]

For some theologians and even poets, the physical manifestations of the plague were directly linked to maladies of the soul, a physical synonymy: "All these blowes are intended to be the remainders of sinne in us, not to our selves, but that the spots of the soule may be drawn forth by these plague spots on the body, and the sinne-sores of the soule may runne and be cut out of these bodily sores."[26] The poet John Davies wrote, "Our sins (foule blots) corrupt the Earth and Aire; / Our sins (soules blotches) all this All defile." For Davies, they were not "remainders" but one and the same.[27]

The rhetorical association between plague and ambition, and ambition as a disease of the soul, can be found in antiquity. In the fourth century, Saint Ambrose referred to ambition as a *pestis occulta*, or "hidden plague."[28] This ancient association now resurfaced in England. References to ambition as a disease of the soul are noted as early as 1563, immediately following the outbreak of plague, one of the most devastating plague years in English history. In the late 1560s Tudor interlude "Inough Is as Good as a Feast," in a debate between Wordly Man and Heavenly Man, Heavenly Man asks:

What men are more wicked, wretched and miserable:
Then those that in riches account their blisse,
Beeing infected with Ambition that sicknes uncurable.[29]

Further, ambition is described as:

this canker pestilent
Corrupting our Realm to our utter decay,
   Ambition I mene which cheefly dooth reign.[30]

In the interlude *Triall of Treasure*, of 1567, ambition is associated with plague in much the same manner and language:

What men are more foolish, wretched and miserable,
Then those that in these treasures accompt their whole blys,
Being infect with ambition that sickness incurable.[31]

And again, ambition and the cankers of the plague are rhetorically associated:

We have sene of late daies this cancar pestilent,
Corrupting our realme, to our great decaie,
Ambition I meane, which chiefly did raigne
Among those that should be examples to others.[32]

A "rebellious and stifnecked people," then, were suffering from a sickness incurable as just punishment for their ambition. For the first time, though, ambition had a visible, physical manifestation in the forms of "cancars" and other plague symptoms. Ambition, too, formerly an abstraction but now linked with disease, adopted the physical characteristics of illness. Recall that the Water Poet, John Taylor, describes ambition as "the greatest plague that ever came from Hell."[33] In the *Anatomy of Melancholy*, Robert Burton, citing Ambrose, refers to ambition as "a canker of the soul, an hidden plague," and, citing Saint Bernard, as a "secret poison."[34]

In 1616 Thomas Adams published *Diseases of the Soule: A Discourse, Divine Morall and Physicall.*[35] The book illustrates the transition from sin to illness as it names several diseases of the soul and links them to bodily illness. It discusses the causes, symptoms, and cures of each. Among the diseases of the soul, Adams includes an "Immoderate thirst and Ambition" as "Disease Number 10."[36] Adams characterizes ambition as a "disease of the soul." The cure for this disease is humility: "For the bodily disease, caused of heate and drinesse, Physicians prescribe *Oxicratum*, a drinke, made of vinegar and water sodden together. . . . To *cure* the immoderate *Thirst of Ambition*, let him take from God this prescript: *He that exalteth himselfe, shall be brought low: but he that humbleth himselfe, shall be exalted.* . . . That a glorious Angell by ambition became a Divell . . . the first step to heaven's court is *humilitie.*"[37] As sin was one of the major causes of disease, repentance was thought to be among the cures. In fact, a prayer against the plague includes a renunciation of the sin of ambition in hopes of winning God's mercy and an abatement of the scourge of pestilence. In the title of Anthony Anderson's "Approved Medicine against the Deserved Plague: A Prayer against the Plague," of 1593, the plague is acknowledged to be of divine origin and a just manifestation of God's indignation.[38] The prayer acknowledges a sinful nation, one marked by "wanton appetites & carelesse abuse" that invites the "threatened Judgements" of God's displeasure. Among the appetites acknowledged and renounced in the prayer is ambition. Noteworthy, the prayer itself is described in medical scientific terms as *medicine.* This medicine was to be applied to a nation of sinners suffering from the plague, which they had brought upon themselves:

> But O swéete Father haue mercie, and pardon our sinnes, (euen the whole trée, with hir braunching fruits,) which at this present, we heartely disclayme, and wherewith, euen the téeth of the whole Land, hath béene set on edge, namely infidelitie, incredulitie, and all impietie. No faith, no truth, no mercy, no knowledge of thée in our harts, though great pretence of thy Religion in our lippes, but by falsehood, and cunning circumuention, one of another, by lying lips, and decitfull tongues, vanitie, hath béene tossed, one to another, pryuat pilffrie, and open stealth, robbing at home, and rouing abrode, swearing, forswaring, whorring and killing, oppressing, & deuoureing, to all our powers and pollicies, euen blood vnto blood, passing by pleasure to pleasures, from profite to pride, *from pride to ambition, and in ambition, to inward contempt,* & outward disdaine, each one of another.[39]

The prayer places blame for the plague on a society that has lost sight of God. It is acknowledged that the origin of the plague was not mysterious but an angry God's judgment on a sinful nation. But as there was growing recognition that contact with the ill enabled its spread, there was a growing risk, too, that the ill themselves would come to be the embodiment of sin. As sin was tantamount to a spiritual isolation from God, the victims of the plague, the "King of Terrors," suffered the actual isolation of quarantine.[40] The Plague Orders, instituted from the 1580s on, were "set down of the Lord Mayor for repressing of disorders."[41] These laws were accompanied by threat of severe legal retribution, including hanging.[42] Sufferers were shut in houses, with red crosses painted to mark their isolation and ultimate dissolution. Daniel Defoe, though writing of the plague that struck England later in the century, depicted the breakdown of community and the solitude of the sufferers: "Now many houses are shut up where the plague comes and the inhabitants shut in. . . . It was very dismal to behold the red crosses, and read in great letters, 'Lord, have mercy upon us,' on the doors, and watchmen standing before them with halberd; such was the solitude about those places, and people passing by them so gingerly and with such fearful looks, as if they had been lined with enemies in ambush that waited to destroy them."[43] In the time of plague, the ill became the embodiment of sin itself.

But as the laws dictating quarantine indicate, there were other causes of the plague besides sin. Drawing on Galen and Hippocrates, among others, early modern philosophers of medicine speculated on the "corruption of the air" and "the imbalance of the humors" as the two other principal causes of the plague.

Air could be corrupted by a number of factors, not only by the dead and dying. "The first cause whereby the aire may bé corrupted," proclaimed Thomas Thayre in 1606, "is through the unwholesom influence of the planets; who by their malitious disposition, qualitie, and operations, distemper, alter and corrupt the aire, making it unwholesom unto humane nature."[44] Most philosophers of medicine accepted the role of the planets in both illness and cures. Even the efficacy of bleeding was predicated in part on timing the treatment with proper planetary alignment.[45] But "aire" could be corrupted, too, by the "venomous evaporation arising from the earth, as from fennes, moores, standing muddie waters, and stinking ditches . . . or dead bodies unburied."[46] Francis Bacon writes that the "aptness or propension of air or water to corrupt or putrefy, (no doubt) is to be found before it break forth into manifest effects of diseases, blastings, or the like."[47]

But signs and signals, natural and otherwise, were imbued with the mystery of vague comprehensive incomprehension and the surety of a proud, authoritative unknowing. Their prognostications were like those of astrologists or fortune-tellers, speaking in the most general terms and therefore never wrong. Consider, for example, William Bullein's late sixteenth-century treatise, A *Dialogye Bothe Pleasaunte and Pietifull Wherein Is a Goodly Regiment against the Fever Pestilence*. The presages of the plague included: "eclipses in the Sunne and Moone . . . or muche Southe Wind . . . and verie colde nightes, and extreame hotte daies, and much chaunge of weather in little time, or when birdes do forsake their egges, flies or thinges bredyng under the ground, doe flie high by swarmes into the ayre, or death or fishe or cattell, or any dearth goyng before, these are the sygnes of the Pestilence, and evident presages of the same."[48]

The alternative was far more awful—helplessness in the face of devastating illness. One somewhat perplexing aspect of plague, given the external factors and causes, was why some people would be struck by the illness and others not, even within the same household. Along with God and corrupted air, the third reason offered an explanation: internal factors, specifically, the individual's internal logic, or what was theorized, at the time, as a balance or imbalance of humors.

Humoral theory originated in antiquity. The Greek philosopher Empedocles theorized a world constructed of four elements: earth, air, fire, and water.[49] From the four elements, Hippocrates and later Galen and the Arabic philosopher Avicenna comprised a theory of medicine predicated on four humors.[50] From their writings, a set of hypotheses generally referred to as humoral theory suggests that human beings are made up of these four essential components: yellow bile, black bile, phlegm, and blood.[51] These elements are ideally in balance, but in any individual, one humor could be slightly dominant. According to the theory, the dominance of any humor led to a behavior or a certain recognizable set of personality traits. An excess of any one humor, however, led to an unhealthy imbalance that could result in illness. The skilled physician recognized the imbalance and treated the patient accordingly. In some cases, the imbalance could be treated through drawing off an excess of any one humor through bleedings or purges. Other times, diet and herbs could influence humoral balance or the restoration of any imbalance.

"This is the reason that divers persons living together in one aire," reasoned Thomas Thayre in the early seventeenth century, "that one is infected and not another, namely, the disposition of the body: for those naugtie, corrupt & superfluous humors." Balance was the key, what the Greeks called *eucrasia*. The imbalance, or *dycrasia*, occurred when individuals were at risk.[52] "As for example," Thayre continued, "*if choler do putrifie within the vesselles*, it ingendreth *febris ardens* or *febris causon*, a hot and a dangerous fever, working his malice in the concavite of the liver and lunges and about the heart."[53] This imbalance, according to the theories expounding in plague literature of the early seventeenth century, created a susceptibility to the corrupted air:

> Now such bodies, (I say), wherein there is such superfluous humors abounding, in the time of any infection, receiving into their bodies the corrupt and venomous aire, are thereby infected . . . whereas in bodies voide and frée from such superfluous humors, there the infectious aire hath not such matter to worke upon: and againe, nature is more strong and forcible to resist and expell a corrupt and infectous aire although received. . . . Here the reason is apparent why one person is affected and not another.[54]

An excess of any humor, as with choler in the example Thayre gives, created a dangerous imbalance, allowing corrupted air to turn an otherwise healthy individual into a disease-stricken soul.

The medical philosophical speculation that illness could be caused by a humoral imbalance had its correlation in the passions. Francis Bacon, in his essay *Of Ambition*, frames ambition in terms that are strikingly similar to those of the dominant plague theories of his time. Bacon writes, "*Ambition is like choler.*"[55] Bacon here is describing ambition not as sin but as a humor, the excess or "stoppage"[56] of which could, as Thayre describes, "putrifie the vessels" and cause illness. Bacon wrote extensively on the plague. It preoccupies him in seven out of ten chapters of his work *Sylva Sylvarum: A Natural History in Ten Centuries*.[57] In these chapters he considers common causes and treatments, as well as the philosophical bases for illness and its remedies. Of particular significance to the connection between countervailing passions and plague is his discussion of treatments for the plague. In chapter 10, Bacon addresses the theoretical basis behind treatments for illness in a section titled: "Experiments in consort touching the secret virtue of sympathy and antipathy." Bacon writes of "little bladders of quicksilver, or tablets of arsenic, as preservatives against the plague." The fundamental principle for this practice, as Bacon explains, is "not as they conceive, for any comfort they yield to the spirits, but for that being poisons themselves, they draw the venom to them from the spirits."[58] That is, poison was used to counteract poison.

The notions of sympathy and antipathy are not unique to Bacon. Mercury was used in treating a number of different ailments, including syphilis and the plague, predicated on this fundamental theoretical basis.[59] One common treatment for the plague was the Italian treacle, a concoction made in part of the poison of the viper's flesh. The plague's poison was often imagined in terms of *dycrasia*, or humoral imbalance, which could be neutralized with amulets of arsenic or other strong herbal concoctions worn around the neck "for the purgeing of all cholericke and melancholy humors."[60] The theory of sympathy and antipathy may be traced to antiquity.[61] But it was Bacon who extended these treatments to the passions and to whom I now turn.

Bacon's significance in the construction of an ideological modernity is almost axiomatic. John Locke, Isaac Newton, and Bacon were considered as almost a secular philosophical trinity in the late eighteenth century.[62] Thomas Jefferson was particularly taken with Bacon.[63] In an 1811 letter to Benjamin Rush, Jefferson recalls a meeting from his time in George Washington's cabinet. Vice President John Adams and Treasury secretary Alexander Hamilton met with Jefferson at his lodgings to discuss an urgent matter, as directed by Washington, who was away from Philadelphia at the time. "The room being hung around with a collection of the portraits of remarkable men," Jefferson continues, "among them were those of Bacon, Newton and Locke. Hamilton asked me who they were. I told him they were my trinity of the three greatest men the world had ever produced, naming them."[64] For Jefferson, these three were the minds against which all others might be measured. In his 1814 biographic sketch of Washington, he wrote: "I think I knew General Washington intimately and thoroughly; and were I called on to delineate his character, it should be in terms like these. His mind was great and powerful, without being of the very first order; his penetration strong, though not so acute as that of Newton, Bacon or Locke."[65] In fact, Jefferson was said to keep a picture of Sir Francis Bacon with him, in Douglass Adair's words, "much as a devout Roman Catholic maintains a shrine with images and pictures in his home."[66]

Yet Bacon's contribution to the founders extends to a fundamental concept with the English and later the American system of government—namely, the notion of "countervailing passions." In Federalist No. 51, *The Structure of Government Must Furnish the Proper Checks and Balances between the Different Departments*, James Madison recognizes ambition's potential to destroy even liberty. But he realizes that warnings alone are inadequate to the task of curbing its devastating potential. He expounds on the necessity of "separate and distinct" departments of government as essential for the survival of the Republic. Madison writes, "In order to lay a due foundation for that separate and distinct exercise of the different powers of government, which to a certain extent, is admitted on all hands to be essential to the preservation of liberty. . . . *Ambition must be made to counteract ambition.*"[67] Ambition counteracting ambition, the countervailing of passions, finds its essential place in American history at the very roots of the American system of government.[68] This reflects what can be considered a dominant strategy or philosophical paradigm in the late eighteenth century, not only found in Madison's writing, but also reflected in the works of David Hume, Henry Home (Lord Kames), and Paul-Henri Thiry, Baron d'Holbach.[69]

Although the notion of countervailing passions became dominant in the late eighteenth century, Hirschman and others recognize it roughly a century earlier, in Spinoza's *Ethics* (1675): "An affect cannot be restrained nor removed unless by an opposed and stronger affect. . . . No affect can be restrained by the true knowledge of good and evil insofar as it is true, but only insofar as it is considered as an affect."[70] Perhaps because scholars ignore the connection of the passions and their fundamental relation to sin, they likewise ignore how countervailing made its way into mainstream seventeenth-century theology. The assumption is static. Sin can only be repressed. Once vice is teased from theology to secular philosophy, new strategies are realized, but only within the secular realm. But in the sermons of Thomas Manton, a seventeenth-century puritan divine and chaplain to Oliver Cromwell, one discovers a theological manifestation of countervailing expressed before the publication of Spinoza's *Ethics*. In a sermon on Ecclesiastes, Manton, though not advocating the countervailing as a strategy for managing sin, nonetheless recognizes the ways in which poison can counteract poison, sin can contradict sin: "*Whence come Wars and Fightings among you? Come they not hence, even of your Lusts, which war in your Members?* Desire of Riches contradicts Idleness; and the toilsom Cares and Labours of this World, that Ease which the Flesh affecteth; disgraceful Lusts are contradicted by Ambition and Pride."[71] But the emergence of countervailing, as I mentioned earlier, has been traced to the writings of Francis Bacon. Scholars, such as Hirschman, cite a single work—Bacon's *Advancement of Learning*—in delineating the origins and development of countervailing passions in Anglo-American thought.[72] Scholars, however, largely overlook the proposition of countervailing passions in Bacon's other works, some of which enjoyed a much wider circulation, including *The Essays, Novum Organum,* and *Sylva Sylvarum.*

Advancement of Learning is generally recognized as the ideological progenitor of countervailing passions. In some ways, Bacon's treatment of ambition is consistent with the dominant ideology of the time, reflective of the Genevan biblical denunciations of ambition as sin. In other passages, his intent is less clear. In book 1, Bacon discusses original sin. Recall that in the marginal notes in the Geneva Bible at Genesis 3:22 specify that "Adam ate the fruit not to please his wife, but because he was moued by ambition." Bacon describes the motivation in different terms; he attributes man's fall to the desire for "the moral knowledge of good and evil."[73] This is a subtle shift. One might argue that the moral knowledge of good and evil constituted Adam's desire for a higher estate, a forbidden knowing. But Bacon makes no explicit attribution to ambition as one finds throughout the religious and secular writings at the time. In addition, Bacon later remarks that God's "first great judgment" against "the ambition of man" was not the eating of the forbidden fruit but "the confusion of tongues."[74] This interpretation is consistent with a Genevan biblical interpretation regarding the Tower of Babel as an expression of ambition as I discussed in chapter 1.

Bacon then moves away from a discussion of ambition specifically, and away from references to specific passions as sin, to a discussion of the passions in general. In book 2, Bacon writes about the "affections," which he uses broadly and somewhat synonymously with the passions. Bacon writes of "medicining the mind" against the "perturbations and distempers of the affections."[75] This is consistent with a Stoic interpretation. Recall that Seneca speaks of ambition as a *mala mentis humanae,* and Robert Burton similarly conceives of ambition and the passions in terms that modern psychiatrists might refer to as a psychological imbalance.[76] Bacon considers the affections to be the cause of this imbalance, as minds without affections are calm. In the following passage,

Bacon likens a mind without passions to a calm sea and the affections to tumultuous winds: "For as the ancient politiques in popular estates were wont to compare the people to the sea . . . the mind in the nature thereof would be temperate and stayed, if the affections, as winds, did not put it into tumult and perturbation."[77] This metaphor is not original to Bacon. From antiquity, passions or affections had been imagined in terms of winds or storms in the air and sea. What is important and fundamentally relevant to our discussion of ambition is that there were principally two interpretations of the winds, one derived from Aristotle, the other from the Stoics. Aristotle saw the passions as winds that acted as motivating forces, moving men or ships from inertia to an active state. The Stoics, on the other hand, considered the passions, imagined as winds, as destructive forces.[78] This latter interpretation is reflected in Bacon, who writes of the ill winds that disrupt the health of the mind in terms that are strikingly similar to his description of the ill winds that preceded the plague. Recall that Bacon, when writing about the plague, states, "Aptness or propension of air . . . to corrupt or putrefy, (no doubt) is to be found before it break forth into manifest effects of diseases, blastings, or the like."[79] This was a fundamental theory of New Galenism, that bad air or bad winds could disrupt the humoral balance, leading to contagion.[80]

But unlike the corrupt and venomous air that could only be avoided, Bacon believed the tumultuous winds of the affections could be placated. To mitigate the dangers of the passions, like ambition, Bacon believed that it was possible to discern "how affections are kindled and incited; and how pacified and refrained; and how again contained from act and further degree; how they disclose themselves, how they work, how they vary, how they gather and fortify, how they are inwrapped one within another and how they do fight and encounter one with another, and other the like particularities: amongst the which this last is of special use in moral and civil matters."[81]

It was in "moral and civil matters" that Bacon believed special attention should be given to how different affections interact, how they "fight," the fields of their engagement. Here Bacon recognized the potential efficacy of "bridling one faction against another" and "using hope and fear" to suppress what remained. He wrote in hunting terms, affections now like not winds but birds of prey or dogs of war: "How (I say) to set affection against affection, and to master one by another; even as we use to hunt beast with beast and fly bird with bird, which otherwise percase we could not so easily recover: upon which foundation is erected that excellent use of *praemium* and *poena*, whereby civil states consist; employing the predominant affections of *fear* and *hope*, for the suppressing and bridling the rest."[82] Then Bacon, in comparing state government to governing one's passions wrote, "For as in the government of states it is sometimes necessary to bridle *one faction with another, so it is with the government within.*"[83] Recall that Bacon spoke of the curative properties of sympathy and antipathy in his writings on the plague in *Sylva Sylvarum.* This antipathy and sympathy of passions, likewise, produces a "medicining" of their destructive potential. This, however, was written in 1623 and published in 1627. If in fact theories of the plague influenced theories of the passions, one could reasonably expect some articulation of those theories in the work that is generally recognized as the genesis of countervailing passions. In fact, in *Advancement of Learning* one finds exactly that: "Pride is inconsistent even with vice; and *as poison expels poison,* so are many vices expelled by pride."[84] While scholars recognize *Advancement of Learning* when discussing the emergence of countervailing passions, they ignore this central passage and the importance of his theoretical basis for the treatment of illness in general and the treatment of the plague specifically. Here, then, is direct evidence. When Bacon discusses poison expelling poison as passion can expel passion, he directly links theories for treatments of disease with what later came to be called countervailing passions.

Hirschman asserts that Bacon's suggestion of countervailing passions in *Advancement of Learning,* written in Latin, had limited impact and was recognized only with historical hindsight and resurrected by scholars who sought to identify ideological precursors to Hume and Spinoza.[85] But he and others overlook additional expressions of a simi-

lar sentiment in Bacon's other works.[86] Perhaps it is because they search
for the passions in general rather than reading them through specific
passions, like ambition, and then drawing more general conclusions.
That said, they ignore how Bacon employed the formulation in more
specific ways in what was his most popular work, his *Essays*.[87]

Bacon's *Essays* were inspired by Montaigne's *Essais*, which were
first published in France in 1580 and later in an expanded multivolume
form in 1588, and finally in a third edition published posthumously in
1595.[88] Bacon's first edition, published in 1597, includes ten essays.[89]
His second edition of 1612 expands the topics to forty-eight.[90] The
work reaches its fruition with fifty-eight topics in 1625.[91]

Adair refers to Bacon's essays as "a Renaissance equivalent of Dale
Carnegie's success manual showing how to win powerful friends and
influence the top people in a fiercely competitive hierarchical society."[92] This estimate seems a bit dismissive. The *Essays* are a wonderful
collection of wisdom, learning, and common sense drawn from real-
world living on certain universal moral and civil topics. They are like
François de La Rochefoucauld's *Maxims* or Benjamin Franklin's aphorisms in essay form.

Bacon wrote the *Essays* in the vernacular, adopting a somewhat
informal tone, bordering on conversation, with long compound and
complex sentences with subordinate clauses. But his informality is
tempered somewhat by its educative aspect. Bacon's *Essays* were his
means of holding a glass to humanity and society, so that we might see
in those reflections our flaws, our hopes, the hunger of human imagination, and the vanity of human aspiration. Bacon at times achieves a
certain Aristotelian poetic excellence, in that the universal wisdom in
his essays can still be appreciated in the twenty-first century. For example, in his essay "Of Friendship," Bacon writes on the nature, the
"fruit" of true friendship, "There is no such flatterer as is a man's self;
and there is no such remedy against flattery of a man's self, as the liberty
of a friend."[93] In his essay "Of Regiment of Health," he writes: "Physicians are some of them so pleasing and conformable to the humour of
the patient, as they press not the true cure of the disease; and some other

are so regular in proceeding according to art for the disease, as they re-spect not sufficiently the condition of the patient."[94] In "Of Anger," he notes, "No man is angry, that feels not himself hurt."[95]

But in addition to those essays that offered educative observations for individuals, Bacon wrote others for the purpose of advising the lead-ers of civil nations, for princes and states, in a manner that recalls Machiavelli.[96] In these essays one sees little of Adair's Dale Carnegie. These essays are quintessentially the reflections of a shrewd politi-cian and statesman whose insights were written with every expectation that they would be read and considered by the leading men of his time.[97] Perhaps this is in part due to the transformation of the collec-tion, reflected in title as well as substance. The initial subtitle of the essays was *Religious Meditations; Places of Perswasion & Disswasion; Seene and Allowed.* The subtitle of the later edition became *Counsels, Civill and Morall.* In his later essays Bacon transforms himself from an observer to a self-conscious counselor, and his essays reflect this objective.

"Of Ambition" is one such essay. Far from winning friends and influencing people, or offering personal advice on managing one's own ambition, "Of Ambition" casts ambition as a fundamental threat to the stability and health of the state and suggests strategies for managing that threat.[98]

Given that Federalist No. 51 has received such considerable atten-tion, especially the famous passage on ambition counteracting ambi-tion, it is surprising that Bacon's "Of Ambition" has eluded scholarly consideration. Scholars who cite Bacon as the ideological father of countervailing passions and trace him to Federalist No. 51 ignore the popular work in which Bacon expands on what he merely suggests in *Advancement of Learning.* For the purposes of this study, "Of Ambi-tion" marks a shift in both the strategies for managing ambition and an understanding of the quality itself. "Of Ambition" is remarkable as much for what was written as for what was disregarded. Given the con-text provided in the previous chapter and the fact that Bacon identifies ambition as sin in *Advancement of Learning*, one might expect Bacon to follow this course in an essay on ambition.

The 1605 *Advancement of Learning* recognized this theological construct. Yet by the 1612 publication of the *Essays*, Bacon chose to ignore any theological implications of the quality. This is a remarkable departure from mainstream thought. Instead of sin, ambition is first identified as "choler."[99] Recall the plague tract of Thomas Thayre in which he warns, "If choler do putrifie within the vesselles, it ingendreth *febris ardens* or *febris causon*, a hot and a dangerous fever."[100] Bacon similarly warns of the dangers of the "putrification" of choler: "If it be stopped, and cannot have his way, it becomes adust, and thereby malign and venomous."[101] Here Bacon suggests that it is not choler, and by extension ambition, that is inherently dangerous. It is the dream deferred, the desire thwarted that leads to a humoral imbalance, a dangerous malignancy.

But ambition, this illness, this "canker on the soul" can be treated.[102] The philosophers of medicine provide the theoretical framework in their theories of antipathy and sympathy. As poison counteracts poison, ambitious men could be used to counteract other ambitious men. In *Advancement of Learning* Bacon writes, "As in the government of states it is sometimes necessary to bridle one faction with another," and later, "As poison expels poison, so are many vices expelled by pride."[103] In "Of Ambition," Bacon recommends to princes the efficacy of using vice to expel the viscous, in this case ambitious men: "There is use also of ambitious men in pulling down the greatness of any subject that overtops; as Tiberius used Macro in the pulling down of Sejanus."[104] Lucius Aelius Sejanus, who was head of the Praetorian guard, charged with the protection of the emperor Tiberius, ultimately sought to supplant him as emperor. The most effective way of mitigating the danger was by using another ambitious man, Macro, to arrest Sejanus. Macro was named Praetorian prefect after Sejanus's execution.[105] As I discussed in chapter 2, Ben Jonson invokes Sejanus as an emblem of ambition.[106] But unlike Jonson, who condemns Sejanus for this quality, Bacon, instead, draw-

ing from Tacitus, to whom John Donne referred as the oracle of statesmen, observes the skillful way Sejanus's danger was mitigated through
countervailing. Bacon, later in the essay, reiterates: "Another means to
curb them, is to balance them by others as proud as they."[107]

But the use of these ambitious men was dangerous business. Bacon
urges caution, stating, "It were good not to use men of ambitious natures, except it be upon necessity."[108] That said, he offers suggestions
for the ways in which they were to be "bridled." Bacon's first suggestion
was to make sure that the ambitious were unaware they were being
used, especially in matters of "danger and envy." Ambitious men, Bacon
writes, should be "like a seeled dove, that mounts and mounts because
he cannot see about him."[109] "Seeling," or blinding, birds was a technique used in training falcons. The bird's eyes were sewn shut with
thread to keep it docile during training, a practice later replaced by the
use of a hood.[110] When a dove's eyes are seeled and it is allowed to fly,
the disoriented bird will "mount and mount," in a primal urge to rise
above the clouds that obscure its vision, until exhausted, it plummets
to the earth and death.[111] John Ford later adopts the "seeled dove" as an
image for ambition:

> Ambition, like a seeled dove, mounts upward,
> Higher and higher still, to perch on clouds,
> But tumbles headlong down with heavier ruins.[112]

Bacon recognized the inevitability of ambition and the futility of simply denouncing it as a dangerous passion that must be repressed. In "Of
Ambition" he recognizes, like Machiavelli, not what men ought to be
but what they are. Only with this recognition could practical strategies
be suggested.

But there are other strategies that Bacon suggests in addition to
countervailing, strategies that recognize that ambition might actually
have a positive aspect. In identifying ambition as choler, Bacon knew
that in a state of *eucrasia*, or health, "choler . . . is an humour that maketh men active, earnest, full of alacrity, and stirring."[113] But he quali-

fies his celebration of this choler with the conditional "if it be not stopped."[114] As those who wrote of ambition as sin suggested that ambition was a vice of excess, Bacon applied this theological concept to theories of medical science. Choler makes men "active" and "earnest." But let us return to the qualifier at the end of the characterization, "if it not be stopped." To Bacon ambition is both part of human nature, a part that must be given an outlet, an object. Ambition must be drawn off, given an outlet, released: "So, ambitious men, if they find the way open for their rising, and still get forward, they are rather busy than dangerous; but if they be checked in their desires, they become secretly discontent, and look upon men and matters with an evil eye, and are best pleased when things go backward; which is the worst property in a servant of a prince or state."[115] In order for the individual or the state to be healthy, the humors must be in balance. An excess of choler can produce the plague, a sickness in man, a *dycrasia* in the state.[116]

But in condemning ambition, the question is, to what extent is Bacon redefining it? While he recognizes its destructive potential and fundamental nature, is he suggesting that ambition may in fact be a productive quality, provided that it is given an outlet? If Bacon is, in fact, recognizing the dual nature of ambition, he is among the first in Anglo-American thought to do so. He may, in fact, be implying that ambition is not necessarily dangerous, provided that individuals are permitted to express it, if they "find their way open." This suggestion is later clarified. Bacon's intention is clear, as is his explicit redefinition of ambition as a quality that can, in fact, be beneficial to the state. This is the origin of the "private vice, public virtue" paradigm that has traditionally, and incorrectly, been associated only with the eighteenth century. It is also a watershed in ambition's trajectory. From vice to two-headed passion: "He that seeketh to be eminent amongst able men hath a great task; but that is ever good for the public."[117]

In *Novum Organum*, Bacon goes even further, suggesting, for what I believe is the first time in Anglo-American thought, the possibility of "noble ambition." While recognizing the negative qualities of ambition, he actually posits three "species or degrees of ambition":

The first is of those who desire to extend their own power in their native country; which kind is vulgar and degenerate. The second is of those who labour to extend the power of their country and its dominion among men. This certainly has more dignity, though not less covetousness. But if a man endeavour to establish and extend the power and dominion of the human race itself over the universe, his ambition (if ambition it can be called) is without doubt both a more wholesome thing and a more noble than the other two.[118]

Bacon, too, seems unsure of whether noble ambition itself is a contradiction in terms. In the passage he is unsure whether he may term this endeavor *ambition* at all. But in this expression, ambition makes an enormous leap, from vice to potential virtue, depending on the ends to which it is applied. Herein is an emergent suggestion, one that will soon become the dominant understanding of ambition within Anglo-American thought.

Bacon's emergent strategies for managing ambition represent a watershed in the trajectory of the idea. What was once a vice or sin that might be repressed becomes, in Bacon, an illness that can be treated. Countervailing ambition with ambition was born from treatments for disease in the time of the plague and in recognition of the inevitability of human nature. But countervailing the passions was simply one strategy. In the next chapter, we will explore the possibility of harnessing ambition for noble ends.

4

Harnessing Ambition in the Age of Exploration

Tres maneras para medrar, iglesia, casa real
o mar. *There are three ways to prosper, the
church, royal patronage, or the sea.*
— Sixteenth-century Spanish proverb

Ambitious men . . . are to be bridled, that
they be less dangerous.
— Francis Bacon, "Of Ambition"

The Kinges wants might be much relieved
out of the vanities and ambition of the
gentrie.
— John Chamberlain to Sir Dudley
   Carleton, June 15, 1615

Where was ever Ambition baited with greater
hopes then here, or where ever had Vertue so
large a field to reape the fruites of Glory.
— Sir William Alexander, *An
   Encouragement to the Colonies*

Recall the *Hortus Deliciarum*, the medieval manuscript of Herrad of Landsberg mentioned in chapter 1. In the *Hortus Deliciarum*, ambition is depicted as a lion yoked to a chariot. The message was simple: while ambition might be powerful enough to draw a chariot, those who harness ambition harness their own destruction. As tempting as bridling its force might have seemed, repression was the only strategy for managing ambition's devastating potential.

But by the early seventeenth century, new strategies emerged. In the last chapter I discussed what is commonly termed countervailing and suggested one possible origin of this new strategy in the work of Francis Bacon. In this chapter, I turn to harnessing. Harnessing ambition not only became a potentially virtuous undertaking but official state policy in England.

The dominant scholarly literature attributes the origins of harnessing to the eighteenth-century works of Bernard Mandeville,[1] Giambattista Vico,[2] and Adam Smith,[3] and later, in the nineteenth century, to the works of Johann Gottfried von Herder[4] and G. F. W. Hegel.[5] Scholars of the transformation of the passions from the sixteenth to the eighteenth centuries owe a profound debt to Albert O. Hirschman, who first limned this ideological trajectory. It would be difficult to overstate his contribution and influence.

That said, while Hirschman recognizes countervailing in the early seventeenth century, he incorrectly dismisses harnessing the passions from the early seventeenth century. He writes: "Given the overwhelming reality of restless, passionate, driven man, both the repressive and the harnessing solutions lacked persuasiveness. The repressive solution was a manner of assuming the problem away, whereas the greater realism of the harnessing solution was marred by an element of alchemical transformation rather out of tune with the scientific enthusiasm of the age."[6]

What Hirschman fails to note is that this was not just an age of scientific enthusiasm; it was an age of exploration. Roughly one hundred years before Mandeville wrote of transforming private vices into public benefits, and more than two hundred years before Hegel's cunning of reason, ambition implicitly spurred New World settlement and was explicitly harnessed by the state.

Ambition was harnessed, specifically, through the use of titular incentives created to encourage potential emigrants to undertake colonization. While titular incentives are most commonly associated with Spain's colonization efforts, scholars have largely overlooked England's similar efforts, incorrectly assuming this practice to have been a salient feature of Spanish colonization exclusively. J. H. Elliot, in his innovative integrated study of British and Spanish colonization, a narrative of early America that in many ways transcends traditional narrow limits of geography and period, notes Spain's use of title and honor as an incentive to colonization. However, he contrasts this tendency with the British settlements.[7] In so doing, Elliott overlooks the explicit use of noble title in certain English settlements used much in the same way as in the Spanish settlements. Spanish colonization was both a model and an anti-model for English colonization. Although many consider Spain only through the context of the Black Legend, I argue for its importance in English expectations of realizing ambition. In fact, in explicit imitation of the Spanish, a new noble title, "Knight Baronet of Nova Scotia," was created specifically to provide "bait" for ambition, to offer certain Englishmen the opportunity to be "the author of their nobility."[8] Unexpectedly, though titular incentives were most commonly associated with Spain, they were more widely realized in England.

The new incentives for colonization had a profound impact on the idea of ambition and the rights of the king. Once ambition was harnessed with the object of planting flags and saving souls, individual aspiration conflated with virtuous goals, both Christian and national. Could ambition retain its sinful associations if suddenly it was not only no longer against God and crown but for the glory of God and country? In addition, once the king harnessed ambition, transformed it from a sin to an act of virtue, he unintentionally challenged the hierarchy on which his own authority rested. With the creation of a new noble title for sale, even for virtuous ends, nobility was no longer predicated on the immutable blood. One logical result of the legitimation of ambition (given its well-emphasized connection to rebellion), was the possibility of a justifiable rebellion and ultimately the invalidation of the king.

But irrespective of titles conferred by crown, America was often imagined as a place where ambition could be safely realized, fundamentally ennobling, a place where individuals could become approximate nobility, regardless of birth. This was due not only to perceived availability of wealth, land and opportunity but also to the presence of a native population imagined in ways that reinforced an innate European superiority, further fueling European ambition.

This chapter captures a watershed in the trajectory of ambition from Christian sin to problematic virtue. In it, I illustrate how ambition was harnessed and the ways in which it was transformed. As Christian, national, and individual interests harmonized in New World settlement, ambition became not only a necessary evil but a Christian good. Ambition suddenly saved souls of pagan Indians and Africans, planted flags and won riches for kings. As men rose, so, too, did God and country.

In 1605, on the eve of England's sustained American colonization efforts, the most distinguished playwrights of the day likewise turned their attention to America. London's elite crowded the fashionable Blackfriars Theatre to see popular actors, players in the Children of Her Majesty's Revels, perform *Eastward Hoe*, a new work by John Marston, George Chapman, and Ben Jonson.[9]

Shortly after its performance, the playwrights were imprisoned. In jail, Jonson was told that his punishment would be the removal of his nose and ears.[10] It has been suggested that the performance included numerous offensive comments about the Scots that were interpreted as aimed at the new king, James I.[11] Infrequently observed is that the play parodied the promises of the New World and an English colonial expansion with which some of the most powerful men of the day, including the king himself, had aligned their interests. Despite the play's conservative sentiment, an unabashed condemnation of ambition, *Eastward Hoe* was even denounced explicitly from the pulpit. In 1609 William Crashaw addressed his congregation. "As for *Plaiers*," he began, "(pardon me right Honourable and beloued for wronging this place and your patience with so base a subject,) . . . they abuse *Virginea*, but they are but *Players:* they disgrace it: true, but they are *Players*, and . . . if they speedily repent not, I dare say, vengeance waites for them."[12]

Why then did a play with a conservative Christian agenda receive such scorn? Why was this condemnation of ambition so different than the many others I treated in chapter 2?

In *Eastward Hoe* the vanity of human ambition is directly linked to Virginia. In condemning ambition, the playwrights condemned colonization and the emerging delusion that somehow harnessing ambition was anything other than pure folly. Neither in England nor in America could ambition transform base metal into gold, the common into the noble.

The play is the tale of two apprentices, one humble, the other ambitious, who serve a master with two daughters who parallel the apprentices in comportment and expectations. In the second chapter I discussed ambition in Elizabethan and Jacobean tragedy and illustrated how ambition drove men and women to create selves that could not be sustained. These were tragedies of protagonists whose selves made did not match the station to which they were born. A similar theme is evident in this comedy and presented early in act 1, scene 2. In this scene, Mildred, the heroine of the play and embodiment of Christian virtue, attempts to warn her ambitious older sister Gertrude: "Where titles presume to thrust before fit meanes to second them, wealth and respect often growe sullen, and will not follow. For sure in this, I would for your sake I spake not truth. *Where ambition of place goes before fitnesse of birth, contempt and disgrace follow*" (1.2.38–43).

In *Eastward Hoe*, ambition of place takes a geographic as well as a titular aspect. In the play, one of the first in English literature to imagine Virginia, America is represented and parodied as ambition writ large. In act 3, scene 3, three adventurers significantly named Scapegoat, Spendthrift, and Seagull gather in a tavern to ready themselves for the voyage to Virginia. Virginia in 1605 was broadly construed to include the territory between Florida to Newfoundland.[13] To the would-be voyagers, it is a place where:

golde is more plentifull there then copper is with us; and for as much redde copper as I can bring, I'le have thrice the waight in golde. Why, man, all their dripping-pans and their chamber pottes are pure gold; and all the chaines with which they chaine up their streetes are massy gold; all the prisoners they take are fetterd in gold; and for rubies and diamonds, they goe forth on holydayes and gather hem by the sea-shore, to hang on their children's coates, and sticke in their capps, as commonly as our children weare saffron gilt brooches and groaets with holes in 'hem.
(3.3.29–41)

Yet Virginia is not only parodied as a place of gold chamber pots but satirized as a place where "meanes to advancement" are simple, where ambition may be realized without impediment:

And then you shall live freely there, without sargeants, or courtiers, or lawyers, or intelligencers. . . . Then for your meanes to advancement, there it is simple, and not preposterously mixt. You may be an alderman there, and never be scavinger: you may be a nobleman there, and never be a slave. You may come to preferment enough, and never be a pandar; To riches and fortune inough, and have never the more villanie, nor the lesse wit. Besides there we shall have no more law then conscience, and not too much of either; serve God inough, eate and drinke inough, and inough is as good as a feast.
(3.3.46–68)

The voyage never reaches Virginia but is, instead, shipwrecked. Yet this passage on Virginia reflects and parodies the perception of the New World as a land of riches where natives use gold chamber pots and lay treasures before the English. It is a place where preferment is self-directed, where any man might simply choose to be an alderman or officer. It also mocks the sort of person who would undertake the

colonization: only knaves or fools, scapegoats and spendthrifts, counterfeit knights, the greedy or ambitious. Virginia is a land where those
ambitious of "place goes before fitness of birth," and as Mildred warns,
as any good voice of an ambition parable would, disgrace can only
follow.

Scholars have traced the sources of *Eastward Hoe* to Richard Hakluyt and Sir Thomas More. But they have largely ignored the influence
of Spanish colonization that preceded and informed the English expectations reflected in this play.[14] While More may have imagined
golden chamber pots in 1516, the English well knew that the Spanish
had subsequently discovered some approximation of what More intended as hyperbole. And there was no telling what more remained.
For any satire to be effective, there must be a grain of truth. For the
English, the Spanish experience, the incredible discoveries of Columbus, Hernán Cortés, and Francisco Pizarro, among others, were truth
enough. The other truth was the moral of this parable—that all the
hopes invested in America, satirized in *Eastward Hoe*, included the im-
possible and inevitable expectation that in Virginia any man might be
a Pizarro or Cortés.

It is perhaps not surprising that few scholars look to Spain as a
source for the English dramatic imagining of Virginia in 1605. Most
often the infamous Black Legend is identified with England's view of
Spain in the Americas. The term the Black Legend (La leyenda negra)
was coined in the early twentieth century by Julián Juderías.[15] His
work, as well as that of Rómulo D. Cabria and Edward Peters, delin-
eates the propaganda campaign in England and elsewhere in early
modern Europe to define the Spanish colonization efforts as the embodiment of a rapacious, brutal conquest.[16] Largely because of this
campaign, Spain became, in the words of Peters, "the symbol of all
forces of repression, brutality, religious and political intolerance, and
intellectual and artistic backwardness for the next four centuries."[17]

That is not to say that there was no truth to the accusations. The
Spanish treatment of native peoples was often marked by savage exploitation and violence. In fact, much of the English propaganda drew on

Spanish self-critical eyewitness accounts, notably that of Bartolomé de las Casas. In 1552, the former New World colonist, Dominican friar, and self-proclaimed protector of the Indians published a work that castigated Spain for its treatment of Native Americans. In *Brevísima relación de la destrucción de las Indias* (A short account of the destruction of the Indies), Las Casas wrote,

> Our fellow-countrymen have, through their cruelty and wickedness, depopulated and laid waste an area which once boasted more than ten kingdoms, each of them larger in area than the whole of the Iberian Peninsula. . . . At a conservative estimate, the despotic and diabolical behavior of the Christians has, over the last forty years, led to the unjust and totally unwarranted deaths of more than twelve million souls, women and children among them, and there are grounds for believing my own estimate of more than fifteen million to be nearer the mark.[18]

Las Casas's work, though published in 1552, was not translated into English until 1583, when England was preparing for war against Spain.[19] In his *Discourse on Western Planting*, Richard Hakluyt excoriates the Spanish for their treatment of the Indians, and in chapter 11 he translates Las Casas. Though *Discourse* was a private work prepared for the government of England and was not published until the nineteenth century, it both reflected the anti-Spanish sentiment held by many in England at the time and helped perpetuate it.[20] Hakluyt wrote: "So many and so monstrous have bene the Spanishe cruelties, suche straunge slaughters and murders of those peaceable, lowly, milde, and gentle people."[21] Hakluyt, drawing from Las Casas, reported that these monstrous cruelties were responsible for the deaths of some twelve million people over forty years.[22]

Fueling the fire of what would be later known as the Black Legend were the popular later engravings by Theodorus de Bry. De Bry's depictions of the Spanish conquest are often graphic portrayals of an inhuman and barbaric genocide.[23] Even though De Bry never traveled to

Theodor de Bry's engravings of Spanish colonization fueled the Black Legend.
Bartolomé de las Casas, *Narratio regionum Indicarum per Hispanos quosdam
deuastatarum verissima . . .* (Frankfurt, 1598).

the Americas, his accounts persisted well into the seventeenth and
eighteenth centuries as accurate portrayals of Spanish conquest and
colonization and as plausible visual explanations for the disappearance
of the native peoples. As Stephanie Moser writes, "The significance of
de Bry's engravings for the development of an iconography of the past
cannot be overemphasized."[24]

People in early modern England, of course, were unaware of germ
theory and the impact of a global pandemic on the Native American
population. Although the exact pre-Columbian population is a subject
of dispute, scholars agree that it was germs, not Spanish exploitation,
that were largely responsible for decimating the native populations.[25]
Yet partially due to the depictions of Spanish depravity, some English

The seal of the Massachusetts Bay Colony. Used
with permission from the Massachusetts
Archives.

evangelical colonizers regarded themselves as saviors of the natives, as
illustrated by the seal of the Massachusetts Bay Colony. The seal prom-
inently depicts a native with a bow and arrow, his nakedness discreetly
covered by edenic leaves, with a bubble and the words "Come over
and help us," a visual plea for protection from the Spanish and for a
path to God.[26]

   Considerably less scholarly attention is paid to the sixteenth- and
seventeenth-century celebration of the Spanish men who first ventured
to America and were transformed by it. It is important to remember
that the Black Legend was a historical reconstruction traced to the late
sixteenth and early seventeenth centuries. As Jonathan Hart notes, most
Spanish works translated into English were not those that helped create the Black Legend but in fact described Spain and its early explorers in laudatory terms.[27] As I mentioned, Hakluyt's translation of Las
Casas appeared in a private report prepared for the crown.[28] Before Las

Casas was translated, popular histories, myths, and accounts translated from the Spanish had already reached England. These stories glorified Spain and its conquerors and were extremely influential in shaping English attitudes toward Spain and informing English expectations of colonization.

John Smith, for example, far from condemning the Spanish con-quistadores (save his reservation regarding their Catholicism), held Spain as worthy of emulation. According to Hart: "The class mobility, skill as soldiers and captains, and the memory of their great glory as servants to the king of Spain all presented Smith with a personal and national model. America would allow scope to men of merit and daring."[29]

According to Leo Lemay, Smith established what Lemay refers to as a "platonic genealogy" consisting of Columbus, Cortés, Pizarro, Hernando de Soto, and Ferdinand Magellan.[30] These are the men that Smith admired and hoped to emulate for the glory of England. But Smith also recognized that, in America, these men procured honor and status as a result of their achievements. In his A Description of New England (1616), Smith wrote:

> Columbus, Cortez, Pitzara, Soto, Magellanes, and the rest served more then a prentiship to learne how to begin their most mem-orable attempts in the West Indies: which to the wonder of all ages successfully they effected, when many hundreds of oth-ers, farre above them in the worlds opinion, beeing instructed but by relation, came to shame and confusion in actions of small moment, . . . brave spirits that advanced themselves from poore Souldiers to great Captaines, their posterity to great Lords, their King to be one of the greatest Potentates on earth, and the fruites of their labours, his greatest glory, power and renowne.[31]

In this passage, Smith valorizes the ambition of these Spanish men. These were "prentices" who achieved what those "farre above them" in rank could not. In America, a "poore Souldier" could become a "great

Captaine," and in their posterity, even "Lords." Elsewhere Smith compared the Spaniards to classical models of ambition, as in this promotional tract on Virginia: "Why should not the riche haruest of our hopes be seasonably expected? I dare say, that the resolution of *Caesar* in France, the designes of *Alexander,* the discoueries of *Hernando Cortes* in the West, and of *Emanuel* King of *Portugal* in the East, were not encouraged vpon so firme grounds of state and possibilitie."[32] Smith emphasized the transformative possibilities of America, the ambition realized, rather than the gold that waited. Cortés and Pizarro were valorized for their personal transformations and the glory they brought to their nation rather than for the riches they discovered. As it became increasingly clear that the English would not find another Mexico in Virginia, Smith harnessed the alchemy of personal transformation.

How is it, given the Black Legend, that Smith lavished praise on the Spanish and the captains of its New World explorations and conquest? Smith's account suggests the existence of counternarratives with which to construct his beliefs. In fact, there were heroic popular portrayals of Spain's conquerors, those figures in Smith's "platonic genealogy," some drawn from written histories and others from cultural myths.

Perhaps the most significant source was the work of historian Francisco López de Gómara's *Historia general de las Indias.* Gómara's work was published in 1552, shortly after the famous debates between Juan Ginés de Sepúlveda and Bartolomé de las Casas at Valladolid.[33] It was what scholar Glen Carman describes as "an instant success." He writes, "Within two years of its release, there were eight Spanish printings of part one, the *Historia general,* and nine of part two, the *Historia de la conquista de México.* During the rest of the sixteenth century the *Historia general* was published eight times in Italian, eight times in French, and twice in English, while the *Historia de la conquista de México* saw ten printings in Italian, nine in French, and two in English."[34]

Despite its enormous success, Gómara's work and its translations have received scant scholarly attention. Carman notes: "Cortés's writings have been the subject of intense critical scrutiny since the time of their publication. . . . Gómara's work, by contrast, has yet to receive the attention it deserves, especially considering the initial success and lasting influence of his *Historia general de las Indias* and *Historia de la conquista de México*."[35]

While scholars of colonial Latin America tend to devalue Gómara, scholars of colonial North America tend to disregard his influence completely.[36] This is surprising considering that a popular English translation of Gómara was published in England in 1579, four years before Las Casas, and was followed by a popular second edition in 1596. Even so, it is Las Casas and the origins of the Black Legend that some scholars tend to accept as the sole or dominant narrative.[37] The Black Legend, though it becomes the dominant narrative in Anglo-American thought, does not do so until the seventeenth century. Las Casas, for example, never received a second printing of the 1583 English translation.[38] Gómara and his translators suggest a popular and competing narrative, one that helped Smith lionize the achievement of Spain's explorers and conquerors.

It was with Thomas Nicholas's translation that England received its first full written account of Cortés's conquest. The translations of Nicholas, though rough hewn, were popular celebrations of Spain's conquest and conquerors, on which Smith, Jonson, Marston, and Chapman may have drawn.[39]

Thomas Nicholas had been a merchant trading with Spain. There he came to know Gómara's history. In 1560 he was arrested by the Inquisition on charges of speaking against the Mass. He was imprisoned in chains for nearly two years.[40] When he finally made his way back to England, he published *Pleasant Historie of the Conquest of the West India, now Called New Spaine*.[41]

Nicholas begins his work by noting the accuracy of Gómara's account: "Conference with auncient gentlemen which had serued in the Conquest of the West India, now called new Spaine, vnder the princely Captaine *Hernando Cortez*. By whom as present witnesses at many of the actes herein contained, I was credible informed, that this delectable and worthie Historie is a most true and just reporte of matter of past in effect."[42] He then suggests that Spain's example should be emulated: "For here they shall behold, how Glory, Renowne, and perfect Felicitie, is not gotten but with great paines, travaile, perill and daunger of life: heere shall they see the wisdome, curtesie, valour and pollicie of worthie Captaines, yea and the faithfull hearts whiche they ought to beare vnto their Princes service."[43] In these early laudatory accounts of Spain's conquest, before Smith's alchemy of personal transformation, gold, and the probability that more remains as yet undiscovered, is understandably a central preoccupation of the English. Nicholas suggests:

> And where it was supposed, that the golden mettall had his beginning and place in the East and West *India*, neare vnto the hote Zoane [hot zone], (as most learned writers held opinion) it is nowe approoued ... that the same golden mettall dooth also lie incorporate in the bowels of the Norweast parties, environed with admirable Towers, pillers and pinacles, of rockes, stone and Ise, possessed of a people bothe straunge, and rare in shape, attire and liuing, yea suche a Countrey and people, as all *Europe* had forsaken and made no account of, except our most gracious Queene and her subjects, whom vndoubtedly God hath appointed, not onely to be supreme Princesse ouer them, but also to be a meane that the name of Christ may bee knowne vnto this heathenish and sauage generation.[44]

Far from denouncing the Spanish treatment of the native peoples, Nicholas praised their gift of Christianity; he did not denounce Catholicism but celebrated the light it brought to the Indians:

> In this historie doth appeare the simplicitie of those ignorant Indians in time past, yea and how they were deluded in worshipping Idolles and wicked *Mamon*, their bloudie slaughter of men in sacrifice, and now the greate mercie of Jesus Christ extended upon them in lightning their darkenesse, giving them

knowledge of the eternitie, and holy trinitie in unitie, whereby they are nowe more deueute unto heavenly things then we wretched Christians, (who presume of auntient Christianitie) especially in Charitie, humilitie, and liuely workes of faith.[45]

Nicholas imagined the Indians as purer Christians, despite their instruction in Catholicism. The introduction was not altered in 1596 in the second English edition. This passage and the popularity of the text, even the fact that the introduction was not changed after the failed Spanish invasion of England, challenges the assumption of the dominant Black Legend associated with Spain and its treatment of the Indians. Likewise, it describes Spain's conquerors in celebratory terms. Cortés was a man who won glory and renown not only by wisdom, courage, and valor but, remarkably, given the assumption of the ubiquity of English disregard for brutal Spaniards, by courtesy.

The account reads like a nonfiction adaptation of a chivalric tale, its heroes Cortés and his men. But most astounding, perhaps, are the descriptions of the incredible wealth and gilded pomp that Cortés discovered. The gold chamber pots of *Eastward Hoe* do not seem as much of a stretch of the English imagination given the descriptions found in Gómara's text, both in the original and in Nicholas's translation. When Cortés first meets Montezuma, it is described as follows:

At this bridge came *Mutezuma* to receyve *Cortez* under a Canapie of greene feathers & gold, with much argentery [silver] hanging thereat, which Canapie foure noble men did carry. . . . All . . . were riche apparelled & all of one fashion, except *Mutezuma*, which had a paire of shoes of golde beset with pretious stones. . . . *Cortes* put about Mutezuma his necke a coller of margarites, Diamonds, & other stones all of glasse. *Mutezuma* received it thankfully, . . . The coller of glasse pleased well *Mutezuma*, and because he woulde not take without giuing a better thing, as a great prince, he commaunded to be brought two collers. . . . From every one of them hanged

eight shrimpes of gold of excellent workemanship, & of a fin-
ger length every one.[46]

But this was only the beginning. In a chapter titled "The Golde
and Iewels that Mutezuma gave vnto Cortez for tribute," Nicholas details the incredible wealth lain before Cortés's feet:

> golde in planches like bricke battes, Jewels, and pieces wrought
> in a hall and two chambers, which were opened. . . . *Mute-*
> *zuma* gave vnto him rich clothes of cotten and feathers, mar-
> velously woven in figures and colours, it seemed without co-
> parison, for the Spaniardes had never seene the like: he gave
> unto him more, twelve shooting tronkes, wherewith he him-
> self was wont to pastime: some of them were painted with
> birdes, beasts, floures & trees very perfite, a worke surely much
> to be commended: and some of them were engraven very curi-
> ously, with their mouldes and pellets of golde. . . . Cortes re-
> ceived all that they brought, and caused it to be molten, out of
> the whiche was had in fine golde, 1,600,000 Castlins, of the
> value of seven shillings and five pence the peece, and rather
> more, and also five hundred markes of plate.[47]

Nicholas, however, wrote about more than just wealth. In Nicholas's translation, the English learned of Cortés's meteoric rise. The account speaks of the explorer's childhood, claiming that Cortés was
from an ancient, noble, and honorable lineage and, though poor in
goods, was rich in virtue. Cortés was sent to university in Salamanca,
where he remained for two years, and then left for Medellin, "wearie of
his studie."[48] He then tried the law but found that equally uninspiring.
He "caused much strife in his father's house," for he was a "very un-
happie ladde, high minded, and a lover of chivalrie, for which cause he
determined with himselfe to wander abroad to seeke adventures."[49]

By the time his adventures ended, this failed university student was
opulently rewarded by his king with lands and noble title:

The Emperour received Cortes magnificially, and to give him the greater honour he went & visited him at his owne lodging. The Emperour being in a readines to passe into Italy, to be ther crowned with the Emperiall crowne, *Cortes* went in his maiesties company vnto the Citie of *Saragoza*, whereas his Maiestie calling to remembrance his worthie service, and valor of his person, made him Marques del Valle de Huaracac, according to his desire . . . and Captaine general of the newe Spaine, with all the provinces and coast of the south sea, chiefe discoverer and inhabiter of the same coaste and landes, with the twelfth parte of all that after that time shoulde be discovered, for a sure inhabitance to him and his discendentes, he offered unto him also the habite of the order of knighthoode of Saint Iames, which Cortes refused, because there was no rent giuen with the habite. . . . He likewise gave unto Cortez all the kingdome of Michuacan but hee had rather had divers other townes which he demanded, many other great favours and rewards he received at the Emperours hands.[50]

In this remarkable passage, Cortés accompanies his king on his journey to Rome to be crowned Holy Roman Emperor. The implication is clear that the king of Spain is making this journey largely because of Cortés's discoveries. Remarkably, this failed law student from a poor, though hidalgo family, not only receives the favor of the king but refuses honors bestowed and makes demands of his sovereign, demands that are then granted. Cortés's discoveries have legitimated his ambition.

The question remains, given his rise, was Cortés ambitious or simply the passive recipient of God's favor? If rising to a higher station than "God hath geven or appoynted" was the sixteenth-century English definition of ambition, what can one make of the rise of a sixteenth-century Spanish captain?

We are unsure of the English view of Cortés's rise (though we might suspect that if God did not like Catholics much, God was unlikely to

favor them, unless, perhaps, to serve as a model for English emulation).
The Spanish sources written by those who were not in the employ of
Cortés make it clear that he was a profoundly ambitious man with all
the negative associations that one finds in English sources.[51] In his
Conquest of New Spain, Bernal Díaz del Castillo denounces Cortés's
assumption of noble rights that were not his due.[52]

The criticism of Cortés's ambition begins early in Díaz's account.
Díaz marvels at the ways in which, almost simply through the act of
coming to the New World, Cortés was transformed. He writes, "It was
here in Havana that Cortes began to form a household and assume the
manners of a lord."[53] Throughout Díaz's work there are numerous accounts of Cortés's inappropriate assumption of noble rights with the
imputation that his rank was substantiated neither by wealth nor by
birth, pretense without substance, self-made and unnatural. For example, when Cortés is made a general, Diaz writes: "He began to adorn
himself and to take much more care of his appearance than before. He
wore a plume of feathers, with a medallion and a gold chain, and a
velvet cloak trimmed with loops of gold. In fact he looked like a bold
and gallant Captain."[54]

This was not a medal earned but a medal purchased. It was not
that Cortés was a bold and gallant captain, simply that he fashioned
himself to appear as such. Díaz details Cortés's inability to afford these
trappings of office, principally due to his need to adorn himself and his
wife in finery commensurate with his new station: "But he had nothing
with which to meet the expenses I have described, for at that time he
was very poor and in debt, despite the fact that he owned a good *encomienda* of Indians and was getting gold from the mines. But all this he
spent on his person, on finery for his newly married wife, and on entertaining guests who had come to stay with him."[55]

Was this ambition? Cortés's men seemed to think so. Near the end
of his account Díaz writes:

> While Cortes was at Coyoacan, he lodged in a palace with
> whitewashed walls on which it was easy to write with charcoal

and ink; and every morning malicious remarks appeared, some in verse and some in prose, in the manner of lampoons. One said the sun, moon, and stars, and earth and sea followed their courses, and if they ever deviated from the plane for which they were created, soon reverted to their original place. *So it would be with Cortes' ambition. . . . He would soon return to his original condition.*[56]

This account shares some of the elements of Elizabethan tragedy and of the satire *Eastward Hoe*. The passage implies that Cortés manufactured a self that was insubstantial. A self made is not a self born, and the natural order would certainly overwhelm Cortés's manufactured self. Birth and blood, like the "sun, moon, and stars, and earth and sea," dictate a place in the world. The early modern graffiti artist mocked the vanity of Cortés's ambition. Thomas Nicholas, however, celebrated it for an English audience eager for more.

After the popularity of his translation of Cortes's conquest, Nicholas turned to Francisco Pizarro and Peru. In his translation of Agustín de Zárate's history of the conquest of Peru, England learned of another stunning example of the transformative possibilities of America.[57] But Pizarro's story and his spectacular rise were informed as much by written histories as by popular myth drawn from a propaganda campaign to disparage him. Much of this effort was made by Francisco López de Gómara. Gómara glorified the actions of his patron, Hernán Cortés, and often disparaged the actions of Cortés's rivals, one of whom was the rival conqueror Pizarro. Gómara even maligned Pizarro's family and origins, starting the "porcine legend," the myth through which most early modern English readers, like John Smith, encountered Pizarro.[58]

Gómara claimed that Francisco Pizarro was abandoned at the door of a church, survived by nursing on a pig, and only later, and with great reluctance, was reclaimed by his father, who then put him to work as a swineherd.[59] James Lockhart, in his study of Pizarro, states unequivocally, "There is not the slightest reason to believe any part of Gómara's story."[60] Lockhart interrogates this myth and illustrates that it is at odds with the historical record, inspired by a vindictive competition for fame between the conqueror of Mexico and the conqueror of Peru.

But there may be other implications to the slander that Lockhart ignores. *Pig* had more than one implication. In Spanish, it could mean the farm animal, but *pig* could also signify, through the derogatory term *marrano*, a recently converted Christian who was believed to be practicing Judaism in secret.[61] The term *marrano* is thought to be of Arabic origin, originally ascribed to Jewish people who did not eat pork and later, ironically, denoting those who were no longer Jewish.[62] The dominant medical theories in Spain at the time, informed largely by the enormously popular work of Antonio de Guevara, maintained that an adult's personality could be directly formed by the wet nurse, who was thought to transfer parts of her personality and beliefs through breast milk.[63] One wonders if Gómara was not cleverly impugning not only Pizarro's childhood but his adulthood through the transference of crypto-Jewish ideology in his wet nurse's milk. Given the evangelical imperative of New World conquest and the persistent and widespread fear of the pernicious influence of the *marrano*, or recently converted Jew, in the New World, the suggestion of a false or suspect faith would be quite a damning implication.[64]

The Pizarro story, its myth and subtle implications for double meaning, of course, has a historical precedent in Rome's founding. Like Pizarro, Romulus and Remus were suckled by an animal, in their case a she-wolf. Livy suggests that the woman who cared for the twins, Acca Larentia, was called Lupa, the Latin slang word given to both women of "loose" morals and female wolves.[65] Rome's mythic origins were disparaged by this recognition, as its corruption was suggested by its founders' wet nurse. We know that Gómara was classically trained. His work is subtle, clever, and marked by use of puns and double entendres. One Gómara scholar identifies "irony" as "one of Gómara's favorite and most successful devices, sometimes used playfully and sometimes [used] as a weapon wielded with devastating effect against Cortés' enemies."[66] Adding evidence to this speculation is a recent archaeological find that revealed that Pizarro's ossuary may have been marked by his relatives with symbols consistent with those used on other Jewish ossuaries and in ancient funerary markings.[67]

Regardless of the speculation, the historical record is clear that Peru, not Mexico, and silver, rather than gold, became the bullion that funded the rise of the Spanish Empire. But whether or not it was due to the rich silver mines of Potosí (now in Bolivia but during the colonial period part of the viceroyalty of Peru), "Peru" was often used by the English as a synonym for the wealth, mystery, and marvelous in the Spanish New World settlements.[68] As its founder and conqueror, well-compensated and rewarded until his death, Pizarro became one of the most famous rags-to-riches tales in early modern Europe, one that obviously captured the imagination of John Smith and suggested to others that, in America, ambition could be realized beyond one's wildest dreams, even by a child suckled by a sow.

This is cited not to challenge the significance of the Black Legend and Spain as an anti-model for English colonization. For many English colonizers, the perception of the destruction of the Indies and the treatment of the Native Americans as depicted in the work of Las Casas was potent evidence of the righteousness of the English cause in the New World. But, also, Spain and the men who conquered and explored the New World served Captain John Smith and others as hope for a geographic place where ambitions might be realized. As the English came late to the colonization of the Americas, many of their expectations were, therefore, informed by the Spanish experience, not only those of the great men but of the colonists, too, who would risk all. English hopes were shaped by Spanish experience but also by Spanish expectations of the New World.

These Spanish hopes were perhaps exemplified best by the common phrase explaining their motivation for leaving the surety of the Iberian Peninsula: *Vale mas*, "to be worth more."[69] For the Spanish, noble status, land, and vassals (in the form of *encomienda*) were often used as incentives for those who would risk overseas adventure. A popular saying from the time captures the spirit: "Tres maneras para medrar, iglesia, casa real o mar."[70] In other words, there were three methods for gaining preferment or rank: the church, the royal house, or the sea.[71]

The sea, and America, Asia, and Africa, the overseas discoveries of Spain and Portugal, represented a substantial opportunity for individuals to garner rank and preferment from a crown that required administration and colonization of newly discovered lands. The religious imperative, saving souls, the conversion of others to Christianity, conflated with conquest and discovery, as personal achievement, ambition, became a means by which God and nation could likewise be elevated. The overseas discovery of the Americas coincided with the reconquest of the Iberian Peninsula and the expulsion of the Jews and Moors, lending a swagger of divine favor to the Catholic king and queen of Castile and Aragon bent on the delusion of purity of Spain and its purpose.[72]

It is in this context that Columbus sailed. In his *Diario* he reflected the dominant spirit of national, Christian, and individual ambition.[73] At the time, his journal was intended not only for the king and queen but was written with the expectation of its importance. It was a formal and ultimately public declaration.[74] Ultimately, not only was the diary published in Spain, but it was read throughout Europe and intended to convey a divinely favored national destiny.[75]

Columbus's narrative begins with a letter to Ferdinand and Isabella. Las Casas would later frame the letter as a prologue to the diary and publish Columbus's account in his *Historia de las Indias*.[76] But whether Columbus intended it to serve that function is unclear. The letter itself, as I mentioned, was widely published, its function as performative as substantive, the assertion of Spain's prerogative announced throughout Europe.

It makes sense, then, that the letter, one intended for the world stage, begins with a historic context full of national and religious import that extended to Columbus's voyage. Columbus wrote to the king and queen: "This present year of 1492 . . . on the second day of the month of January I saw the Royal Standards of Your Highnesses placed by force of arms on the towers of the Alhambra . . . and I saw the Moorish King come out to the gates of the city and kiss the Royal Hands of Your Highnesses."[77] By beginning the account of his first voyage within the context of the reconquest, Columbus lends both a historic and a religious gravity to his endeavors. Columbus writes:

> Your Highnesses, as Catholic Christians and Princes, lovers and promoters of the Holy Christian Faith, and enemies of the false doctrine of Mahomet and of all idolatries and heresies, you thought of sending me, Christóbal Colón, to the said regions of India to see the said princes and the peoples and the lands, and the characteristics of the lands and of everything, and to see how their conversion to our Holy Faith might be undertaken. . . . So, after having expelled all the Jews from all of your Kingdoms and Dominions, in the same month of January Your Highnesses commanded me to go, with a suitable fleet, to the said regions of India.[78]

Columbus ennobled his voyage by contextualizing his efforts. But then, with decorum and deference, reminds Ferdinand and Isabella that he has been likewise officially ennobled with title, both present and hereditary.

> And for that you granted me great favors and ennobled me so that from then on I might call myself "Don" and would be Grand Admiral of the Ocean Sea and Viceroy and perpetual Governor of all the islands and lands that I might discover and gain and [that] from now on might be discovered and gained in the Ocean Sea; and likewise my eldest son would succeed me and his son him, from generation to generation forever.[79]

This formula of God, crown, and individual aspiration became a potent incentive that drove colonization and conquest of the Americas. It is perhaps surprising that a letter with an ostensible performative intent and evangelical air would include specific references to the benefit that Columbus himself would receive in service of God and crown. The letter, a private missive to the sovereigns, may easily have been edited before publication. Many scholars believe that it was in fact published with revision. Why, then, the deviation from the historical and evangelical to the decidedly personal benefit that Columbus would receive?

One possible answer is that the publication of the rewards of title and status for those who would hazard a New World adventure might serve as a potent incentive, bait for the ambitious men of Spain. Titular incentives were to become official policy in New Spain, lending support for this speculation. Historian Stuart Schwartz notes that the adoption of titular incentives became the "standard formula" for enticing Spanish colonists to the New World. These incentives were offered to encourage individuals to "serve, populate and remain in the said land."[80]

Perhaps the first explicit effort to bait ambition was made in 1519–1520 by Bartolomé de las Casas. Following on the heels of his failed efforts to recruit simple farmers to colonize the New World, Las Casas adopted a different tactic for his proposed colony in Tierra Firme, in present-day Venezuela. Las Casas proposed that a new knighthood be formed as an incentive to colonization. The newly knighted men were to be known as the Knights of the Golden Spur. Among the advantages to obtaining the title was the right to wear a distinctive white cloth with a red cross. The advantages for the king were two hundred ducats per new knight. This would provide the capital necessary to form the new colony, pacify the Indians, and organize them into towns so that they could pay taxes. This system would ultimately provide a return to the king on an investment that required only the conferment of a title rather than capital investment. The Knights of the Golden Spur and Las Casas were committed to the proposition of peaceful colonization. But ultimately his colony was a failure, as he was unable to maintain his utopian vision in the face of a rapacious appetite for trade and native slaves. In a final irony, while Las Casas was in Santo Domingo or Hispaniola (today the Dominican Republic and Haiti), pleading for the rights of his colony to develop without interference, some seven hundred native men, women, and children were captured by a Spanish slave raiding expedition.[81]

Though the colony at Tierra Firme was a failure, officials recognized the efficacy of using noble titles and the trappings of noble entitlements to entice prospective colonists. In 1528 the *Relacion de los oidores Licenciado Espinosa y Licenciado Zuazo al Consejo de Indias*, two royal governors suggested substantive means to tempt colonists to leave the relative safety of the Iberian Peninsula for the island of Hispaniola. Sickness and natives who resisted incursion destroyed some early colonial efforts. Stories of their failure soon reached Spain and served as a powerful disincentive for many to try what then seemed to be an adventure not worth the potential risk. The two administrators in 1528 suggested that the crown grant certain incentives: the right to import African slaves, the waving of taxes, certain monetary rewards, and a noble title. Suddenly men of meager birth could become a *hidalgo* or a *caballero* simply by agreeing to come to Hispaniola.[82]

These measures were adopted by the crown and enhanced further with the promise of the creation of entails, titles of *hijosdalgo de solar conicido*, and even the coat of arms of their choice. As Schwartz notes, this became "more or less a standard formula in the Spanish Indies as a means to stimulate colonization. They are found in the Ordinance of Population of Hispaniola (1560), and were later incorporated in the general Ordinances for New Conquests in 1573."[83] James Lockhart, in his study of the men of Cajamarca, likewise studied the use of distinctions once reserved for those of noble blood to encourage conquerors to become colonists, to remain in Peru, and to encourage colonization. His research indicates that individuals were promised inducements including escutcheons, habits in the military orders, and titles.[84]

While titular incentives are most commonly associated Spain's colonization efforts, scholars have largely ignored England's similar efforts, incorrectly assuming that this was a salient feature of Spanish colonization exclusively. While a fear of leveling and a rather traditionally Genevan biblical denunciation of ambition were evident in New England settlement, in other English colonies, noble title was explicitly contemplated and later employed for the purposes of encouraging New World colonization.[85]

David Beers and Nicholas Canny, among others, have noted that England's expansion into Wales, Scotland, and Ireland established certain precedents for New World colonization.[86] This was certainly the case with the knight baronet of Nova Scotia, which was modeled on the knight baronet of Ulster. But what scholars often ignore is that Spanish colonization in the New World also informed the English colonization of Ireland, establishing certain precedents before the English New World settlements. England looked to Spain's use of titular incentives as a model for what might be effective in encouraging colonization and settlement. England, like Spain, endeavored to bridle ambition as a means to advance the nation's overseas expansion.

One finds evidence for this contention and the proposal for harnessing ambition for the purposes of benefiting the state in the works of Francis Bacon. It is not surprising, given the discussion of Bacon's essay "Of Ambition" and the new strategies that he suggested for harnessing the passions, that his political philosophy would find some practical application. As a councillor to Queen Elizabeth and later to King James I, Bacon's theory of the passions found a practical application in the use of titular incentives in the settlement of Ulster that later became a model for the proposed plantation in New Scotland. Recall that in his essay "Of Ambition," Bacon suggests that princes, from time to time, need to "bridle" ambition. Bacon writes: "So ambitious men, if they find the way open for their rising, and still get forward, they are rather busy than dangerous. . . . Therefore it is good for princes, if they use ambitious men, to handle it so as they be still progressive and not retrograde. . . . For if they rise not with their service, they will take order to make their service fall with them. . . . They are to be bridled, that they may be less dangerous."[87] Due to the hazardous nature of their passion, Bacon advises, "it is good not to use such natures at all." But he recognizes that even certain imprudent steps might at times be necessary, so he qualifies his assertion by adding, "except it [using ambitious natures] be upon necessity."[88]

Bacon applies this philosophy of the passions and suggests one such "necessity" in a letter to the king, in a series of specific recommendations for the plantations in Ireland. He recognized that convincing people to emigrate was one of the most formidable challenges the king had to overcome in order to make the colonization of Ulster a success. Or perhaps Bacon realized that the challenge was not just convincing people to emigrate but convincing the right sort of people to do so. Bacon recognized that it was "necessary to allure by all means undertakers." By "all means" because "those men will be least fit, which are like to be most in appetite of themselves; and those most fit, which are like least to desire it."[89] All means, in this case, included "bridling ambition."

Much of the historiography of early America is dedicated to explaining the motives for the founding of the North American colonies.[90] There is far less scholarship on Bacon's theory of colonization, one that privileged human nature over religious or national ideals.[91] Bacon recognizes three major motives for emigration: pleasure, honor, and profit.[92] When it came to Ireland, for Bacon, pleasure was simply absent. "There are no warm winters, nor orange-trees, nor strange beasts, or birds, or other points of curiosity or pleasure." But as he continues his discussion of Ireland's lacking, he suggests that there might be another motive for colonization, a certain sort of human nature: "so as there can be found no foundation made upon matter of pleasure, otherwise than that the very general desire of novelty and experiment in some stirring natures."[93] One might, then, add "curiosity" or a restless nature to a motive for colonization, but Bacon categorizes curiosity under pleasure.

He then turns to "honor." He suggests that the king create a new title, the "earldom of Ulster," to add to the prince's titles, to put "more life and encouragement into the undertakers."[94] Here, he cites King Edward I, who did so with Wales, and "the Prince of Spain" who "hath

the addition of a province in the kingdom of Naples."[95] Bacon here suggests the creation of a new earldom, citing Spain as one of the precedents that the king should consider.

But then, in order to further encourage "undertakers," in hopes of
"bridling" their ambition, Bacon suggests the "raising of some nobility
here," as it "may draw some persons of great estate and means into the
action." His suggestion comes with qualifications. As with Spain, Bacon
intends these titles to be carefully circumscribed: "If it be done merely
upon new titles of dignity, having no manner of reference to the old;
and if it be done also without putting too many portions into one hand:
and lastly if it be done without any great franchises or commands, I do
not see any peril can ensue thereof."[96] In addition, Bacon suggests
"knighthood to such persons as have not attained it; or otherwise knighthood with some new difference and precedence, it may no doubt work
with many."[97]

Bacon's general recommendations were later adopted with the creation, in the spring of 1611, of a "new Dignitie between Barons and
Knights" and designated with a new noble title, "baronet."[98] Scholars
who have studied the origins of *baronet* in the early seventeenth century emphasize the financial motivation for its creation and tend to ignore the importance of the object and ostensibly the primary justification for its inception.[99] The state papers of the time contain numerous
similar proposals for raising funds for the crown by the use of the sale
of titles, but not one of these is adopted.[100] Yet conferral of titles for
the purposes of bridling ambition to encourage colonization is embraced. That is not to minimize the financial motivation for the crown
to adopt the program. James's reign was marked by financial difficul-
ties and distress. The baronetage provided him with necessary funds
without the need to call a Parliament. George Calvert captured this
sentiment when, in 1611, he wrote: "If this take good effect, your old
Parliament men think the King will not call a Parliament in haste
for a new subsidy, for this will amount to much and more."[101] John
Chamberlain, an acquaintance of Francis Bacon and contemporary
observer of the court of James I, characterized these efforts as "the

Kinges wants might be much relieved out of the vanities and ambition of the gentrie."[102]

In fact, the sale of baronets was a financial boon to the crown. But it was also a revolutionary step, both in English history and in the history of ambition. For the first time there was a price tag on nobility. Historian Katherine Van Eerde writes, "Men had bought titles before . . . but this was England's first (and only) experiment with an honor clearly marked with a price tag."[103]

The nobles responded angrily, concerned that the wrong sort would be elevated. James was irked that his prerogative was challenged. Ultimately, he brushed aside the concerns of the existing nobility and many new knights baronets were named.[104] But by putting a price tag on title, James unintentionally challenged the premise on which his own authority rested—noble blood. In offering nobility for sale by proclamation of the king, the wellspring from which nobility was supposed to flow, the "fountain of honor," nobility was effectively deracinated. This, then, was a watershed in ambition's trajectory. If the elevation to nobility is no longer barred by the immutable, the unchangeable—to wit, blood—then the path for the ambitious, even to nobility, has been cleared. Can the king's crown be far off? This policy became increasingly perilous as baronetage became detached from colonization. The crown began to use the sale of baronetcies for paying debts and rewarding courtiers.[105] An account of the degradation of the title and its disassociation from its original intent is captured in an official book of crown revenues compiled after James's death:

> It is to be observed that since this first institution of this honour of baronets, and after the first number completed, infinite number of baronets were made and had the like patents for that honour, as those eminent gentlemen of first rank had; although they maintained not one footman in Ireland. . . . The reason is, the King to gratify Scottishmen and other needy courtiers gave them the nomination and presentment of such persons as they could find out to be baronets . . . so that many

men of base birth and weak estate (*ambitious of place* and dignity) had this honour conferred on them, to the disgrace of the
first institution.[106]

The nobles, protective of their distinction, complained to the king. An
anonymous petition denounced the ambition of men of "mean birth
and many of them but lately tradesmen . . . have by indirect means
slipped themselves into this title of honor."[107] There is evidence that
these charges were not without merit, as the title, originally intended
to be significantly limited to those of gentle birth and large estate, had
been more liberally bestowed. Even recusants and alleged Catholics
had joined the ranks of the baronets.

Harnessing ambition through baronetcy reattached to colonization late in James's reign, in 1621, with the creation of the knights
baronets of Nova Scotia. Bacon may have been one of the first English
proponents of harnessing ambition for colonization, but it was Sir William Alexander, the principal projector of an English colony in Nova
Scotia, who seized upon his acquaintance's proposition. Ambition might
have been a sin in the early seventeenth century, but Alexander, like
Bacon, and like the Spanish before them, recognized the utility in harnessing it. He does so explicitly, unabashedly referring to the conferral
of noble title for the colonization of Nova Scotia as ambition's "bait."[108]

William Alexander was a Scot, a poet, and the tutor of James's
son Henry.[109] When James was crowned king of England, Alexander
accompanied his court to England, where he was knighted. While in
London, Alexander became "exceedingly inflamed" with American colonization.[110] On August 5, 1621, James granted Alexander the "lands
lying betweene New England and Newfoundland."[111] His stated motivation was "sovereign anxiety to propagate the Christian faith, and to
secure the wealth, prosperity and peace of the native subjects of our
kingdom of Scotland, as other foreign princes in such cases already
have done."[112] Here in the royal charter, James cites "foreign princes"
as precedent for his decision. James created one hundred new baronets
for the purposes of encouraging colonization of Nova Scotia.

But James died before the order could be executed. When Charles I ascended to the throne, he confirmed Alexander's charter and his father's creation of the knights baronets of Nova Scotia. Charles I proclaimed his purpose in so doing: "Whereas, upon good consideration, and for the better advancement of the Plantatioun of New Scotland, which may much import the good of Our service, and the honour and benefite of Our auncient Kingdome, Our Royall Father did intend, and Wee have since erected, the Order and Title of Barronet in Our said auncient kingdome."[113]

The challenge for Alexander was how to convince "undertakers" to settle in the land he was granted. Despite the incentive that baronetcy provided, the response in Scotland was less than enthusiastic. Alexander recognized the virtue of publicizing his colony and the spiritual, national, and titular rewards for those who would undertake it. One way he sought to accomplish this goal was with the 1624 publication of his *Encouragement to the Colonies*.[114] With *Encouragement*, Alexander joined other English travel and promotional authors who sought to promote colonization in their descriptions of the New World. Again the tripartite incentives of God, nation, and self are clearly evident. Alexander writes that "the greatest incouragement of all for any true Christian is this, that heere is a large way for aduancing the Gospel of Jesus Christ, to whom Churches may bee builded in places where his Name was never knowne."[115]

The planting of churches and the advancing of the Gospel were accompanied by the conversion of the "Sauage people" who "doe now liue like brute beasts."[116] David Brion Davis has written extensively on the connection between slavery and animalization or bestialization as central to the master class ideology.[117] While Alexander explicitly suggests only conversion, by stating that the natives live like beasts, he subtly undermines any claim they may have to land or control over their own potential labor. Oddly, earlier in *Encouragement*, Alexander suggests that that the natives are gone and that the land awaits the arrival of the Scottish or English colonizers. So this passage seems largely rhetorical, a noble justification for the colonization effort. While Bacon suggested honor, profit, and pleasure as the three main incentives, Alexander pleads that the potential colonizers leave "these dreames of Honour and Profit, which doe intoxicate the braines, and impoyson the minde with transitory pleasures."[118] The pleasures of honor and profit are transient, and the colony should be formed "to begin a new life, seruing God more sincerely then before, to whom we may draw more neere, by retyring our selues further from hence."[119]

Despite his urging that "serving God more sincerely" should be the most potent encouragement and that one should set aside transitory motives, Alexander recognizes the more worldly motives for colonizers and for Scotland. For the nation it is beneficial "by reason of her populousnesse being constrained to disburden her selfe (like the painfull Bees) did every yeere send forth swarmes." Alexander suggests that this might be a way of "disburdening the Countrey of them." But in the "disburdening" they might have been able to "deserve of their Countrey, by bringing vnto it both Honour and Profit."[120]

As for the incentives for the colonizers, the means by which they might win both honor and profit, Alexander extolls the virtues of Nova Scotia's abundant natural resources, a place ripe for trade and export. But what perhaps distinguishes Alexander from other promoters is that while other authors implied a quasi-noble New World status, suggesting large tracts of land, abundant resources, and willing vassals, Alexander explicitly engages titular incentives. More remarkable is that Alexander, a poet and playwright, elsewhere denounces ambition in predictable terms as vice, consistent with the dominant ideology of the time. For example, in his poem *A Paraenesis*, he writes:

If I would call antiquity to minde,
I, for an endlesse taske might then prepare,
But what? ambition that was ever blinde,
Did get with toyle that which was kept with care,
And those great States 'gainst which the world repin'd
Had falls, as famous, as their risings rare:

And in all ages it was ever seene,
What vertue rais'd, by vice hath ruin'd been.[121]

But when it comes to the colonization of Nova Scotia, ambition is suddenly transformed from a vice, ever blind and destructive, into a virtuous undertaking. Alexander suggests that ambition can be harnessed. In his work we see a microcosm of the transformative possibilities of the New World. What was vice or sin in England was transformed by the act of colonization into a national, Christian, and personal virtue. In this incredible passage, Alexander suggests not only that the New World is "ambition's bait" but that ambition itself might become a virtue through the act of emigration. "Where was euer Ambition baited with greater hopes then here, or where euer had Vertue so large a field to reape the fruites of Glory."[122] The "bait" here is to become a "great man" and, remarkably, a self-created noble, a self-made aristocrat:

> Since any man who doth goe thither of good qualitie, able at first to transport a hundred persons with him furnished with things necessary, shall have as much Bounds as may serve for a great Man, wherevpon hee may build a Towne of his owne, giuing it what forme or name hee will, and being the first Founder of a new estate, which a pleasing industry may quickly bring to a perfection, may leaue a faire inheritance to his posteritie, who shall claime vnto him as the Author of their Nobilitie there, rather then to any of his Ancestours that had preceded him, though neuer so nobly borne elswhere.[123]

Alexander, through extending the king's offer of baronetcy and through the grants of land, offered émigrés the chance to become nobility, though "never so nobly borne elswhere."

Encouragement allows us insight into an English rationale for colonization — harnessing or "baiting ambition" as an outlet for the state and for individual, national, and Christian glory. With the creation of the knights baronets of Nova Scotia, England, like Spain before it, created a new noble title for the explicit purpose of encouraging New World colonization.

Surprisingly, though titular incentives are most often associated with Spain's colonization efforts, Stuart Schwartz's research indicates that few promised titles were actually granted. In his words, though the "promise of noble status was used as an inducement to service, reasons were always found to prevent full compliance," and, if granted, "the history of these early grants of nobility was generally one of legal arbitration in a continuing effort to reduce their powers. . . . Noble or *hidalgo* status in sixteenth-century America was far more ephemeral than real."[124] In the case of England, not generally known for using noble title as an incentive, a number of baronets were eventually created for the purposes of colonizing Nova Scotia, Newfoundland, and Maine, with family names including Agnew, Barclay, Elliot, Forbes, Kirkpatrick, and Stewart. In 1580, when the Spanish crown was in desperate financial need, several proposals for the sale of *hidalgo* status were considered and rejected.[125] In England, as mentioned, the crown accepted similar proposals. A comparison of noble titles granted in Peru and Nova Scotia (which includes Newfoundland and parts of what is now Maine) is illustrative. For the English, as for the Spanish, America became a place where ambition not only could be safely realized but could be harnessed for the benefit of God and the crown.[126]

This suggests a certain dual nature of ambition now emerging, a potentially virtuous vice, a sin that might be harnessed for God and country. In What Alexander decries as sin in poetry becomes, in colonization, a large field for virtue to be realized. Even for a puritan divine, one for whom ambition as sin is firmly rooted in his Calvinist theology and Genevan biblical and homiletic associations, ambition is likewise converted by the New World. In 1609, four years after the first performance of *Eastward Hoe*, William Symonds preached a sermon at Whitehall on the subject of colonization of Virginia.[127] In Symonds's sermon, he promises that the New World is a place where individual virtue is magnified. But as a result of this magnification, remarkably, he

Comparison of Grants of Noble Titles in Peru and Nova Scotia, 1532–1660

Peru		New Scotland	
1532–1600	1	1625	19
1600–1630	3	1626	9
1631–1660	10	1627	13
		1628	22
		1629	7
		1630	10
		1631	4
		1633	2
		1634	4
		1635	8
		1636	9
		1637	3
		1638	5
Peru total: 14		New Scotland total: 115	

promises worldly fame and eminence, the realization of individual ambition. This ambition could never be realized in England. He states: "Manie a man, while he staieth at home, liveth in obscuritie, as in the darkest night, though his vertues and worth deserve better respect. For at home what can bee a mans regarde, where there be millions of his rank, though not better deserving, yet better favoured."[128] He contrasts this with Virginia and from his pulpit urges: "Get abroad where vertue is skant, and there, by the advancing of thy wisdome and vertue, thou shalt bee more eminent and famous in a yeare, then at home halfe of thy rank shall bee all their daies: hidden vertue is neglected, but abroade is magnified."[129]

Formerly a sin that might only be repressed, ambition is now recast as a passion that can be harnessed for a potentially virtuous undertaking. The harnessing of ambition for colonization redefined it in fundamental ways that would have been unimaginable a century before: as a vice with virtuous possibilities, as a virtue with a dark side. Ambition assumes a duality, a passion that can be good or bad depending on the object to which it is applied.

But regardless of titles conferred, there was a widespread perception in both Spain and England that America offered an opportunity to realize ambition in ways that were unavailable in Europe. Anthony Pagden captures this preoccupation when he writes: "These new men had come to New Spain to act out the role of the great magnates of the Old Spain. Like nearly all the colonists in the Atlantic world, they had come to found a new society where their otherwise hopeless social ambitions might be fulfilled."[130] The sources are filled with disparaging accounts of their presumption. Viceroy Núñez Vela of Peru sarcastically observed that in the Indies, Spaniards were "all gentlemen, sons of magnificent fathers."[131] One contemporary observer even went so far as to describe the process of their self-making as a rebaptism by the ocean so that they might be "born again" in nobility: "on landing in Panama, the Chagres River and Pacific Ocean baptizes them so that arriving in this city of Lima all are dressed in silk, descendants of Don Pelayo and the Goths and Archgoths: They go to the palace seeking fees and offices and in the churches. . . . They order masses said for the honored Cid."[132] "The Spaniards," complained the procurator general of Peru in 1619, "from the able and the rich to the humble and the poor all hold themselves to be lords and will not serve."[133] Often, Spaniards in the New World chose poverty over "common" labor. Chroniclers remark on the frequency of ragged Spanish vagabonds wandering the roads of Mexico trailed by native women as early as 1529.[134] This unwillingness to work and the assumption of a quasi-gentleman status conferred by the mere act of emigration may also have been present at Jamestown. During the "starving time," men preferred starvation to the labor of planting, even when it might have saved their lives.[135]

Land and the opportunity for wealth and rank, including actual title, fueled the ambition of many prospective colonists. However, there is another essential element that is unique to the New World: a large native population, which functioned, in part, to elevate these American self-made aristocrats and Europe as a whole in the presumption of a cultural superiority. From the time of Columbus, an elevation to a higher status for Europeans was achieved through the Indians' very existence, both the ways in which they were imagined and the ways in which they in turn imagined the European newcomers. Through myth, marriage, and ultimately a process of both cultural and legal subordination, Europeans realized their ambition of a higher estate through the permanent degradation of a racialized indigenous people.

But first to the myth, the widely publicized European belief that the Native Americans viewed the Europeans as gods among them. This belief, the Euro-god myth, begins early in contact with the New World, present in Columbus's account. Columbus describes how he and his crew were magically transformed from mere men to gods in the eyes of the people, the inhabitants of the New World. Columbus describes the elevation of his men, both literally and figuratively, in the following passage:

> Later, when it was afternoon, the lord gave them three very fat geese and a few small pieces of gold; and a large number of people came and carried for them everything that they had received in trade there; and they insisted on carrying the Spaniards on their backs; and in fact they did so through some rivers and muddy places. The Admiral ordered that they give the lord some things, and the lord and all his people, with great contentment, truly believing that the Christians had come from the heavens, considered themselves very fortunate in seeing them.[136]

The perception of the New World deification of Spanish adventurers was perpetuated through the accounts of Cortés's conquest of Mexico. In the accounts of Gómara and in popular myth, Cortés and his men are seen as the long-prophesied return of the god Quetzalcoatl. Gómara writes:

> The Indians stared at the dress, fierce countenances, and beards of the Spaniards; they were astonished to see the horses eat and

run; they were frightened by the flashing of the swords; and
they fell to the ground at the roar of the cannon, for it seemed
to them the sky was falling upon them with its thunder and
lightning. They said of the ships that the god Quetzalcoatl
had come, bearing his temples on his shoulders, for he was the
god of the air who had gone away and whose return they were
expecting.[137]

In Gómara's account, Cortés then, realizing the advantage of this misconception, attempts to perpetuate it. He tells the natives to send word
to Montezuma to send gold because he and his companions "suffer
from a disease of the heart which can be cured only with gold."[138] With
this lie, or metaphorical use of the word *disease*, Cortés implies that
they are not mortal men; they are not like the Native Americans but
gods, perhaps, with strange ailments and remedies. Throughout the
accounts of the conquest, both in Díaz and Gómara, the Spanish are
referred to as *teules*, the Spanish corruption of the Nahuatl word *teoles*,
"gods." Bernal Díaz recounts that Cortés is told by two caciques of
Tlaxcala the myth of a god from the East that was prophesied to arrive
and conquer the land.[139] Historians have attributed Montezuma's reluctance to make war against the Spaniards to the acceptance of the
Spaniards' arrival as the return of the god Quetzalcoatl and the acceptance of the futility of acting against a prophesied inevitability.[140] In
his second letter, Cortés recounts Montezuma's speech to him, though
mediated through translators and Cortés's recollection. According to
Cortés, Montezuma suggests that Cortés, though not a god, might be
the descendent of a mythic godlike ancestor who it was foretold would
one day come from the East to reclaim the throne.[141]

Other historians have challenged the Quetzalcoatl myth as func-
tioning as a plausible explanation for Montezuma's strategic decision.
Stuart Schwartz and J. H. Elliott, among others, suggest that the myth
was likely a mid-sixteenth-century retrospective reconstruction among
both the Spanish and the Aztecs. Schwartz notes that preconquest myths
were strongest where the Spanish impact was greatest, suggesting the

people's need to provide a narrative to accommodate the cataclysmic changes to which they were subjected. The *Florentine Codex* recounts eight omens that foretold the coming of the Spanish. They included a comet, a woman weeping, a temple struck by lightning, and a bird with the head of a mirror.[142] But Schwartz notes that the Spanish commonly included preconquest omens in their accounts of conquest. He suggests that they did so to "as a way of underlining the preordained nature of their conquest," which made "the beliefs of the indigenous peoples of Mexico appear even more exotic to European readers."[143] This is a fascinating suggestion. The Catholic conquerors considered the pagan beliefs as adding value or imbuing the conquest with meaning, a pre-ordination of their destiny conferred not from the God of the Christians but from the indigenous prophecies. Perhaps this would have served to underline their arrival not for the Europeans but for the indigenous peoples themselves. The Spaniards may have included preconquest omens in their accounts of conquest in order to reinforce their delusion of entitlement and mastery. It is an interesting example of syncretism that runs against the assumption of the normal flow of culture, the indigenous incorporation of European ideology. Here the Europeans appropriate an indigenous myth in the service of their ambition for supremacy.

Yet in addition to believing that the native peoples saw them as gods, some Europeans believed that their ambition to higher status could be realized through marriage as well as myth.

The men of Cortés's and Pizarro's armies sought marriage to members of Indian nobility to realize certain social ambitions, as well as to obtain land grants through dowries. While in some cases there was the assumption of empty land, or land uncultivated, in the case of the *conquistadores*, there was a recognition not only of ownership but also of the noble prerogative to transfer it through a daughter's dowry. A document of June 27, 1526, serves as a challenge to the assumption of Indian barbarity. In it, Montezuma grants a dowry for the marriage of his eldest daughter to Alonso Grado, one of Cortés's captains.[144] Juan Cano de Saavedra, who accompanied Cortés, married Montezuma's daughter Tecuichpotzin in 1532. When he returned to Spain, he appended the name Moctezuma to his own name, as did his Spanish descendants, who later built their family seat and named it the Palacio Toledo-Moctezuma.[145]

Intermarriage with Native American nobility was also used as justification for usurping the authority of the Iberian crown in the New World, as ambition turned to rebellion in both Mexico and Peru. Gonzalo Pizarro spoke of marrying an Inca princess in order to legitimate his ambition to become king of Peru.[146]

But legitimation of the rights of New World nobility could be conferred by Native American approbation as well as intermarriage. Martin Cortés was accused by the crown of proclaiming himself king of Mexico in what was known as the "conspiración del marques." It was said to be spurred by the refusal of the crown to extend the rights of the Indian labor, the *encomienda,* to the heirs of the conquistadors. The refusal of hereditary rights to labor was one way the crown curtailed the nobility of the New World elite. Martin Cortés was accused of plotting to kill the king's men and "to make a great fire in the plaza of all the papers and writings which were in the archives and offices so that there should remain no written memory of the name of the king of Castile."[147] Part of what validated Martin Cortés's claim were the exploits of his father, who won the land by his own ambition. His nobility, then, was one procured by achievement and imagined to be passed to his son. In a further attempt to legitimate Cortés's son's right to claim sovereignty over the land, several of his alleged coconspirators masqueraded as Indian chiefs and warriors who, in an elaborate public procession, marched to the gates of Cortés's house to implore him to be their king. They handed him a crown of flowers inscribed, "Do not fear to fall, for by this act you shall rise higher."[148] The judges in the trial understood that this was meant to indicate that "the Marqués was to be king of this land."[149] The crown responded to this presumptuous ambition by executing the conspirators and expelling Martin Cortés from Mexico. Whether Martin Cortés actually planned to proclaim himself king of Mexico is unclear. His prosecution might simply have been a way of mitigating the ambition of the heirs of the conquistadors. They might claim hereditary rights, the rights of a noble of Spain, but the rights of these new nobles of New Spain, as the research of Stuart Schwartz indicates, were severely curtailed. Nonetheless, the fascinating account of Martin Cortés implies that the Indians possessed an authority to confer the rights of king. This of course complicates the statistics compiled in the chart delineating New World nobility, as it was also established de facto by the natives, as well as by the Iberian crown.

Intermarriage was important as well in the colonization of Brazil. The nation was originally divided into fifteen captaincies, or land grants (*donatarios*). Of the fifteen, two were successful. Schwartz notes that the success of these two was largely due to intermarriage between the Portuguese and the Native American inhabitants.[150] In fact, as Charles Boxer observes, "Portuguese colonists of either sex who intermarried with Brazilian Indians would not only nothing in the way of social status, but would improve their chances of official preferment and promotion."[151]

In Virginia, John Rolfe married Pocahontas. When Rolfe returned to England with his native bride, King James was vexed. The cause of his annoyance was not that Rolfe had married an Indian but that Rolfe, a commoner, had married the daughter of a foreign prince, a woman therefore of noble blood, without his express permission.[152]

In the colonies of Spain, intermarriage for the purposes of realizing an ambition to noble status was a social dynamic that did not persist long past the first generation of conquerors and settlers. Pagden summarizes the situation as follows: "The idea that Indians were noble barbarians like the Moors or the Turks, together with the idea that Indian blood might confer some degree of nobility on a plebeian Spaniard did not, however, last long. Although some of Cortes's and Pizarro's men had been proud to marry into the ancient Indian aristocracy, they were not keen to associate themselves with their successors, the *curacas* and *caciques*, who were little more than tribute collectors for the encomenderos."[153] But early in the conquest and colonization,

Native Americans were capable of conferring status to lowly European soldiers and adventurers or, as in Mexico and Peru, legitimating even the ambition to become New World kings.

But as Pagden's remarks imply, this phenomenon was relatively short-lived and by no means the dominant understanding of the Indians. In the Europeans' efforts to make sense of the New World, the legal and cultural status of its inhabitants was a topic of considerable debate. But even within the debates, there was a common ground—a racial or cultural hierarchy in which Native Americans were to occupy a subordinate position. As Magnus Mörner notes in his work on race mixture in Latin America, a decided racial hierarchy soon emerged in Latin America in which whiteness or Spanish origin became synonymous with a New World nobility regardless of profession.[154] Pagden, citing Mörner, notes that "most Spaniards were more willing to marry white prostitutes than Indians," even the daughters of chiefs, or caciques.[155] This was later reflected in the law that codified these racial distinctions in a hierarchy in which "white" occupied the top rung.[156]

Interestingly, both the nobility and the subordination of the Native Americans are a product of the same ideological contradiction, what has been referred to as the early modern paradox of "knowing the unknown." That is, in response to the contact and "discovery" of this new land and its peoples, a debate ensued as to what exactly these people were. Hypotheses were proposed and debated, but from a flawed initial assumption: that European theologians and philosophers already knew all that could be known, or, as Anthony Pagden writes, "All that could be known had to be made compatible with recognized canon of sacred and ancient authors."[157]

Within the relatively closed cosmology of theories of knowing, Europeans attempted to accommodate the discoveries of the New World. Imagining the native chieftains as foreign nobles was one way in which new experience could be accommodated to canonical knowledge. But so, too, was subordination of the indigenous population.

Stephen Greenblatt and others have referred to this process as *mimesis*, often writing of these marvelous possessions in spatial terms.

But I would argue that the mimesis was a temporal as well as a spatial mimesis. That is, in the closed cosmography of the European imagination, America and its inhabitants were often imagined as a time in the European past from which the Europeans themselves had advanced. For many Europeans, Columbus had discovered a "when" as much as he had discovered a "where."

In the debates between Las Casas and Sepulveda in Valladolid, Las Casas, as David Brion Davis notes, considered the Indians to be the "equal to the primitive Europeans of antiquity, and could thus be considered raw material for a Christian civilization."[158] Similarly, the English imagined the native peoples as not yet English. Thomas Scanlan, in his study of the De Bry engravings, notes that "by Europeanizing the Indians . . . Indian culture is simply a lesser developed version of English culture."[159]

This took its most extreme form in the Edenic references in some European accounts. Not only was America a distant past, it was a world just after man's fall, and its inhabitants had not progressed far past it. Columbus, in fact, believed he had found the site of the "terrestrial paradise." The Garden of Eden was believed to be located somewhere in the world, occluded from man by God's will. Medieval travel narratives held that Eden, the terrestrial paradise, would be revealed to God's chosen pilgrim. Columbus believed himself to be that chosen pilgrim.[160] Las Casas supports Columbus's interpretation, writing of the "fresh lands, and such green and delightful groves." He continues extolling not only the virtue of the land, but the goodness of the people in support of America as the site of the terrestrial paradise:

> So much clemency and amenity in the subtle breezes, so much and such rapturous grandeur and [rapturous] lake and capacious and so large a union of such slender and sweet waters; and moreover, the goodness, generosity, simplicity, and gentleness of the people. What else could he judge or conclude but that there, or around there, or even close to that place, the Divine Providence had constituted the Terrestrial Paradise, and

that that freshwater lake was where the river and fountain of Paradise emptied and where the four rivers Euphrates, Ganges, Tigris, and Nile originated?[161]

The English, too, in their promotional tracts depicted America in Edenic terms. Arthur Barlowe, in an attempt to attract prospective colonists to Roanoke, wrote, "The earth bringeth forth all things in abundance, as in the first creation, without toil or labor."[162]

Like the rivers, humanity, too, had originated in the Americas. But unlike with the Spanish, their "simplicity," had remained such that they were often imagined as what humanity might have looked like before it had progressed, or been fully corrupted. The idealization of the Native Americans often informed European depictions, as the writings of Las Casas indicate. Elsewhere in the Americas there emerged a similar idealization of native peoples. They were imagined as simple, closer to nature, less well developed, later what is referred to as "natural man." It was a state of man that is not now, but a then, an earlier time in man's development, a picture of European man as he once existed, before civilization corrupted him. That is not to say that the Indians were not free from evil. They were considered in need of true religion. Some speculated that the land had been hidden from the European Christians by the Devil so that he could have free reign over its inhabitants. But other evils, sins of a world corrupted, were often thought to be inapplicable to them. Often, native peoples were seen as incapable of "ambition." Las Casas wrote, "They are neither ambitious nor greedy, and are totally uninterested in worldly power."[163] This seems to have been a fairly common European interpretation. The French Jesuit Paul Le Jeune in 1634 wrote: "If it is a great blessing to be free from a great evil, our Indians should be considered fortunate. For there are two tyrants, ambition and avarice, who distress and torture so many of our Europeans but have no dominion over these great forests."[164]

According to Columbus, Las Casas, Le Jeune, and others, the Native Americans were a simple people free from the evils of a corrupted European world, free from ambition and avarice. Arthur Barlowe, in his *First Voyage to Roanoke*, states, "We found the people most gentle, loving and faithfull, voide of all guile and treason, and such as live after the manner of the golden age."[165] In this case, Barlowe invokes "the golden age," an idyllic past from Greek mythology. This age, a pre-Christian Edenic parallel, was used to describe an age of bliss and harmony for humanity that ended when Prometheus brought fire to the earth, and Zeus allowed Pandora to open the box that unleashed evil on the world to destroy that bliss and end that age. Virgil depicts it in *The Georgics*. In the Golden Age,

> Fields knew no taming hand of husbandmen;
> To mark the plain or mete with boundary-line —
> Even this was impious; for the common stock
> They gathered, and the earth of her own will
> All things more freely, no man bidding, bore.[166]

Here, before English colonization, the natives have not subdued the earth, not because of some inherent deficiency but because of some uncorrupted excellence that resembles a time before corruption. Ovid, with whom many sixteenth-century English would have been familiar, describes the Golden Age in terms that closely resembled Eden:

> Golden, that first age, which, though ignorant
> of laws, yet of its own will, uncoerced,
> fostered responsibility and virtue; . . .
> . . . without warfare, all
> the nations lived, securely indolent.[167]

This rapturous secure indolence was possible as:

> No rake had been familiar with the earth,
> no plowshare had yet wronged her; untaxed, she gave
> of herself freely, providing all essentials.
> Content with food acquired without effort.[168]

Later English poets would describe the golden age as an age in which "ambition was not known."[169]

The absence of ambition and the armor of their "innocence" had helped maintain the "simplicity" of the Native Americans. Later, however, the absence of their ambition, their "secure indolence," that very simplicity, helped justify their displacement and the English entitlement to their lands. The grounds for this displacement were established on the basis of native inferiority, evidence of which could be found in theories of law and understandings of sin. Paradoxically, in denying the possibility of American Indian ambition and avarice, both sins widely accepted as fundamental to human nature, Europeans failed to regard the Indians as more godly, instead seeing them simply as less human.

This took an extreme form early in the Spanish conquest. Some argued that in the Indians, they might have discovered the "natural slave" suggested by Aristotle. In Aristotelian theory, true slavery was a reflection of a condition that was innate and immutable. David Brion Davis notes that "for Aristotle true slavery derived from an innate deficiency in the beauty and inner virtue of the soul," and he cites Aristotle as writing, "From the hour of their birth, some are marked out for subjection, others for rule."[170]

The bishop of Darien, Juan Queveda, is thought to have been the first to apply the Aristotelian theory of natural slavery to the American Indians.[171] Las Casas, among others, debated the issue, but the theory was given full expression between 1550 and 1551, when theologians, jurists, and officials gathered in the city of Valladolid to determine the nature of native people's humanity and their place within an imposed European hierarchy. In that debate, Juan Ginés de Sepúlveda advanced theories of the Spaniards' natural superiority and the natives' natural inferiority, their relative lack of humanity. He writes that the Indians are:

> as children are to adult, or women as to men. Indians are as different from Spaniards as cruel people are from mild people. Compare then those blessings enjoyed by Spaniards of pru-

dence, genius, magnanimity, temperance, humanity, and religion with those of the homunculi (little men) in whom you
will scarcely find even vestiges of humanity, who not only possess no science but who also lack letters and preserve no monu-
ment of their history except certain vague and obscure reminiscences of some things in certain paintings. Neither do they
have written laws, but barbaric institutions and customs. They
do not even have private property.[172]

Clearly, this passage ignores Cortés's dowry arrangement with Montezuma. If there was no notion of private property, then how could Cortés claim land bestowed to him by virtue of his written arrangement
with Montezuma? Las Casas, as David Brion Davis notes, did not refute the Aristotelian notion of "natural slave," but he simply argued
that Native Americans were not the group that fit that designation. Las
Casas imagined the native peoples not as a group permanently assigned
to that place outside the social order but as good raw material for Christianity. Again, not a what but a "when," a "not yet quite Spaniard" but
with all the potential to become every bit as prudent, brilliant, and
magnanimous one day. The superiority of the Spanish was not a subject of debate.

Nor was the subject of English superiority, once colonization began
in earnest. For the English, the presence of a large, indeterminate
group of native people had been greatly reduced through the unfore-
seen devastation of disease. Even before the seventeenth century, disease had ravaged the North American native population. As such, there
was often the perception that the land was empty or that the native
people were impediments or unwanted growth, weeds in an otherwise
healthy garden, fecund for English planting. John Winthrop, in a 1634
letter, conveys this sense: "[As] for the natives, they are near all dead of
smallpox, so the Lord hath cleared our title to what we possess."[173]

The land, however, was not as empty as Winthrop imagined. The
English developed legalistic justifications for Amerindian usurpation.
The doctrine of "vacuum domicilium" was one such theory, most often

attributed to the writings on jus gentium (the law of nations) as espoused by Hugo Grotius and John Locke.[174] Perhaps the best known
justification is John Locke's *Second Treatise*. This holds that property
rights do not extend to man in a state of nature. Value and ownership
are created by "the labour of his body, and the work of his hands. . . .
Whatsoever then he removes out of the state that nature hath provided,
. . . he hath mixed his labour with, and joined to it something that is
his own, and thereby makes it his property."[175] By imagining the Native
Americans as living in a state of nature, a state without ambition or
avarice, Europeans had the ideological imperative for the usurpation
of their lands and the establishment of empire.[176] The colonizers themselves often used biblical passages to justify the precedent for the plantation of their colonies and the displacement of the native populations
from their lands. Most often cited was Genesis 1:28, in which God commands Adam and later reiterates to Noah to "fill the earth and subdue
it." John Cotton writes in this vein of "vacant soil," arguing that "in a
vacant soyle, hee that taketh possession of it, and bestoweth culture
and husbandry upon it, his Right it is. And the ground of this is from
the grand Charter given to *Adam* and his posterity in Paradise, *Gen.*
1.28. *Multiply, and replenish the earth, and subdue it.* If therefore any
sonne of *Adam* come and find a place empty, he hath liberty to come,
and fill, and subdue the earth there. This Charter was renewed to *Noah*,
Gen. 9.1."[177]

The previous passage begs the question as to what is intended by
"vacant" earth and what exactly is intended by God's injunction to
"subdue it." John White in his 1656 commentary writes that subduing
the earth "is, by Culture and Husbandry, to Manure and make it fit to
yield fruits and provision . . . which is done by Planting, Earing, Sow-
ing, and other works of Husbandry."[178] George Hughes likewise explains
that subduing the earth could be understood to mean "plowing, tilling,
and making use of it." John Winthrop, when writing about the native
tribes' right to their land, states that they had "only a natural right to
so much land as they had or could improve."[179] In Virginia, the lack of
ambition and avarice was accompanied by a lack of industry, which

disqualified the natives from ownership. Robert Gray writes: "These Sauages have no particular propriety in any part or parcell of that Countrey, but only a general recidence there, as wild beasts have in the forest . . . so that if the whole land be taken from them, there is not a man that can complaine of any particular wrong done unto him."[180]

Their participation did not include "subduing" the land through cultivation, and therefore their presence could be discounted, as could their ownership. The Presbyterian Scots-Irish also used the Bible to denounce the Delaware Indians, who they believed were guilty of ignoring the Parable of the Talents.[181] The Delawares had no right to their land because of their failure to improve it.

The Spanish and English were superior by virtue of their comparative excellence, as judged by their own cultural criteria. In this case, as in other cases throughout human history, superiority requires inferiority to substantiate it—the *Übermensch* cannot proclaim itself *über* without the presence of an *Untermensch*, as ambition, both individual and national, is historically realized at the expense of a degraded other. While Native Americans served this purpose initially, Africans would soon become the more fundamentally degraded other.

That said, the Americas presented for both the English as for the Spanish, in the words of Amerigo Vespucci, a *Mundus Novus*, a New World. In this New World commoners could become kings, cities could be planted on "empty" hills, and laborers could be reborn as New World nobility, with vassals, title, land, and wealth. For the English, as for the Spanish, America became a place where ambition could be not only safely realized but harnessed to benefit God and crown, even at the expense of others. What was once a sin had become a virtuous vice, as the Icaran sun had suddenly distanced itself from European waxen wings and moved west to the New World.

Epilogue

We have not raised armies with the ambitious designs of separating from Great-Britain, and establishing independent states.
—A Declaration . . . Setting Forth the
   Causes and Necessity of Their Taking up
   Arms, 1775

When in the course of human events it becomes necessary for a *people to advance from that subordination in which they have hitherto remained, & to assume among the powers of the earth the equal and independent station* to which the laws of nature & of nature's god entitle them, a decent respect to the opinions of mankind requires that they should declare the causes which impel them to the change.
—Thomas Jefferson, "original Rough
   draught" of the Declaration of
   Independence (emphasis added)

By ambition, I meane the unlawful and restles desire in men to be of higher estate then God hath geven or appoynted unto them.
—*An Homilie against Disobedience and
   Wylfull Rebellion*

W here does one end a history of ambition in early America? Perhaps the best place to end is at America's beginning: "When in the Course of human events, it becomes necessary for one people to dissolve the political bands which have connected them with another, and to assume among the powers of the earth, the separate and equal station to which the Laws of Nature and of Nature's God entitle them." These are the words that introduce our American scripture, our "in the beginning" of a self-fashioned heaven on earth, our Genesis, our Declaration of Independence. Thomas Jefferson is acknowledged to be the principal author, but perhaps *author* is the wrong word, as it fails to convey the import that the document has assumed in American culture, its elevation to a near sacred text.[1] Perhaps *prophet* would be a better word—Jefferson, the chosen one and, like all prophets, the instrument of divine will, a conduit of God's intent.[2]

But as with all myths national and otherwise, the history behind them is messier. The Declaration, of course, was not handed to Jefferson from God but incorporated significant editorial input first from John Adams and Benjamin Franklin and later from other members of Congress.[3] Jefferson was, in fact, frustrated that his work was torn at by Congress, though he sat quietly through the editorial debates. Franklin tried to console him with a story about a hatter who painted a signboard to advertise his shop: the hatter solicited input from well-intentioned friends whose zeal to assist left the sign so well "edited" that all that remained was the hatter's name and a picture of a hat.[4]

This anecdote may be indicative of the eighteenth-century attitude toward the document, not a sacred scroll, but a hat, something to warm the nation's head, chilled by the last resort of independence. Or perhaps our Declaration was a fashion statement or a theatrical prop. Adams referred to the publication and proclamation of the Declaration of Independence as a stage event: "The Declaration was yesterday published and proclaimed from that awful Stage, in the State-house yard."[5] Jay Fliegelman observes that "American independence coincides with a theatricalization and commercialization of private life in America, phenomena reflected in the very marks on the manuscript of the Declaration."[6] The marks were intended to guide the performance of the Declaration. If Franklin is any indication our nation's stage prop, our hat was one made of fur rather than silk.

The historical record indicates that Jefferson was not entirely consoled by Franklin's fable, as Jefferson sent copies of his first, carefully constructed document to several friends. Well, almost his original, but more on that in a bit. On the rest, Richard Henry Lee commiserated, writing back to Jefferson after receiving a copy of the draft, "I wish sincerely . . . that the Manuscript had not been mangled as it is."[7]

Modern scholars, however, do not share Lee or Jefferson's opinion. With the exception of the passage on slavery, most historians believe that the Declaration of Independence was improved by editorial input. In 1948, Pulitzer Prize–winner Dumas Malone wrote, "There can now be little doubt that the critics strengthened [the Declaration of Independence]," attributing a weakness of rhetorical excess to Jefferson's unedited drafts.[8] I am invariably drawn to assertions where "little doubt" is coupled with little evidence. Historians have in the past misjudged even Jefferson, guided by truths they believed to be self-evident.[9]

Pulitzer Prize–winning historian Garry Wills, in *Inventing America: Jefferson's Declaration of Independence*, writes, "I have found no scholar who argues that the congressional changes altered Jefferson's message in any substantial way." Wills follows this statement with a chapter explaining several important, though overlooked, "substantial" changes that Congress made in editing Jefferson's draft.[10] But what he misses is the fundamental change in the opening sentence of Jefferson's "original Rough draught" before it is given to the Congress. Despite their importance as the first words intended to proclaim independence, they have been largely ignored by scholars.

Of the scholars who do write about the changes made to Jefferson's "original Rough draught," only Pauline Maier engages the first sentence directly. In her Pulitzer Prize–winning *American Scripture: Making the Declaration of Independence*, Maier attributes the rewrite to the old formula of rhetorical excess. She writes that Jefferson's original first line was "more awkward and also harder to say than the revised version," noting that it was a document that was intended to be orated.[11]

I would argue that the rewrite of Jefferson's "original Rough draught" was made for reasons not stylistic but, in fact, substantive. As Stephen Lucas correctly observes: "British leaders and American Tories had long claimed Congress did not represent the true wishes of most colonists, and Congress knew its enemies would condemn the quest for independence as a desperate measure forced on the majority of Americans by a handful of 'artful, ambitious, and wicked men.' If the charge took hold, it would alienate many citizens from Congress and 'raise up such a Schism as would prove more dreadful than any outward Enemy.'"[12] Justifying independence meant guarding against charges that it was inspired by a small group of men driven by wickedness and ambition.

A careful consideration of Jefferson's "original Rough draught" reveals that it was rewritten to mitigate potential charges of a declaration not of independence but "of ambition," one with the potential to destroy the moral claims on which the Declaration hoped to rest.

We know the words of our scripture. Let's turn now to Jefferson's "original Rough draught" and look for evidence of ambition: "When in the course of human events it becomes necessary for a *people to advance from that subordination in which they have hitherto remained, & to assume among the powers of the earth the equal & independant station* to which the laws of nature & of nature's god entitle them, a decent respect to the opinions of mankind requires that they should declare the causes which impel them to the change."[13] I would like to review the charges against this original, which are twofold: the final draft "sounded better" than Jefferson's original; and the final draft was easier to say, especially as it was intended to be orated.

There is an inherent problem in assessing whether American scripture "sounds better" than any other written version that we know less well, with words less enshrined in our national origins. Does "four score and seven years ago" sound better than "eighty-seven years" or "nearly ninety years have passed"? It does to me, but it is difficult to evaluate

Jefferson's "original Rough draught" of the Declaration of Independence. Library of Congress.

objectively. It may simply sound "better" because it has always sounded that way, the gravity of the inevitable and expected too strong, as in music, when the melody returns to the home key, we expect it to return to that tonic. It is challenging to forget "scripture" and view the words with a fresh eye, one that looks past the imposing facade of the presumptions of origin.

But let us suspend, as much as possible, what we know and argue the contrary. When I do, though it takes some doing, I happen to find the original more mellifluous. With its clause architecture, parallelism, rhythm, and internal rhyme, it is music. Maier rightly observes that "attention to the cadences of language was natural for Jefferson, a committed violinist fascinated with music. He also studied classical oratory and rhetorical theory, employed several known rhetorical strategies in composing the Declaration, and 'wrote for the ear as well as for the eye.'"[14]

In Jefferson's original he creates an elegantly parallel architecture through the use of phrase/clause construction with correspondence further solidified through an internal rhyme that is absent in the revision. Note that in Jefferson's original "subordination" rhymes with "station" and "remained" and "change" form approximate rhymes, while repeated "which" clauses create a further rhetorical parallel.

Guided by Fliegelman's work on Jefferson's pauses, let's carve Jefferson's original into segments to better view its architecture.[15] For the purposes of illustration, I have labeled the "subordination/station" rhyme A and "remained/change" rhyme B and have emphasized the "which" clauses.

to advance from that *subordination* (A)
 in *which* they have hitherto *remained,* (B)
& to assume among the powers of the earth the equal and independent *station* (A)
 to *which* the laws of nature & of nature's god entitle them,
a decent respect to the opinions of mankind requires that they should declare the causes
 which impel them to the *change.* (B)

Parallelism is a fundamental technique of eighteenth-century English rhetoric and oratory. As Jim Engell notes, part of Jefferson's stylistic excellence may be attributed to his knowledge of the rhythms and possibilities of parallelism.[16] The *Oxford Dictionary of Literary Terms* defines *parallelism* as: "The arrangement of similarly constructed clauses, sentences, or verse lines in a pairing or other sequence suggesting some correspondence between them. The effect of parallelism is usually one of balanced arrangement achieved through repetition of the same syntactic forms."[17]

Other examples of the use of rhyme to create parallelism in the eighteenth century include Edmund Burke's letter to the Duke of Bedford: "Such are their ideas; such their religion, and such their law. But as to our country and our race, as long as the well-compacted structure of our church and state, the sanctuary, the holy of holies of that ancient law . . . shall stand inviolate on the brow of the British Lion."[18] And elsewhere Jefferson writes: "If a nation expects to be ignorant and free, in a state of civilization, it expects what never was and never will be."[19] Oration, the music of its form, admits the opportunity to borrow from verse, using rhyme to create a musical effect. We hear the rhyme that creates a rhythm and a parallel.[20] As John Sitter notes, for "eighteenth-century readers (as well as for us) [rhyme] calls attention to itself and to the words it links through sounds."[21] In his theory of rhyme, linguist Maurice Grammont's observations on French poetry are equally applicable to Jefferson's original prose. Grammont writes that rhyming "warns the ear that one rhythmic group is complete and that another is coming. As long as the second rhyme has not been heard, the mind remains expectant. Once the rhyme has been heard, the ear reposes with a feeling of satisfaction born of a harmonious combination that is recognized as perfect."[22]

To me (and perhaps to Grammont), Jefferson's original sounds better. But ultimately this assessment is subjective.

I'd like to turn now to the assertion that the finished draft was easier to orate and provide more objective evidence to the contrary. Jefferson changes "advance from that subordination" to "connected them with another." Try saying, "connected them with another." Speak it aloud. Now annunciate it as if you are speaking to a large audience without the modern convenience of amplification. When I do, I stumble on the consonant combination "c-t" in "connected." I find my lips pulled awkwardly back, teeth bared; my airflow, which wants to project, is interrupted by the need to raise my tongue to the roof of my mouth to produce the sound. In linguistic terms, the "c" makes a /k/ sound and forms a velar stop, or a plosive midword, as my airflow is constricted. But this is not simply my opinion. The science of acoustic phonetics demonstrates that velar stops like the one found in "connected" involve a total occlusion of the vocal tract. The result is a period of silence in the spectrogram, known as a "gap." This gap as measured by a spectrograph indicates that during a velar stop, in the words of linguistic theorist Rob Hagiwara, "there's no useful sound coming at you— there's basically silence."[23]

Silence is antithetical to the basic premises of good oration (save pauses full of pregnant possibility). The words from Jefferson's original draft, "advance from that subordination," produce no velar stops, and simple consonant vowel combinations are more easily projected. Here is objective evidence that Jefferson's original was easier to orate.

Leaving aside the debate over "sound," I'd like to now turn to "sense." The first line of the Declaration of Independence changes from: "advance from that subordination . . . the equal and independant station" to: "dissolve the political bands . . . the separate and equal station." When Jefferson finished his "original Rough draught," John Adams and Benjamin Franklin reviewed it before it was then submitted for congressional "mangling." The Declaration went to Congress with the alteration. So either Adams or Franklin (or Jefferson himself) saw the line and suggested the change that was adopted.

At this juncture, let us review some of the central arguments of this book. Recall that *ambition* is earlier defined in Anglo-American culture as "the unlawful and restles desire in men to be of higher estate then God hath geven or appoynted unto them."[24] It condemned those men and women "clymyng up of theyr owne accorde to dominion."[25] Ambition was directly linked to sin, Satan, and, perhaps more relevant at the time of the American Revolution, to rebellion.

This point is explicit in *An Homilie against Disobedience and Wylfull Rebellion.* Tudor homilies were required reading from the pulpits of sixteenth- and seventeenth-century England.[26] They were composed to help local parish priests, who were often less learned in liturgy or interpretation, disseminate the official religious doctrine. The audience was the common person or "middling" man and woman. Unlike many sermons or theological tracts, the homilies eschewed scholastic or "high" pretension. The language was simple, clear, often redundant, full of straightforward directives and unambiguous "take home" messages. The homilies are, then, both an elite source and a common source, and they are extremely relevant in a social history of ideas. Literacy rates are less relevant in evaluating this source because people are being read to, in "their" language, each week.[27]

While the homilies are traditionally seen as a primarily "Elizabethan" source, this is simply not the case. According to Millar MacLure, the homilies were "the single greatest influence" on Jacobean and Caroline divines. In the early eighteenth century, Bishop George Bull urged the clergy to rely on the homilies, rather than "trust at first to their own compositions, but to furnish themselves with a provision of the best sermons, which the learned divines of our church have published . . . use the Homilies of the church."[28] Pollard and Redgrave's *Short-Title Catalogue* and Wing's *Short-Title Catalogue* list roughly fifty editions of the homilies. Candidates for the Anglican clergy as late as the eighteenth century were compelled to read *An Homilie against Disobedience and Wylfull Rebellion* on the anniversary of the regicide of Charles I.[29]

There is evidence of their extensive use in Anglican churches in eighteenth-century America as well. The extant parish and county records of Anglican Virginia indicate that the homilies were still read by laymen "readers" or "clerks" who assisted in worship. In 1698 a parish paid one "Will Clapton" 250 pounds of tobacco for "reading Homilies there being noe minister."[30] With a noted shortage of qualified ministers, there "being" none, the homilies as set pieces were to take on a much more prominent role. The vestry from a church in Middlesex County, Virginia, describes the clerk's role to "Duely on the Lords Day Read Divine Service, and a Homily."[31] Because of a shortage of priests, Anglican parishes relied on clerks who could be "of good character . . . and read tolerably."[32] The homilies were prepackaged and preapproved; no background in theology was required and seldom demanded.

Despite their significance, the homilies have been "unaccountably neglected by students of literature and the history of ideas," writes literary scholar Donald Greene.[33] They are ignored by scholars of the American Revolution. But recognizing their importance helps unlock a crucial link between ambition, sin, and rebellion in the eighteenth century.[34] This link is often as misunderstood by historians of religion as by historians of early America. In fact, one scholar of religion and law in early America even refers to ambition as a "traditional Puritan virtue."[35]

This ambition, this climbing to dominion, is inveighed against in part because it is at the root of both rebellion and the damnation that will result from it. In fact, *An Homilie against Disobedience and Wylfull Rebellion* tells us that there are "many *causes of rebellion* . . . almost as many as there be vices in men and women. . . . The principall and most usuall causes [are] *ambition and ignoraunce*."[36]

Further, rebellion is "an abominable sin agaynst God and man," and "horrible plagues, punishemenets and deathes, with death everlasting finally, doth hang over the heades of all rebels." Though the Geneva Bible tells us that Adam was fallen by ambition in his rebellion against God, in the homilies Satan is most often identified as the "first aucthour" and chief embodiment. In Lucifer, rebellion is identified as the "root of all vices and mother of all mischiefes." In the act of rebellion, even the best and most excellent are damned: "Lucifer, first Gods most excellent creature and most bounden subject, who by rebelling against the majestie of God, of the brightest and most glorious angell is become the blackest most foulest feende and devill, and from the height of heaven is fallen into the pit and bottome of hell."[37]

According to the homily, there are "two sortes of men in whom these vices [ambition and ignorance] do raigne." The "restles ambitious" who cannot "by lawfull and peaceable meanes clime so high as they do desire, they attempt the same by force and violence." The "restles ambitious . . . when they cannot prevayle agaynst the ordinarie aucthoritie and power of lawful princes and governours them selves alone, they do seeke the ayde and helpe of the ignoraunt multitude, abusing them to their wicked purpose."[38]

But what about the link between ambition and rebellion in the eighteenth century at the time of the drafting of the Declaration of Independence? One cannot assume a cultural link between the two still persisted despite the suggestion of the homiletic influence.

One obvious place to turn for clues is Samuel Johnson's *Dictionary of the English Language* of 1755. As Jack Lynch notes in an op-ed piece in the *New York Times*, "The dictionary was first extensively revised in 1773, so it was the most influential and up-to-date language guide at that pivotal time." George Washington owned a signed copy. In 1771 Thomas Jefferson elevates Johnson's work to the level of secular bible of sorts, giving a friend a list of books to "fix us in the principles and practices of virtue," among which was Johnson's *Dictionary*. Lynch further notes that from as early as 1785 and as recently as late twentieth century, American legal scholars, including Supreme Court Justices Ruth Bader Ginsburg, John Paul Stevens, Clarence Thomas, and William Rehnquist have used Johnson to try to better understand the intent of the Founders.[39]

Johnson's dictionary defines *ambition* as follows: "The desire of something higher than is possessed at present. (1) The desire of preferment or honour. (2) The desire of any thing great or excellent. (3) It is used with *to* before a verb, and *of* before a noun." He defines *ambitious* as follows: "Seized or touched with ambition; desirous of advancement; eager of honours; aspiring. It has the particle *of* before the object of ambition, if a noun; *to*, if expressed by a verb. (2) Eager to grow bigger; aspiring." Further, many of Johnson's definitions contain pithy and illustrative usage examples. While justices may look to Johnson's dictionary for the Founders' intent, they and we must steep ourselves in Johnson's meanings and examples to determine significance. As Johnson suggests, through Imlac the poet, "Example is always more efficacious than precept."[40]

It is in his example that Johnson recognizes ambition's residual meaning and historical and religious antecedents. For his entry Johnson cites the late sixteenth- and early seventeenth-century metaphysical poet John Donne: "We seem ambitious God's whole work t'undo." Donne's words, drawn from his 1611 poem "An Anatomy of the World," reflect the destructive and sinful import of ambition, still present in the eighteenth century, though dominant in the late sixteenth and early seventeenth centuries. In defining ambition with Donne and ambition's capacity to undo "God's whole work," an Eden, God's brightest angel, the sinful associations are reiterated.[41] In Johnson we glimpse the eighteenth-century ambivalence toward ambition. It was a virtuous vice, a vitiating merit, Janus-like, a two-faced passion that could be good or bad depending on the ends to which it was applied.[42] And ambition with rebellion in its sights was unequivocally vicious.

Johnson's dictionary was originally published in 1755. An American Revolution by most scholars' accounts was a distant, nearly unimaginable, possibility. In the age of revolution there is evidence that ambition, rebellion, and sin were "remembered" and reinvigorated.

In an effort to gauge this I turn to the *Pennsylvania Gazette*. The *Pennsylvania Gazette*, often referred to as the *New York Times* of the eighteenth century, is an interesting source. What makes it relevant for my purposes, and different from today's *New York Times*, is that the majority of its revenues came not from advertisements but from subscriptions. A subscription-based publication is likely to have paid a greater attention to the views of the public than a publication funded primarily by advertisements. Further, it is estimated that up to 70 percent of the content of the *Pennsylvania Gazette* was culled from other newspapers. Colonial newspapers had a reciprocal free postage arrangement, which permitted news to circulate through the colonies. Considering this source provides insight into much more than what

Ambition in the Pennsylvania Gazette
(1728-1800)

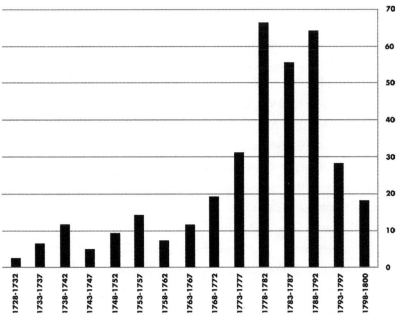

Uses of *ambition* or *ambitious* in the *Pennsylvania Gazette* in the eighteenth century. Note the increased use of the words in the decades of "rebellion."

Pennsylvanians thought; it gives us information on the colonial population as a whole.[43]

To track *ambition*, I looked at every use of *ambition* and *ambitious* between 1728 and 1800 and plotted their use over time. Data visualization, while often the exclusive purview of scientists and statisticians, can be a powerful, elegant, illustrative narrative medium, a powerful device for telling stories.

So I thought, why not see if there is a story to be told here? Why not plot the uses and see what it looks like? What I found was quite exciting (see chart above). This visualization tells us that cultural associations die hard. Although the use of *ambition* is negligible in the early eighteenth century, it explodes suddenly and dramatically around the time of rebellion, from the time just before the onset of open armed conflict and through the following decade.

But what of meaning? Qualitative evidence, both in the *Pennsylvania Gazette* and beyond, also supports my claim. In 1773, a notice mourns the death of Francis Gardner, "a stranger to malice, pride, and ambition, (vices so prevailing in this awful age of degeneracy)." This was an age of revolution to some, an awful age of degeneracy to others.

A May 1776 document titled "To the Freeholders and Electors of the City of Philadelphia" warns against rebellion, calling those who "scheme to independence" "ambitious innovators," and referring to "ambitious republican schemes of a sett of men, whom nobody knows." Further, the writer argues that they have entered into armed rebellion via deception, driven by "republican ambitious partisans."[44] The House of Peers in an address to the king could not "forbear to express our detestation and abhorrence of the audacious and desperate spirit of ambition, which has at last carried those leaders so far, as to make them openly renounce allegiance to the crown."[45]

In 1776, at the nadir of America's revolutionary fortunes, an anonymous play titled *The Battle of Brooklyn* was published and featured none other than George Washington and his commanders Israel Putnam, John Sullivan, and Lord Stirling. Published only a few months after independence was declared, the work might technically be America's first play. It has been virtually ignored, in large part because this was not a drama that celebrated the patriotic efforts of the brave heroes of the newly independent nation. Instead, it was a two-act loyalist work, often attributed to James Rivington.[46] As rebellion at this point was open and much blood had been shed, a work written about the battle and rebellion might be expected to convey a certain poignancy. The Battle of Brooklyn was among the most terrible defeats of Washington's army, one characterized by brutal hand-to-hand combat with little quarter given.[47]

Yet *The Battle of Brooklyn* was not a tragedy but a farce. Farce, though often treated as a genre not worthy of scholarly study, dismissed as appealing to the lowest or basest elements, is elevated in our search for meaning outside traditional "elite" sources. Laughter is predicated on the assumption of a group recognition of the absurd. Because farce is drama written for the masses, we can recognize an echo of the vox populi in the dramatists' efforts to get a laugh. In this case there is the "group recognition" of what was driving George Washington specifically, and the leaders of the American Revolution by extension, to an act of rebellion. In a soliloquy reminiscent of Macbeth's murdered sleep, George Washington laments his decision to bring ruin to his "native country." "Oh!" he begins, "Could I congratulate myself, on finding my lost peace of mind!—on the restoration of my honor!" And what is Washington's tragic flaw? "O! cursed ambition!" he cries, "what have I sacrificed to thee?"[48] But the laughter that is encouraged here is a bitter, caustic laughter. While most assumed that the rebellion would soon end, at a time when rebel fortunes ebbed, in those "times that tried men's souls," when the colonial population seemed "strangely contaminated" as they flocked to the side of king, when the real George Washington wrote to John Hancock of the "very gloomy prospect upon the appearance of things," America's first play blasted Washington and a movement for independence inspired by thoughts of elevation from subordination, spurred by this ambition.[49]

Earlier religious connotations of ambition, sin, and man's first rebellion within popular perceptions are echoed, too, in a well-known loyalist ballad. The ballad is titled "Adam's Fall: The Trip to Cambridge" and is sung to the tune of "Yankee Doodle."[50] It lampoons Washington's assumption of power as head of the rebel army. This ballad implies that Washington, "clothed in power and breeches," falls from God's grace like Adam by his act of irreconcilable disobedience to George III. Recall that in the marginal notes of the Geneva Bible, the dominant biblical translation for a century in colonial America, it is explained that "Adam . . . was fallen by ambition." If Adam ate the fruit because he was moved by ambition, what was Washington's "fruit"?

Jonathan Boucher, loyalist minister and tutor to George Washington's stepson, answers this question. Boucher was the minister of the Anglican church of Saint Barnabas in Upper Marlborough, Maryland. His loyalist sympathies were met with threats of violence. In 1775 an angry crowd of two hundred, led by Osborn Sprigg, uncle of the future governor of Maryland, filled Saint Barnabas. They told Boucher that if he tried to preach he would not "come out alive." But enter the church he did, and with one hand on the pulpit and the other on one of the loaded pistols he kept near his Bible, he faced them with the words, "No power on earth should prevent [me] from praying and shouting 'God Save the King.'"[51] He then grabbed Osborn Sprigg at gunpoint and with his hostage beat a hasty retreat to his waiting horse. Boucher escaped unharmed. Almost perfectly paraphrasing the Geneva marginalia, Boucher considers the rebels as Adam and independence as the "forbidden and accursed fruit."[52] In many ways he reflects Johnson's dictionary definition perfectly. He was by many accounts desirous of a higher station and later writes in his *Reminiscences:* "Determined always to raise myself in the world, I have not patience to wait for the slow savings of a humble station; and I fancied I could get into a higher, only by my being taken notice of by people of condition."[53] But the line between virtue and vice is drawn in rebellion, still forbidden fruit, still fecund with sinful import.

Loyalist minister Jonathan Odell, too, recognized ambition as the spur to rebellion in his verse.[54] Odell was closely connected with Benjamin Franklin's son William, the Governor of New Jersey. In his 1776 poem "Inscription," Odell, in an inversion of the Faust myth, celebrates Franklin's scientific achievement and in so doing recognizes ambition's dual nature.[55] He writes:

Like a Newton sublimely he soar'd
  To a Summit before unattained;
New regions of Science explor'd
  And the Palm of Philosophy gain'd.

Celebrating Franklin's experiment with electricity, Odell continues: "With a Spark, that he caught from the Skies, / He display'd an unparallel'd wonder." This is a loyalist minister celebrating Franklin's catching sparks "from the Skies." In Faust this would have been ambition. In Franklin it is sublime and wondrous.

But for Odell, ambition is not purged of sin. Odell recognizes the homiletic connections among ambition, rebellion, and sin, bemoaning that Franklin did not continue to pursue scientific truths:

> O had he been wise to pursue
>   The track for his talents design'd,
> What a tribute of praise had been due
>   To the teacher and friend of Mankind!

Odell then compares Franklin to Lucifer and recognizes that Franklin's spark, like Satan's, was ambition, which set sedition's blaze:

> But to covet a *political* fame
>   Was, in him, a degrading ambition;
> A Spark, that from *Lucifer* came,
>   And kindled the blaze of *Sedition*.

Again, reflecting the homiletic and Genevan notions of ambition, rebellion, and sin in these loyalist tracts, we recognize that at the time of the American Revolution, ambition is still tied to sedition and Lucifer.[56]

Odell returns to the theme in his "Ode for the New Year," of 1780:

> Rebellion madly shakes the land,
> And love is turn'd to hate and fear.
> Here, Britannia, here at last
> We feel Contagion's deadly blast.
> Thus blind, alas! when all is well,
> Thus blind are Mortals here below:
> As when apostate Angels fell,
> Ambition turns our bliss to woe.[57]

The rebels are like the "apostate Angels" fallen by ambition.

The "apostate Angels," too, were acutely aware of the charges of ambition and attempted to guard against them. The accusation of "ambition" was so damning that Congress felt obliged to publicly and explicitly refute it. The problem is, the colonist doth protest too much. In a January "1775 Petition of the Continental Congress to the King," Congress laid out their grievances, with the assurance that these "distresses, dangers, fears, and jealousies" flow from the "system of colony administration," in place since the Seven Years' War, and not from "unjust impulses of ambition."[58]

In July 1775, Congress issued "A Declaration . . . Setting Forth the Causes and Necessity of Their Taking up Arms." One year before the Declaration of Independence, when blood had already been shed on the fields of Lexington and Concord, the July 1775 declaration, as in the January petition, proclaims that the colonists "have not raised armies with *ambitious* designs of separating from Great-Britain, and establishing independent states."[59] This establishes a rhetorical pattern in petitions and declarations from Congress in 1775. The members of Congress are announcing and proclaiming and petitioning and emphasizing that they are doing what they are doing NOT because they are ambitious. Independence is ambitious, and Congress has no choice but to defend itself from the charge and proclaim that it is driven by a motivation less damning.

Which brings us, finally, back to Jefferson's "original Rough draught." It was not rewritten because it sounded better but because "advancing from that subordination" to a more "equal and independant station" was a statement tantamount to an explicit admission of ambition. The Founders are not apostate angels but enlightened patriots. Jefferson, most likely urged by Franklin, would rewrite the "original Rough draught" to mitigate the charges of ambition, replete with residual associations of sin, antithetical to republican ideals of disinterest.

The problem was that their claim was not even remotely plausible. This was a full-blown rebellion, soon to become a revolution, one in which Americans with their Declaration of Independence explicitly stated their intent to wrest control of lands from king and Parliament to form a more perfect union, to relocate sovereignty with "the people." Their action, many scholars believe, was tantamount to regicide. Winthrop Jordan has described the American Revolution in exactly those terms. "One can propose," Jordan writes, "that in 1776 George III was killed in his American provinces vicariously but very effectively."[60] In acts of symbolic violence, effigies of George III were burned on the streets throughout the colonies. Whether or not the king was actually killed was not as important as the fact that sovereignty, as it was understood, was both symbolically and substantively destroyed.

The American Revolution was among the most audaciously ambitious acts in the history of the Western world.[61] The problem was how to reconcile an act traditionally defined as evil with a republic that was intended to convey the essence of virtue. Franklin's "natural man," the simplicity of Jeffersonian architecture, Washington's self-conscious self-identification with Cincinnatus, a figure from antiquity identified as a model of "anti-ambition"—all were attempts to identify the project of independence not as a desire to have a higher station but as a step toward having a more perfect union.[62]

But the requirements of a declaration are not the whole story here. We know that ambition becomes widely celebrated in nineteenth-century America. After independence has been proclaimed, how can Americans not rehabilitate ambition? Is it not an ideological necessity? That is, if ambition is sin, and independence is ambitious (by the colonists' own definition), then either independence is sin or ambition must be redefined. And redefined it is.

Thomas Paine explicitly rejects loyalist definitions of sin and denounces a more profound evil—monarchy—for which independence was the only reasonable recourse. Paine writes in *Common Sense*: "For as in Adam all sinned, and as in the first electors all men obeyed; as in the one all mankind were subjected to Satan, and in the other to Sovereignty; as our innocence was lost in the first, and our authority in the last; and as both disable us from reassuming some former state and privilege, it unanswerably follows that original sin and hereditary succession are parallels."[63] In Paine, original sin was linked no longer to ambition but instead to hereditary succession. This signals a full and explicit rejection of ambition as sin. *Common Sense* was one of the most widely disseminated pamphlets of the Revolution. Estimates vary from tens of thousands to one hundred thousand copies printed. This document marks a watershed in ambition's trajectory, one that explicitly purges ambition as sin, and though it does not celebrate ambition, it renames a lack of ambition born of absolutism as the more damning vice. The influence of *Common Sense* is reflected even in sermons. Unlike Jonathan Boucher, who sees independence as "forbidden fruit," or the Genevan and homelitic sources that recognize "ambition and rebellion as sin," in his 1776 sermon, "American Independence Vindicated," Massachusetts divine Peter Whitney, like Thomas Paine, recognizes monarchical government as sin.[64]

Paine was not alone in redefining ambition. John Adams, too, suggested a radical reinterpretation when he wrote in 1777, "Ambition in a Republic, is a great Virtue, for it is nothing more than a Desire, to Serve the Public, to promote the Happiness of the People, to increase the Wealth, the Grandeur, and Prosperity of the Community. This, Ambition is but another Name for public Virtue, and public Spirit."[65] This is profoundly radical, representing a departure and full purgation of sin. Adams here proclaims ambition a virtue.

But just as Jefferson writes of all men created equal, never intending equality to extend beyond white men, Adams's celebration of ambition and proclamation of its rehabilitation was likewise never intended to extend beyond a small group of white men. Adams often refers to his wife as his "dearest friend." Theories of friendship from Aristotle to Derrida are predicated on assumptions of equality.[66] Yet when Abigail asks John in a 1776 letter to "remember the ladies" in the new laws of the new nation, John refuses, promising instead to fight the "Despotism of the Peticoat."[67] As the nineteenth century was to show, women,

The colonies as serpent by Benjamin Franklin.
Pennsylvania Gazette, May 9, 1754.

African Americans, and Native Americans were never imagined to be part of the celebration of ambition. Self-made men were just that.

But despite the severe restrictions on ambition, the Revolution fundamentally changed and wrote American ambition. Perhaps the most conspicuous symbol of the redefinition of sin is to be found not in a letter but in a flag. Whereas in the Bible Satan was the most extreme embodiment of both sin and ambition, represented by the serpent, in the eighteenth century the serpent becomes increasingly associated with the American colonies, first published in a political cartoon of 1754 by Benjamin Franklin. By 1775, the serpent comes to represent the nation, with images appearing all over the colonies on buttons, flags, and paper money.

While a writer in the *Pennsylvania Journal* of 1775 interpreted the snake's bright eye as representing courage and vigilance, others were fully aware of the sinful implication of the serpent's invocation.[68] James Rivington, the same writer who in his farce accused Washington of ambition, writes:

> Ye Sons of Sedition, how comes it to pass,
> That America's typed by a SNAKE—in the grass?
> Don't you think 'tis a scandalous, saucy reflection
> That merits the soundest, severest correction?[69]

Massachusetts Spy, July 7, 1774.

The Gadsden Flag, c. 1774–1775.

Finally, "Don't Tread on Me" were the words attached. Ambition, once associated with Satan and sin, had become the symbol of the new nation.

Wresting ambition from the panoply of vice and reconstituting it as a virtue was a necessary ideological precondition to the establishment of the United States. Without ambition, there could be no America. Understanding ambition within a historical and ideological context illuminates a facet of our Declaration of Independence, our Revolution, and a fundamental aspect of our national character. The War for Independence was not just a political struggle, it was a contest over the very definition of good and evil. Formerly a manifestation of original sin, ambition was transformed into "another name for Public Virtue." Icarus had been unbound, and ambition's American journey had begun, though it would be another few centuries before everyone could openly avow the doctrines of its scripture.

Notes

Introduction

1. H. W. Brands, *The First American: The Life and Times of Benjamin Franklin* (New York: Doubleday, 2000); Joseph Epstein, *Ambition: The Secret Passion* (New York: E. P. Dutton, 1980), 9.

2. Mark Twain, "The Late Benjamin Franklin," *Galaxy* (1870): 138–140. David Herbert Lawrence, *Studies in Classic American Literature* (New York: Thomas Seltzer, 1923), ch. 2.

3. One of the earliest printed versions of this adage may be found in John Clarke, *Paroemiologia Anglo-Latina* (London, 1639).

4. Benjamin Franklin, "Last Will and Testament," June 22, 1750, in *The Papers of Benjamin Franklin*, ed. Leonard Labaree et al., vol. 3 (New Haven: Yale University Press, 1961).

5. *Merriam-Webster's New Collegiate Dictionary*, 11th ed., s.v. "ambition."

6. This is, of course, provided that the means and ends conform to a carefully circumscribed notion of what it means to dream and to whom certain dreams are allowed.

7. Heinz Kohut, *The Analysis of the Self* (New York: International Universities Press, 1971); Kohut, *The Restoration of the Self* (New York: International Universities Press, 1977). Kohut posited two poles of ambition wherein too much or too little ambition were both problematic. He postulated that in some cases the inhibition of striving may be due to a death wish, preferable to the outdoing of an oedipal rival, which would be tantamount to murder. See Kohut, "The Analysis of Mr. R.," in *The Search for Self: The Select Writings of Heinz Kohut: 1978–1983*, vol. 2, ed. Paul H. Ornstein (London: Karnac, 2011), n12.

8. Anthony Robbins, *Awaken the Giant Within: How to Take Immediate Control of Your Mental, Emotional, Physical and Financial Destiny* (New York: Free Press, 1992); James Champy and Nitin Nohria, *The Arc of Ambition: Defining the Leadership Journey* (Cambridge, MA: Perseus Books, 2000); Epstein, *Ambition*, 3.

9. Robert Burton, *The Anatomy of Melancholy*, ed. Floyd Dell and Paul Jordan-Smith (New York: Tudor, 1927), 243. Edwin Wolf and Kevin J. Hayes, eds., *The Library of Benjamin Franklin* (Philadelphia: American Philosophical Society, 2006), 167. The editors note that Franklin refers to Burton's work in a letter to Jonathan Shipley dated February 24, 1786.

10. Glen Pettigrove, "Ambitions," *Ethical Theory and Moral Practice* 10, no. 1 (2007): 53.

11. Steven Watts, *The Republic Reborn: War and the Making of Liberal America, 1790–1820* (Baltimore: Johns Hopkins University Press, 1987), esp. section 2. See

also Epstein, *Ambition*; and Jason Opal, *Beyond the Farm: National Ambitions in Rural New England* (Philadelphia: University of Pennsylvania Press, 2008).

12. Edmund Burke, *The Beauties of Burke: Consisting of Selections of His Works,* ed. Alfred Howard (London: T. Davison, 1834), 109.

13. The best-known example is Douglass Adair, *Fame and the Founding Fathers* (New York: Norton, 1974). More recent is Joanne B. Freedman, *Affairs of Honor: National Politics in the New Republic* (New Haven: Yale University Press, 2001).

14. Lewis Namier, *The Structure of Politics at the Ascension of George III* (New York: MacMillan, 1957), xi, cited by Paul Rahe, *Republics Ancient and Modern,* vol. 2 (Chapel Hill: University of North Carolina Press, 1994), 149.

15. Alasdair Macintryre, "The Nature of Virtues," in *Virtue Ethics,* ed. Roger Crisp and Michael Slote (New York: Oxford University Press, 1998), 123.

16. Namier cited in Rahe, *Republics Ancient and Modern,* 150.

17. There is a large body of work on language and ideas that spans political theory, philosophy, history, and literature; see Quentin Skinner, "Meaning and Understanding in the History of Ideas," *History and Theory* 8, no. 1 (1969): 3–53; Skinner, "Verbalizing a Political Act: Towards a Politics of Speech," *Political Theory* 1, no 1. (February 1973): 27–45; J. G. A. Pocock, *Politics, Language, and Time: Essays on Political Thought and History* (Chicago: University of Chicago Press, 1972); and Pocock, *The Machiavellian Moment: Florentine Political Thought and the Atlantic Republican Tradition* (Princeton, NJ: Princeton University Press, 1975).

18. I thank Professor John Rogers for calling Raymond Williams's work to my attention. Williams, *Marxism and Literature* (New York: Oxford University Press, 1977), 121–137.

19. For excellent examples of the advantages of understanding American history within a global context, see David Brion Davis, *The Problem of Slavery in Western Culture* (New York: Oxford University Press, 1966); and Paul Gilroy, *The Black Atlantic: Modernity and Double Consciousness* (Cambridge, MA: Harvard University Press, 1993). For an excellent overview of the current trends in the history of the Atlantic world, see Alison Games, "Definitions, Challenges, and Opportunities," *American Historical Review* 111, no. 3 (2006): 741–757. On the need to expand Atlantic history to a global perspective, see Peter A. Coclanis, "Drang Nach Osten: Bernard Bailyn, the World-Island, and the Idea of Atlantic History," *Journal of World History* 13, no. 1 (2002): 169–182.

20. Proverbs 39:6, Geneva Bible, marginal note.

21. See Pierre Force, *Self-Interest before Adam Smith* (New York: Cambridge University Press, 2003), 145. Albert O. Hirschman discusses virtue against vice as a precursor of pitting vice against vice in *The Passions and the Interests: Political Arguments for Capitalism before Its Triumph* (Princeton, NJ: Princeton University Press, 1977), 21.

22. James Madison, Alexander Hamilton, and John Jay, *The Federalist Papers,* ed. and intro. Isaac Kramnick (London: Penguin, 1987), 53.

23. John G. Cawelti, *Apostles of the Self-Made Man: Changing Concepts of Suc-*

cess in America (Chicago: University of Chicago Press, 1965), 9–21, 40–47. There is evidence that the term had been used earlier in the decade, but not by anyone as culturally central as Henry Clay, to whom the phrase is attributed.

Chapter 1. From Vice to Christian Sin

1. Nancy K. Sandars, "Introduction," *The Epic of Gilgamesh* (New York: Penguin, 1972), 22.

2. The most comprehensive study of the influence of antiquity on modern Republican thought is Paul A. Rahe, *Republics Ancient and Modern* (Chapel Hill: University of North Carolina Press, 1992).

3. Carl J. Richard, *The Founders and the Classics: Greece, Rome, and the American Enlightenment* (Cambridge, MA: Harvard University Press, 1994), 31; Thucydides, *History of the Peloponnesian War*, trans. Benjamin Jowett, 2nd ed. (Oxford: Clarendon Press, 1900), 2.65.

4. Robert Faulkner, *The Case for Greatness: Honorable Ambition and Its Critics* (New Haven: Yale University Press, 2007), ch. 3.

5. John Dryden, *Plutarch's Lives* (New York: Collier and Son, 1909), 111.

6. For a comprehensive bibliography on *philotimia*, see Simon R. F. Price, *Rituals and Power: The Roman Imperial Cult in Asia Minor* (New York: Cambridge University Press, 1984), 123, n131, as cited by Erik M. Heen, "Phil 2:6–11 and Resistance to Local Timocratic Rule," in *Paul and the Roman Imperial Order*, ed. Richard A. Horsley (Harrisburg, PA: Trinity Press International, 2004), 128, n9. For a good recent discussion of the importance of *philotimia*, see Darel Tai Engen, *Honor and Profit: Athenian Trade Policy and the Economy and Society in Greece, 415–307 B.C.E.* (Ann Arbor: University of Michigan, 2010), 132–135.

7. M. Hakkarainen, "Private Wealth in the Athenian Public Sphere," *Early Hellenistic Athens: Symptoms of a Change*, Papers and Monographs of the Finnish Institute at Athens, vol. 6, ed. J. Frösén (Helsinki, 1997), 17.

8. Ibid., 19.

9. C. B. R. Pelling, *Literary Texts and the Greek Historian* (New York: Routledge, 2000), 51.

10. Geert Roskam and Luc Van der Stockt, *Virtues for the People: Aspects of Plutarch's Ethics* (Leuven: Leuven University Press, 2011), 219. For a discussion of *philodoxia*, see Klaus Bringmann, "The King as Benefactor: Some Remarks on Ideal Kingship in the Age of Hellenism," in *Images and Ideologies: Self-Definition in the Hellenistic World*, ed. Anthony Bulloch (Berkeley: University of California Press, 1992), 16, as cited by Heen, "Phil 2:6–11."

11. Strong's concordance, at http://concordances.org/greek/2052.htm.

12. Aristotle, *Politics*, trans. Benjamin Jowett (Oxford: Oxford University Press, 1995), book 5, pt. 3.

13. Pierre Grimal, *The Dictionary of Classical Mythology* (London: Blackwell, 1996), 152.

14. William Barclay, *New Testament Words* (Westminster, KY: John Knox Press, 2000), 99–100.

15. Anton-Hermann Chroust, "Treason and Patriotism in Ancient Greece," *Journal of the History of Ideas* 15, no. 2 (1954): 280. William K. Prentiss writes about this period as one not only of economic transformation but also of an "emancipation of men's minds" in "The Fall of Aristocracies and Emancipation of Men's Minds," *Transactions and Proceedings of the American Philological Association* 56 (1925): 162. For a general discussion of Athenian democracy, see Paul Cloche, *La démocratie athénienne* (Paris: Presses Universitaires de France, 1951).

16. In Strong's concordance, *eritheia* is number 2052. James 3:16 is translated: "For where jealousy and selfish ambition are, there is confusion in every evil deed." For parallel Greek, Hebrew, Aramaic, and Latin translations, see Biblos.com.

17. Russell Price looks at *ambitio* in Rome in "Ambizione in Machiavelli's Thought," *History of Political Thought* 3, no. 3 (1982): 384–386.

18. Myles McDonnell, "Amphitus and Plautus' Amphitruo 65–81," *American Journal of Philology* 107, no. 4 (1986): 567. See also J. Hellegouarc'h, *Le vocabulaire latin des relations et des parties politiques sous la République* (Paris: Les Belles Lettres, 1963), 208ff.

19. McDonnell, "Amphitus," 569; for key virtues and vices in Livy, see P. G. Walsh, *Livy, His Historical Aims and Methods* (Cambridge: Cambridge University Press, 1961); and T. J. Luce, *Livy: The Composition of His History* (Princeton, NJ: Princeton University Press, 1977).

20. Livy 4.25.12–23, 7.15.12–13.

21. "Novorum maxime hominum ambitionem," Livy 7. 15.12; McDonnell, "Amphitus," 567. For an alternative interpretation of Lex Poetelia, see Richard Wellington Husband, "The Law of Poetelius on Corrupt Practices at Elections," *Classical Journal* 10, no. 8 (1915): 376–377.

22. Sallust, *Bellum Catilinae* 10.5: "Ambitio multos mortalis falsos fieri subegit, aliud clausum in pectore aliud in lingua promptum habere."

23. Ibid., 11.1–2: "Sed primo magis ambitio quam avaratia animos hominum excercebat, quod tamen vitium propius virtutem erat. Nam gloriam, honorem, imperium bonus et ignavus aeque sibi exoptant; sed ille vera via nititur, huic quia bonae artes desunt, dolis atque fallaciis contendit."

24. Cicero, *De officiis*, trans. Walter Miller (New York: MacMillan, 1913), 1.8.

25. Ibid.

26. Ibid.

27. "Angusta . . . misera, depresa," Seneca, *De ira* 1.21. For the seductive nature of all vices, like ambition, see Seneca, *Epistulae morales* 69.4: "Nullum sine auctoramento malum est. Avaritia pecuniam promittit, luxuria multas ac varias voluptates, ambitio purpuram et plausum et ex hoc potentiam et quidquid potest potentia."

28. Quintilian, *De institutione oratoria* 2.22: "Licet ipsa vitium sit ambitio, frequenter tamen causa virtutum est."

29. For Anglican and Calvinist conceptions of the church fathers, particularly

the claims of the importance of the first five centuries, see Jean-Louis Quantin, "The Fathers in Seventeenth-Century Anglican Theology," in *The Reception of the Church Fathers in the West: From the Carolingians to the Maurists*, vol. 1, ed. Irena Dorota Backus (Leiden: Brill, 1996), 998–1008.

30. For a discussion of *libido spectandi* in the *Contra Julianum*, see Michael P. Foley, "The Other Happy Life: The Political Dimensions to St. Augustine's Cassiciacum Dialogues," *Review of Politics* 65, no. 2 (2004): 174–177.

31. Augustine, *On the Trinity*, intro. Gareth Mathews, trans. Stephen McKenna (Cambridge: Cambridge University Press, 2002). Mathews has a useful introduction contextualizing the work and its influence on medieval philosophy. For a recent examination of the fourth-century Trinitarian debates that precede Augustine's *On the Trinity*, see Lewis Ayres, *Nicea and Its Legacy: An Approach to Fourth-Century Trinitarian Theology* (Oxford: Oxford University Press, 2006).

32. Foley, "Other Happy Life," 174.

33. Augustine, "Our Lord's Sermon on the Mount," in *Select Library of the Nicene and Post-Nicene Fathers of the Christian Church*, 1st ser., 14 vols., ed. Philip Schaff (New York: Charles Scribner's Sons, 1883–1905), vol. 6.

34. For a brief discussion of the emergence of harnessing the passions, see Albert O. Hirschman, *The Passions and Interests: Political Arguments for Capitalism before Its Triumph* (Princeton, NJ: Princeton University Press, 1977), 14–20.

35. Augustine, rather than believing that passions could be directed, believed in the effects of grace. That is, when we write God's law or will on our hearts, we freely choose what is good, which we can not do when we are slaves to sin. Perhaps this is what Foley meant by "directing desires towards their true fulfillment." Perhaps he intends some orderly habituation of cardinal virtues as a progression toward our telos. For a good, though older discussion of the Augustinian and Pelagian controversy, see Benjamin B. Warfield, "The Theology of Grace," in Schaff, *Select Library of the Nicene and Post-Nicene Fathers*, 5:13–71.

36. Cited by Foley, "Other Happy Life," 174.

37. Lester K. Little, "Pride Goes before Avarice: Social Change and the Vices in Latin Christendom," *American Historical Review* 76, no. 1 (1971): 20.

38. Augustine, *Confessions and Enchiridion*, ed. Albert C. Outler (Philadelphia: Westminster Press, 1955), ch. 12, 88.

39. Gregory the Great, "XL Homiliarum," in *Evangelia libri duo* (1761), 123. This passage is discussed in Richard Newhauser, *The Early History of Greed: The Sin of Avarice in Early Medieval Thought and Literature* (Cambridge: Cambridge University Press, 2000), 103. Note that "beyond measure" speaks to ambition and avarice as vices of excess — in other words, the expression of the qualities beyond the limits as defined by the elite. Perhaps this indicated a curtailing of upward mobility, a "know one's place" within antiquity.

40. Gregory the Great, "XL Homiliarum," quoted in Little, "Pride Goes before Avarice," 20.

41. Morton W. Bloomfield, *The Seven Deadly Sins: An Introduction to the History*

of a Religious Concept, with Special Reference to Medieval English Literature (East Lansing: Michigan State College Press, 1952). For several excellent essays on vice and sin in the Middle Ages, see Richard Newhauser, ed., *In the Garden of Evil: The Vices and Culture in the Middle Ages* (Toronto: PIMS, 2005).

42. Bloomfield, *Seven Deadly Sins*, 72–73.

43. For a good introduction to Thomas's ethics, see Ralph McInerny, *Ethica Tomsitica: The Moral Philosophy of Thomas Aquinas* (Washington, DC: Catholic University of America Press, 1997).

44. Thomas Aquinas, "Of Ambition", in *The Summa Theologica of St. Thomas Aquinas*, trans. Fathers of the English Dominican Province (New York: Benziger Brothers, 1922), 273ff.

45. For a subtle discussion of the relationship between Aristotle and Thomas Aquinas, see M. W. F. Stone, "The Angelic Doctor and the Stagirite: Thomas Aquinas and Contemporary 'Aristotelian' Ethics," *Proceedings of the Aristotelian Society*, n.s., 101 (2001): 97–128.

46. Aquinas, "Of Ambition," 274.

47. Ibid. (emphasis added).

48. It begs the question, who exactly determines what constitutes excessive or inordinate desire and to what extent did this serve to maintain a status hierarchy? Discouraging an immoderate desire, but allowing for some desire, affords an avenue for industrious endeavor, while precluding any upward mobility that might accompany that industry.

49. R. Scott Smith, *Virtue Ethics and Moral Knowledge: Philosophy of Language after MacIntyre and Hauerwas* (Hants, UK: Ashgate, 2003), 16.

50. Gérard Cames, *Allégories et symboles dans l' "Hortus Deliciarum"* (Leiden: E. J. Brill, 1971), 1.

51. Paul Pickrel, "Religious Allegory in Medieval England: An Introductory Study on the Vernacular Sermon before 1250" (PhD diss., Yale University, 1944), esp. ch. 1. For a good discussion of medieval allegory in literature, see Edward A. Bloom, "The Allegorical Principle," *ELH* 18, no. 3 (1951): 163–190. Jeffery Burton Russell considers Landsberg as part of a medieval "hinge" between the vernacular and the sacred. See Jeffrey Burton Russell, *Lucifer: The Devil in the Middle Ages* (Ithaca, NY: Cornell University Press, 1984), 213.

52. The most comprehensive study of medieval allegorical images is Adolf Katzenellenbogen, *Allegories of the Virtues and Vices in Medieval Art: From Early Christian Times to the Thirteenth Century* (London: Warburg Institute, 1939).

53. Paul E. Beichner, "The Allegorical Interpretation of Medieval Literature," *PMLA* 82, no. 1 (1967): 33–38.

54. Cames, *Allégories*, pl. 36.

55. George Ferguson, *Signs and Symbols in Christian Art* (New York: Oxford University Press, 1959), 18.

56. Dom Pierre Miquel, *Dictionnaire symbolique des animaux* (Paris: Le Léopard d'Or, 1991), 183–188.

57. Kathryn Ann Lindskoog, *Dante's Divine Comedy: Inferno* (Macon, GA: Mercer University Press, 1997), 23.

58. *The Compact Edition of the Oxford English Dictionary*, s.v. "ambition."

59. Hugh Grady, "Shakespeare's Links to Machiavelli and Montaigne: Constructing Intellectual Modernity in Early Modern Europe," *Comparative Literature* 52, no. 2 (2000): 120.

60. For a discussion of positive receptions to Machiavelli in the early sixteenth century, see Sara Warneke, *Images of the Educational Traveller in Early Modern England* (New York: E. J. Brill, 1995), 119–120. For a good critique of Pocock's estimation of Machiavelli's influence on English republican thinking, see Steve Pincus, "Neither Machiavellian Moment nor Possessive Individualism: Commercial Society and the Defenders of the English Commonwealth," *American Historical Review* 103, no. 3 (1998): 705–736. For Machiavelli's influence on Bacon and colonization, specifically Bacon's "Certain Considerations Touching the Plantation in Ireland," see Vincent Luciani, "Bacon and Machiavelli," *Italica* 24, no. 1 (1947): 33–35.

61. Warneke, *Educational Traveller*, 119.

62. See J. G. A. Pocock, *The Machiavellian Moment: Florentine Political Thought and the Atlantic Republican Tradition* (Princeton, NJ: Princeton University Press, 1975), pt. 3.

63. For a study of Machiavelli's influence on Adams, see C. Bradley Thompson, "John Adams's Machiavellian Moment," *Review of Politics* 57, no. 3 (1995): 389–417; John Adams to Francis Adrian Van der Kemp, August 9, 1813, in *The Papers of John Adams*, 8 vols. to date, ed. Robert J. Taylor et al. (Cambridge, MA: Harvard University Press, 1977–), as cited by Thompson, "Adams's Machiavellian Moment," 390–391. Paul A. Rahe offers an interesting argument for Machiavelli's influence on America's founders in "Thomas Jefferson's Machiavellian Political Science," *Review of Politics* 57, no. 3 (1995): 449–481. He argues that Machiavelli exerted a certain cultural hegemony on Jefferson and others.

64. Robert A. Kocis, *Machiavelli Redeemed: Retrieving His Humanist Perspectives on Equality, Power, and Glory* (Bethlehem, PA: Lehigh University Press, 1998), 198–205.

65. Price, "Ambizione," 384.

66. Benedetto Fontana, "The Political Uses of Religion in Machiavelli," *Journal of the History of Ideas* 60, no. 4 (1999): 639.

67. Price, "Ambizione," 408.

68. Among political philosophers and historians of ideas less concerned with the aesthetics of Machiavelli's verse, "Tercets on Ambition" is noted. For example, see Erica Benner, *Machiavelli's Ethics* (Princeton, NJ: Princeton University Press, 2009), 194–197. That said, despite the statement in the *Cambridge Companion to Machiavelli* that the "Tercets on Ambition" "rehearses several important themes of his later political thought," it remains an understudied text, given its relative importance. See John Najemy, ed., *The Cambridge Companion to Machiavelli* (New York: Cambridge University Press, 2010), 44.

69. Joseph Tusiani, ed., *Lust and Liberty: The Poems of Machiavelli* (New York: Ivan Obolensky, 1963), xiv–xv.

70. Critic Angus Armstrong identifies imitation and universality as the two main propositions of Aristotle's theory of poetry, a fact that "has seemed so shocking to modern aestheticians." "Aristotle's Theory of Poetry," *Greece and Rome* 10, no. 30 (1941): 120. The quotation from Aristotle is cited and translated at 123. The poetry of Machiavelli's time is best known by the "Petrarchists" Ariosto and Bembo.

71. Leonard Tennenhouse, *Power on Display: The Politics of Shakespeare's Genres* (New York: Methuen, 1986), 2.

72. The English translations of the "Tercets on Ambition" are from Allan H. Gilbert, trans., *Machiavelli: The Chief Works and Others*, vol. 2 (Durham, NC: Duke University Press, 1989), 735–739.

73. Price, "Ambizione," 445.

74. Ibid., 386, 389–90.

75. Christopher Hill, *The English Bible and the Seventeenth-Century Revolution* (New York: Penguin, 1993).

76. Harry Stout, "Word and Order in Colonial New England," in *The Bible in America, Essays in Cultural History*, ed. Nathan O. Hatch and Mark A. Noll (New York: Oxford University Press, 1982), 19.

77. Lewis Lupton, *A History of the Geneva Bible*, 7 vols. (London: Fauconburg, 1966).

78. Hill, *English Bible*, 56.

79. Maurice Betteridge, "The Bitter Notes: The Geneva Bible and Its Annotations," *Sixteenth Century Journal* 14, no. 1 (Spring 1983): 41–62; Dan G. Danner, "The Contribution of the Geneva Bible of 1560 to the English Protestant Tradition," *Sixteenth Century Journal* 12, no. 3 (1981): 5–18; Richard L. Greaves, "Traditionalism and the Seeds of Revolution in the Social Principles of the Geneva Bible," *Sixteenth Century Journal* 7, no. 2 (1976): 94–109; Greaves, "Concepts of Political Obedience in Late Tudor England: Conflicting Perspectives," *Journal of British Studies* 22, no. 1 (1982): 23–34.

80. Stout, "Word and Order," 20.

81. For literacy rates, see Kenneth A. Lockridge, *Literacy in Colonial New England* (New York: W. W. Norton, 1974); Richard T. Vann, "Literacy in Seventeenth-Century England: Some Hearth-Tax Evidence," *Journal of Interdisciplinary History* 5 (1974): 292; David Cressy, "Literacy in Pre-Industrial England," *Societas* 4, no. 3 (1974): 234–240; and Cressy, "Levels of Illiteracy in England, 1530–1730," *Historical Journal* 20, no. 1 (1977): 5–10.

82. John Edmund Cox, ed., *Miscellaneous Writings and Letters of Thomas Cranmer* (Vancouver, BC: Regent College, 2001), 121.

83. As cited by E. Brooks Holifield, *Era of Persuasion* (Lanham, MD: Rowman and Littlefield, 2004), 43.

84. William Hunt, *The Puritan Moment: The Coming of Revolution in an English County* (Cambridge, MA: Harvard University Press, 1983), 116.

85. Lupton, *Geneva Bible*; Charles Eason, *The Geneva Bible: Notes on Its Production and Distribution* (Dublin: Eason and Sons, 1937).

86. David Daniell, *The Bible in English: Its History and Influence* (New Haven: Yale University Press, 2003), 311-312.

87. Ibid., 295.

88. For an excellent summary of "vocation," see Robert S. Michaelsen, "Changes in the Puritan Concept of Calling or Vocation," *New England Quarterly* 26, no. 3 (1953): 315–336.

89. Roger Chartier, *The Cultural Uses of Print in Early Modern France*, trans. Lydia G. Cochrane (Princeton, NJ: Princeton University Press, 1987).

90. Ronald B. Bond, ed., *"Certain Sermons or Homilies" (1547) and "A Homily against Disobedience and Wilful Rebellion" (1570)* (Toronto: University of Toronto Press, 1987), 12–13.

91. C. H. Van Tyne, "Influence of the Clergy, and of Religious and Sectarian Forces, on the American Revolution," *American Historical Review* 19, no. 1 (1913): 51.

92. Bond, *"Homily against Disobedience,"* 236.

93. Ibid., 212.

94. Ruth Mazo Karras, in her study of the sins most associated with women, identifies lust as predominant in the thirteenth, fourteenth, and fifteenth centuries. See Karras, *Common Women: Prostitution and Sexuality in Medieval England* (Oxford: Oxford University Press, 1998), ch. 6, "Saints and Sinners."

95. John Knox, *The First Blast of the Trumpet against the Monstrous Regiment of Women* (1558; reprint ed., Whitefish, MT: Kessinger, 2004), 9.

96. Karras argues that when men sin, it is blamed on their humanity, whereas when women sin, it is blamed on their gender. She also notes the "constant presentation of woman as the equivalent of a sinful soul." Given this argument, it is logical to assume that if ambition is identified as a sin, women would not escape indictment. Karras, *Common Women*, 106.

97. For studies of women in the law, see Amy Louise Erickson, *Women and Property in Early Modern England* (London: Routledge, 1993); and Anne Laurence, *Women in England, 1500–1760: A Social History* (New York: St. Martins, 1993).

98. Tim Stretton, *Women Waging Law in Elizabethan England* (Cambridge: Cambridge University Press, 1998).

99. Laurel Thatcher Ulrich, *Good Wives: Image and Reality in the Lives of Women in Northern New England, 1650–1750* (New York: Alfred A. Knopf, 1982).

100. Marie Cioni, in *Women and the Law in Elizabethan England with Particular Reference to the Court of Chancery* (New York: Garland, 1985), argues that women litigants actually shaped certain forms of equitable relief, as cited by Stretton, *Women Waging Law*, 3.

101. As cited in Frank Whigham, *Ambition and Privilege: Social Tropes of Elizabethan Courtesy Theory* (Berkeley: University of California Press, 1984), 162.

102. Bond, *"Homily against Disobedience,"* 236 (emphasis added).

103. Ibid., 210.

104. James Sharpe, *Instruments of Darkness: Witchcraft in Early Modern England* (Philadelphia: University of Pennsylvania Press, 1997); John Demos, *Entertaining Satan* (New York: Oxford University Press, 1982); Keith Thomas, *Religion and the Decline of Magic* (New York: Charles Scribner and Sons, 1971); Marianne Gibson, *Reading Witchcraft: Stories of Early English Witches* (New York: Routledge, 1999). For an excellent consideration of the persecution of women and its relation to witch trials, see Rachel Karlsen, *The Devil in the Shape of a Woman* (New York: W. W. Norton, 1987). None of these studies, however, links ambition to witchcraft.

105. Bond, *"Homily against Disobedience,"* 236–237. This fear of individual ambition combining with populist ignorance and support is an early recognition of what later becomes a potent and often frightening historical phenomenon.

Chapter 2. Ambition as Sin in Early Modern English Culture

1. Raymond Williams, *Marxism and Literature* (New York: Oxford University Press, 1977), 121–137.

2. Ronald B. Bond, ed., *"Certain Sermons or Homilies" (1547) and "A Homily against Disobedience and Wilful Rebellion" (1570)* (Toronto: University of Toronto Press, 1987), 236.

3. Williams, *Marxism and Literature*, ch. 8, 122–127; ch. 4 (on ideology), 55–71.

4. Todd Gitlin, "Television's Screens: Hegemony in Transition," in *American Media and Mass Culture: Left Perspectives*, ed. Donald Lazere (Berkeley: University of California Press, 1987), 240–265.

5. Todd Gitlin, *The Whole World Is Watching: Mass Media in the Making and Unmaking of the New Left* (Berkeley: University of California Press, 1980), 252.

6. Ibid., 252 n7.

7. Ibid., 253. See also Stuart Hall's discussion on Gramsci in Hall and Dorothy Hobson, *Culture, Media, Language* (London: Hutchinson, 1980), esp. 2–37.

8. Antonio Gramsci, *Prison Notebooks*, ed. Q. Hoare and G. Nowell-Smith (London: Lawrence and Wishart, 1971), 326, as cited in David McClellan, *Ideology: Concept in Social Thought* (Minneapolis: University of Minnesota Press, 1995), 26.

9. Stuart Hall, *Critical Dialogues in Cultural Studies*, ed. David Morley and Kuan-Hsing Chen (New York: Routledge, 1996), 424.

10. Nicos Poulantzas, *Political Power and Social Classes*, trans. Timothy O'Hagan (London: New Left Books, 1973), 207.

11. Literary scholar John Huntington, writing on England in the 1590s, maintains that certain poets, including George Chapman, form an emergent challenge to the preeminence of nobility and can "transform cultural capital into social dignity." Huntington, *Ambition, Rank, and Poetry in 1590s England* (Urbana: University of Illinois Press, 2001), 64. I do not dispute this or other challenges but they are just that. For the period see also Frank Whigham, *Ambition and Privilege: The Social Tropes of Elizabethan Courtesy Theory* (Berkeley: University of California Press, 1984).

12. Michel Foucault, *The Order of Things: The Archaeology of the Human Sciences* (New York: Routledge, 2002), xxii.

13. *The Famous and Renowned History of Morindos as King of Spaine; Who Maryed with Miracola a Spanish Witch* . . . (1609).

14. Ibid., ch. 4, 17.

15. Henry Roberts, *A Defiance to Fortune; the Miseries of Andrugio, Duke of Saxonie* (London, 1590), 90.

16. Thomas Heywood, *Troia Brittanica; or, Great Britaines Troy* (London, 1609), 2.11–18.

17. William Herbert, *The Lamentation of Britain* (1604), ll. 799–826.

18. John Donne, the best known of the metaphysical poets, is silent on the topic of ambition in his poetry. It may be that Donne, who has been described as the "poet of ambition" and is reputed to have used his poems for preferment, was reluctant to denounce the very quality that was said to motivate him. See Peter DeSa Wiggins, *Donne, Castiglione, and the Poetry of Courtliness* (Bloomington: Indiana University Press, 2001), for a full exploration of Donne and his ties to the courtier. That said, Donne was a convert from Catholicism and did not receive his doctor of divinity degree until 1618, at a time when ambition as sin was more and more challenged. The 1611 King James Bible, for example, includes only four references to ambition, down from more than seventy in the Geneva Bible. This was largely due to the deletion of the Calvinist marginalia. This will be discussed in greater detail later in this work, but Donne, raised a Catholic and converted later in life, would not have been as relatively steeped in the Calvinist doctrine present in the Geneva Bible and written in English as opposed to Latin. The official Bible of Catholicism was the Vulgate, written in Latin. This, I concede, is speculation. It might mark an emergent shift in attitudes toward ambition. It might simply not have been of interest to Donne.

19. Much of this section is drawn from the biography of Taylor by Bernard Capp, *The World of John Taylor the Water-Poet, 1578–1653* (Oxford: Clarendon, 1994). See also John Chandler, ed., *Travels through Stuart Britain: The Adventures of John Taylor, the Water Poet* (Gloucestershire: Sutton, 1999).

20. Joan Parkes, *Travel in England in the Seventeenth Century* (Oxford: Oxford University Press, 1925). For a discussion of the challenges coaches posed to watermen, see Edwin A. Pratt, *A History of Inland Transport and Communication in England* (New York: E. P. Dutton, 1912). Taylor identified the coach as "a mere engine of pride, which no one can deny to be one of the seven deadly sins" (59).

21. Edwin B. Benjamin, "Fame, Poetry, and the Order of History in the Literature of the English Renaissance," *Studies in the Renaissance* 6 (1959): 64–84. For a discussion of the challenges from the nontraditional poets in the late sixteenth and early seventeenth centuries, see Huntington, *Ambition, Rank, and Poetry*.

22. Robert Zaller, *The Discourse of Legitimacy in Early Modern England* (Stanford: Stanford University Press, 2007).

23. John Dryden, "To My Lord Chancellor," *The Poetical Works of John Dryden*, ed. William Dougal Christie (London: MacMillan, 1874), l. 29.

24. Ibid., ll. 23–28.

25. Capp, *World of John Taylor*, 55.

26. Ibid.

27. Rosalind Mills, *Ben Jonson: His Life and Work* (New York: Routledge, 1986), 187.

28. Capp, *World of John Taylor*, 67.

29. Ibid.

30. Ibid., 66.

31. Ibid., 58. See John Taylor, "The Pennyles Pilgrimage-London to Edinburgh," in Chandler, *Travels through Stuart Britain*, 1–53.

32. Robert Boerth, review of *Travels through Stuart Britain: The Adventures of John Taylor, the Water Poet*, by John Chandler, *Sixteenth Century Journal* 31, no. 3 (2000): 915–916.

33. Ibid., 915.

34. "Vrania," from *All the Works of John Taylor, the Water-Poet Beeing Sixty Three in Number* (London, 1630), ll. 233–240.

35. Stephen Greenblatt, "Invisible Bullets: Renaissance Authority and Its Subversion, Henry IV and Henry V," in *Political Shakespeare: Essays in Cultural Materialism*, ed. Jonathan Dollimore and Alan Sinfield (Ithaca, NY: Cornell University Press, 1994), 18–47; and Steven Mullaney, "Strange Things, Gross Terms, Curious Customs: the Rehearsal of Cultures in the Late Renaissance," *Representing the English Renaissance*, ed. Stephen Greenblatt (Berkeley: University of California Press, 1988). For a challenge to Greenblatt, see Jonathan Dollimore, *Radical Tragedy: Religion, Ideology and Power in the Drama of Shakespeare and his Contemporaries* (New York: Harvester Wheatsheaf, 1989).

36. Ambition reimagined as plague is discussed in greater detail in chapter 3.

37. "Richard the III, King of England, and France, Lord of Ireland & Co.," from *John Taylor's Works*.

38. James S. Amelang, review of *The World of John Taylor the Water-Poet, 1578–1563*, by Bernard Capp, *Sixteenth Century Journal* 27, no. 1 (1996): 194–195.

39. "Letter from Mr. Benjamin Vaughan," January 31, 1738, in Benjamin Franklin, *The Autobiography of Benjamin Franklin, The Harvard Classics*, ed. Charles W. Eliot (New York: Collier, 1909), 77.

40. Benjamin Franklin, *Poor Richard's Almanack*, 1735 (Waterloo, IA: U.S.C., 1914), 20; Max Weber, *The Protestant Ethic and the Spirit of Capitalism* (New York: Routledge), esp. ch. 2.

41. "Earley to bed and early to rise, makes a man healthy, wealthy, and wise," was written in John Clarke's *Paroemiologia or Phraseologia Anglo-Latina: A Collection of English and Latin Proverbs*, published in 1639.

42. Benjamin Franklin, *Poor Richard's Almanac*, in *Benjamin Franklin: His Life as He Wrote It*, ed. Esmond Wright (Cambridge, MA: Harvard University Press, 1989), 102.

43. See Gordon Wood on Franklin's emblematic stature in *The Americanization of Benjamin Franklin* (New York: Penguin, 2004).

44. Even earlier rags-to-riches stories are remarkably similar to Whittington's, including accounts from Danish, Persian, Florentine, and Genoan myths. One involves an account of a cat and the king of the Canary Islands. See Thomas Keightley, *Tales and Popular Fictions; Their Resemblance and Transmission from Country to Country* (London: Whittaker, 1834), ch. 7.

45. T. H., *The History of Sir Richard Whittington* (London: Villon Society, 1885).

46. "Dick Whittington and His Cat," *Bulletin of Historical Business* 16, no. 6 (1942): 105.

47. Venetia Newali, review of *The Leaping Hare* by George Ewart Evans, David Thomson; *The Cat's Got Our Tongue*, by Claire Necker, *Journal of American Folklore* 88, no. 350 (1975): 438; Sylvanus Urban, comp., *The Gentleman's Magazine: And Historical Chronicle*, January to June 1818, vol. 83 (London: Nichols, Son, and Bentley, 1818), 512.

48. Colin Platt, *Medieval England: A Social History and Archaeology from the Conquest to A.D. 1600* (New York: Routledge, 1994), 110; Marl Arvanigian, "Regional Politics, Landed Society and the Coal Industry in North-East England, 1530–1430," in *Fourteenth Century England*, vol. 4, ed. J. S. Hamilton (Rochester, NY: Boydell Press, 2006), 175–191.

49. Richard Grafton, *A Chronicle at Large, and Meere History of the Affayres of England, and Kings of the Same, etc.* (London: H. Denham, 1569), 433.

50. George Chapman, Ben Jonson, and John Marston, *Eastward Hoe* (London: George Eld, 1605).

51. The play has received more attention for evidence of protocapitalism than it has as a great work of literature. Though popular in his time, Heywood's reputation suffered after his death. Samuel Pepys, for example, dismissed Heywood's *If You Know Not Me* in his diary as "the most ridiculous that ever came upon stage . . . a puppet play, acted by living puppets. Neither the design nor language better; and one stands by and tells us the meaning of things." See Louis B. Wright, "Notes on Thomas Heywood's Later Reputation," *Review of English Studies* 4, no. 14 (1928): 136. Mary E. Hazard sees the play as a significant reflection of a shift in cultural attitudes in which "the burse is displacing the parish; the courtier will pay court to commerce; the noble will patronize the bourgeois." Hazard, *Elizabethan Silent Language* (Omaha: University of Nebraska Press, 2000), 151.

52. Thomas Heywood, *If You Know Not Me, You Know No Bodie* (London: Thomas Purfoot, 1608), ix.

53. Adam Fox, *Oral and Literate Culture in England, 1500–1700* (Oxford: Clarendon Press, 2000), 227, 221–223.

54. Ibid., 213.

55. Phillips Barry, "A Garland of Ballads," *Journal of American Folk-Lore* 23, no. 90 (1910): 446.

56. Fox, *Oral and Literate Culture*, 27.

57. Nicholas Bownd, *The Doctrine of the Sabbath* (London, 15??), 241, as cited by Fox, *Oral and Literate Culture*, 38.

58. Ibid., 242; Roger North, *The Lives of the Norths*, 3 vols., ed. Augustus Jessopp (London: George Bell and Son, 1890), 1:184, as cited by Fox, *Oral and Literate Culture*, 41.

59. Fox, *Oral and Literate Culture*, 41.

60. Pieter Zwart, *Islington: A History and Guide* (London: Taylor and Francis, 1973), 165–166.

61. T. H., *History of Whittington.*

62. Vanessa Harding, "London, Change and Exchange," in *The Culture of Capital: Property, Cities, and Knowledge in Early Modern England*, ed. Henry S. Turner (New York: Routledge, 2002), 131.

63. For discussions of work and wages in seventeenth-century England, see Jeremy Boulton, "Wage Labor in Seventeenth-Century London," *Economic History Review* 99, no. 2 (1996): 268–290; and D. C. Coleman, "Labour in the English Economy of the Seventeenth Century," *Economic History Review* 8, no. 3 (1956): 288–292. On the growing importance of wages, see Allan M. Everitt, "Farm Labourers," in *Agrarian History of England and Wales, 1500–1640*, vol. 4, ed. Joan Thirsk, ch. 1.

64. Patrick Wallis, "Apprenticeship and Training in Premodern England," *Journal of Economic History* 68, no. 3 (2008): 831–861. The data are limited in determining a runaway rate of all apprentices. The available data indicate a quit rate of 44.6 percent among London carpenters' apprentices between the years 1540 and 1590. One can assume that a guild might have a lower quit rate, as the promise of a trade would be of greater inducement to stay than would a kitchen scullion as in the case of Whittington. The data on departure within first two years of service are restricted to Bristol; see Illana Krausman Ben-Amos, "Failure to Become Freeman: Urban Apprentices in Early Modern England," *Social History* 16 (1991): 155–172.

65. Later versions attribute the bells to Saint Mary-le-Bow in Cheapside, London. The Bow Bells now are associated with the working class. It was once said that a "true Cockney" includes all those born within hearing range. But in Whittington's time, a time of considerably less din and clamor, earshot was of greater range. The historical Whittington lived in fourteenth-century England. Saint Mary-le-Bow was constructed between 1670and 1683, so obviously the Bow Bells could not have been the ones Whittington heard. But the "poor man's" church speaking to the poor man, though apocryphal, is well suited to the myth.

66. Keith Thomas, *Religion and the Decline of Magic* (New York: Charles Scribner's Sons, 1971), 149, quoting E. Drapes, *Gospel Glory Proclaimed* (1649).

67. As cited by Thomas, *Religion and the Decline of Magic*, 79.

68. Alvin Rabushka, *Taxation in Colonial America, 1607–1775* (Princeton, NJ: Princeton University Press, 2008), 82, n30.

69. Laura Caroline Stevenson, *Praise and Paradox: Merchants and Craftsmen in Elizabethan Popular Literature* (New York: Cambridge University Press, 1984), 51.

Notes to Pages 66–70   205

70. See Thomas Heywood, *Four Prentices of London* (1592); Thomas Dekker, *The Shoemaker's Holiday* (1600); Thomas Deloney, *Thomas of Reading* (1612); and John Stow, *Survey of London* (1598).

71. Stevenson, *Praise and Paradox*, 111.

72. Thomas Deloney, *Jack of Newbury* (1597), cited in Stevenson, *Praise and Paradox*, 89.

73. For a discussion of literature that imbues merchants with chivalric qualities, see Stevenson, *Praise and Paradox*, ch. 6, "The Merchant as Knight, Courtier and Prince," 107–130.

74. In Dick Whittington all the elements of a new sort of ambition emerge— ambition that serves the common good, one that is informed by what later is called Republican virtue. Quentin Skinner and J. G. A. Pocock have argued that republicanism was part of the "intellectual landscape" of pre–Civil War England. The ballad of Dick Whittington suggests that the civic duty embodied in what later became known as English republican virtue extended beyond the intellectual forums, to the taverns, and into songs sung by the everyman. Martin van Gederen and Quentin Skinner, *Republicanism* (Cambridge: Cambridge University Press, 2005), 308; Markku Peltonen, *Classical Humanism and English Republicanism, 1570–1640* (New York: Cambridge University Press, 1995); David Norbrook, *Writing the English Republic, Poetry, Rhetoric and Politics, 1627–1660* (New York: Cambridge University Press, 2000); J. G. A. Pocock, *Machiavellian Moment: Florentine Political Thought and the Atlantic Republican Tradition*, rev. ed. (Princeton, NJ: Princeton University Press, 2003).

75. John Stephens, *Essayes and Characters, Ironicall, and Instructive* (London, 1615).

76. Benjamin Boyce, *The Theophrastan Character in England to 1642* (Cambridge, MA: Harvard University Press, 1947), 123.

77. Joseph Hall, *Character of Vertues and Vices in Two Books* (London, 1608), A4.

78. J. and J. A. Venn, eds., "*Alumni Cantabrigienses . . . ,*" vol. 1 (Cambridge: Cambridge University Press, 1922), s.v. "Hall, Joseph."

79. Hall, *Character of Vertues*, A4–A9.

80. Ibid., 153–160.

81. Boyce, *Theophrastan Character*, 220–228.

82. Stephens, *Essayes and Characters*, 7.

83. Lawrence Stone, "Social Mobility in England, 1500–1700," *Past and Present* 33 (1966): 16–55; Stone, "The Inflation of Honors, 1558–1641," *Past and Present* 14 (1958): 45–70.

84. "Seismic upheaval," however, was not accompanied by social instability until the mid-seventeenth century. I. W. Archer and others argue that the late sixteenth and early seventeenth century was certainly a time of social mobility, but also of a remarkable societal stability. See Archer, *The Pursuit of Stability: Social Relations in Elizabethan London* (London: Cambridge University Press, 1991); and Steve

Rappaport, *Worlds within Worlds: Structures of Life in Sixteenth-Century London* (Cambridge: Cambridge University Press, 1989).

85. Stone, "Social Mobility," 16. For a brilliant discussion of the culture of ambition, drawn largely through "courtesy literature," see Frank Whigham, *Ambition and Privilege: Social Tropes of Elizabethan Courtesy Theory* (Berkeley: University of California Press, 1984).

86. Stephens, *Essayes and Characters*, 8.

87. Ibid.

88. Irving Ribner, *Patterns in Shakespearean Tragedy* (London: Metheun, 1960), 9.

89. Aristotle, *Poetics*, ed. James Hutton (New York: W. W. Norton, 1982).

90. Macbeth comes to mind in espousing this theory. Macbeth never recognizes his fatal flaw. The audience, however, does.

91. Though they are often grouped and taught together, a number of scholars distinguish between the dominant ideology of the two periods. Simply put, Jacobean drama is seen as the more radical of the two, the drama that includes emergent challenges to the dominant ideology. See, e.g., Maurice Hunt, "Elizabethan 'Modernism' and Jacobean 'Postmodernism': Schematizing Stir in the Drama of Shakespeare and His Contemporaries," *Papers on Language and Literature* 31 (1995): 115–144; T. F. Wharton, *Moral Experiment in Jacobean Drama* (London: MacMillan, 1988); David Scott Kastan and Peter Stallybrass, eds., *Staging the Renaissance: Reinterpretations of Elizabethan and Jacobean Drama* (New York: Routledge, 1991); Irving Ribner, *Jacobean Drama: The Quest for Moral Order* (London: Methuen, 1962); and Jonathan Dollimore, *Radical Tragedy: Religion, Ideology, and Power in the Drama of Shakespeare and His Contemporaries* (New York: Harvester Wheatsheaf, 1984).

92. Kristian Smidt, "Two Aspects of Ambition in Elizabethan Tragedy: Doctor Faustus and Macbeth," *English Studies* 1, no. 2 (1969): 236.

93. Leo Kirschbaum, "Marlowe's Faustus: A Reconsideration," *Review of English Studies* 19 (1943): 225–241, cited in Christopher Marlowe, *Doctor Faustus*, ed. David Bevington and Eric Rasmussen (Manchester, UK: Manchester University Press, 1993), 15.

94. James T. F. Tanner, "Doctor Faustus as Orthodox Christian Sermon," *Dickinson Review* 3 (1969): 23–31. See also Ann O'Brien, "Christian Belief in Doctor Faustus," *ELH* 37 (1970): 1–11. But critical interpretation of the play is far from uniform. See Irving Ribner, "Marlowe and the Critics," *Tulane Drama Review* 87, no. 4 (1964): 211–224.

95. Carlo Ginzburg, "High and Low: The Theme of Forbidden Knowledge in the Sixteenth and Seventeenth Centuries," *Past and Present* 73 (1976): 28–41. See also James S. Amelang, *The Flight of Icarus: Artisan Autobiography in Early Modern Europe* (Stanford, CA: Stanford University Press, 1998).

96. Richard F. Hardin, "Ovid in Seventeenth-Century England," *Comparative Literature* 24, no. 1 (1972): 46–62; Niall Rudd, "Daedalus and Icarus (i) From Rome to the End of the Middle Ages and (ii) From the Renaissance to the Present Day," in

Ovid Renewed: Ovidian Influences on Literature and Art from the Middle Ages to the Twentieth Century, ed. Charles Martindale (New York: Cambridge University Press, 1988), 21–53.

97. Peter Harrison, "Curiosity, Forbidden Knowledge, and the Reformation of Natural Philosophy in Early Modern England," *Isis* 92, no. 2 (2001): 270.

98. John Calvin as cited in ibid.

99. Lambert Daneau, *The Wonderful Woorkmanship of the World Wherein Is Contained an Excellent Discourse of Chritian Naturall Philosophie, Concernyng the Fourme, Knowledge, and Vse of All Things Created* (London: John Kingston, 1578), 15.

100. *Shakespeare's Ovid, Being Arthur Golding's Translation of the "Metamorphoses,"* ed. W. H. D. Rouse (London: De La More Press, 1904), 4.

101. Christopher Marlowe, *Tamburlaine*, ed. J. S. Cunningham (Manchester: Manchester University Press, 1999), 154–155.

102. George Chapman and James Shirley, *The Tragedie of Chabot, Admirall of France*, from the 1639 Quarto, *Publications of the University of Pennsylvania Series in Philology and Literature*, vol. 10, ed. Ezra Lehman (Philadelphia: John Winston, 1906).

103. Sallust, *Bellum Catilinae* 10.5.

104. Ben Jonson, *Sejanus*, ed. W. D. Briggs (Boston: D. C., 1911), *The Argument*.15–16. Subsequent citations are to this edition.

105. Ben Jonson, *Catiline His Conspiracy*, ed. Lynn Harold Harris (New Haven: Yale University Press, 1916). Subsequent citations are to this edition.

106. See Annabel Patterson, *Censorship and Interpretation: The Conditions of Writing and Reading in Early Modern England* (Madison: University of Wisconsin Press, 1984), 50–58; and Sean McEvoy, *Ben Jonson, Renaissance Dramatist* (Edinburgh: Edinburgh University Press, 2008), 32–52.

107. Stephen Greenblatt, *Sir Walter Raleigh: The Renaissance Man and His Roles* (New Haven: Yale University Press, 1973), 40. For a discussion of the radical instability of the Renaissance self and the associations between self-fashioning and self-annihilation see Greenblatt, *Renaissance Self-Fashioning: From More to Shakespeare* (Chicago: University of Chicago Press, 1980).

108. Robert N. Watson, *Shakespeare and the Hazards of Ambition* (Cambridge, MA: Harvard University Press, 1984), 3.

109. Dollimore, *Radical Tragedy*, li.

110. Franco Moretti, *Signs Taken for Wonders: On the Sociology of Literary Forms* (London: Verso, 2005), 27.

111. Ibid., 42.

112. Hebert R. Coursen Jr., *Christian Ritual and the World of Shakespeare's Tragedies* (London: Associated University Presses, 1978), 319.

113. A. R. Braunmuller, "Introduction," in William Shakespeare, *Macbeth* (New York: Cambridge University Press, 1997), 8. Subsequent citations are to this edition.

114. Muriel Clara Bradbrook, *Themes and Conventions of Elizabethan Tragedy* (New York: Cambridge University Press, 1980), 43.

115. Bond, *"Homily against Disobedience,"* 225, 210.

116. Derek Cohen points out that the word *slave* is often a term of abuse and coupled with other abusive terms. See Cohen, *Searching Shakespeare: Studies in Culture and Authority* (Toronto: University of Toronto Press, 2003), 49. But elsewhere, Shakespeare uses slave as in *Hamlet*, "Give me that man / That is not passion's slave" (3.2.72–73). Joseph Pearce, in his study of *King Lear*, observes Shakespeare's use of slavery in a similar vein. He suggests that Gloucester's death in act 4 suggests that he that loses his patience and becomes a "slave to his appetites, a slave to sin." Pearce, *The Quest for Shakespeare* (Fort Collins, CO: Ignatius Press, 2008), 313.

117. Lily B. Campbell, *Shakespeare's Tragic Heroes* (London: Methuen, 1986), 101.

118. Bond, *"Homily against Disobedience,"* 236.

119. William Shakespeare, *Hamlet, Prince of Denmark*, ed. Philip Edwards (Cambridge: Cambridge University Press, 1985).

120. Bond, *"Homily against Disobedience,"* 230.

121. Rafael Holinshed, *Chronicles of England, Scotland and Ireland* (London, 1807), 269. To the Elizabethan and Jacobean audience, as mentioned in chapter 1, it is not an exclusively masculine passion. What is interesting is that as it becomes more virtuous in Anglo-American thought, it starts to become defined as a manly virtue, but as long as it retains its sinful connotations, no one seems particularly challenged that it is expressed by women, whether in Eden or in Scotland.

122. Bond, *"Homily against Disobedience,"* 225–226.

123. Maynard Mack, *Killing the King: Three Studies in Shakespeare's Tragic Structure* (New Haven: Yale University Press, 1973), 164, 174; the argument is developed at 138–185.

124. See David Brion Davis, *Inhuman Bondage: The Rise and Fall of Slavery in the New World* (New York: Oxford University Press, 2006), 30; and Davis, *In the Image of God: Religion, Moral Values, and Our Heritage of Slavery* (New Haven: Yale University Press, 2002), 126.

125. Stephen Orgel, "Introduction," William Shakespeare, *Macbeth* (New York: Penguin, 2000), xli. For Davenant and *Macbeth*, see Dennis Bartholomeusz, *Macbeth and the Players* (Cambridge: Cambridge University Press, 1969), 15–27.

126. Hugh F. Rankin, *The Theater in Colonial America* (Chapel Hill: The University of North Carolina Press, 1965), 74–91.

127. Ibid.

128. For a discussion of revising Shakespeare, see Stanley Wells et al., *William Shakespeare: A Textual Companion* (New York: W. W. Norton, 1997); and Grace Ioppolo, *Revising Shakespeare* (Cambridge, MA: Harvard University Press, 1992). For Garrick and *Macbeth*, see Bartholomeusz, *Macbeth and the Players*, 38–81.

129. In Nahum Tate's revision of *King Lear*, 1681, Cordelia lives and the play ends with her marriage to Edgar. An online version of the 1749 edition is available through Google Books.

130. Cited by Orgel, "Introduction," xlii.

131. For an example of this trend, see Jonathan Dollimore in Ewan Fernie, ed., *Spiritual Shakespeare* (New York: Routledge, 2005), 215–216. For a discussion of Nietzsche's theory of tragedy as the unification of passion, beauty, and destruction, see Paul Gordon, *Tragedy after Nietzsche* (Urbana: University of Illinois Press, 2001).

132. Friedrich Nietzsche, *The Dawn or Daybreak: Thoughts on the Prejudices of Morality*, ed. Maudmarie Clark and Brian Leiter (Cambridge: Cambridge University Press, 1997), 243–244.

133. Stone, "Social Mobility"; Stone, "Inflation of Honors."

134. Watson, *Hazards of Ambition*, 85. For an alternative read, see Martha Tuck Rozett, *The Doctrine of Election and the Emergence of Elizabethan Tragedy* (Princeton, NJ: Princeton University Press, 1984). She writes, "Of Shakespeare's great tragic protagonists, Macbeth is least likely to inspire audience identification" (299). *Macbeth* would fall under Stephen Greenblatt's rubric of subversive tragedy, one that requires a certain audience identification, even if the act of regicide itself is, as I argue, the brink, the line. The monologues, the regret, ambition's spur all allow the audience to identify and then retreat safely behind that line of regicide, comforted by the limits of their own ambition. See Greenblatt, "Invisible Bullets."

Chapter 3. The Plague and Countervailing Passions

1. Keith Wrightson, *English Society, 1580–1680* (London: Hutchinson, 1982), 10.

2. Albert O. Hirschman, *The Passions and Interests: Political Arguments for Capitalism before Its Triumph* (Princeton, NJ: Princeton University Press, 1977), 20.

3. Literary critic C. Fred Alford suggests a third strategy that he claims has been ignored by theorists. He writes, "Importantly . . . none of these theorists proposed setting what might be called the civilizing passions, such as love and pity against the uncivilized ones. . . . By civilizing passions I mean those passions that are originally and primarily (but not exclusively) concerned with the welfare of others, such as pity, compassion and some types of love." While Alford is correct, his enthusiasm is misplaced. This certainly is a "strategy" but one that belongs to the medieval age, an age replete with allegories that depict countervailing virtue with vice. This is by no means an emergent strategy in the sixteenth and seventeenth centuries but one well documented and discussed by medieval theorists, as well as by Hirschman. See C. Fred Alford, *The Psychoanalytic Theory of Greek Tragedy* (New Haven: Yale University Press, 1992), 145–147. Hirschman discusses virtue against vice as a precursor of pitting vice against vice in *Passions and Interests*, 21.

4. Alexander Hamilton, James Madison, and John Jay, *The Federalist Papers*, ed. Garry Wills (New York: Bantam, 1982), 316.

5. Hirschman, *Passions and Interests*, 21.

6. Ibid., 22–23.

7. Francis Bacon, *Sylva Sylvarum: or, A Natural History; in Ten Centuries*, in *The Works of Francis Bacon*, ed. James Spedding, Robert Leslie Ellis, and Donald

Denon Heath, 14 vols. (London: Longman, 1858–1874), 2:660 (hereafter cited as Bacon, *Works*).

8. Paul Slack notes that before 1540 it is difficult to measure the severity and frequency of epidemics due to the inadequacy of probate evidence. Slack, *The Impact of Plague in Tudor and Stuart England* (New York: Oxford University Press, 1990), 148.

9. Ibid., 151.

10. Stephen Greenberg, "Plague, the Printing Press, and Public Health in Seventeenth-Century London," *Huntington Library Quarterly* 67, no. 4 (2004): 509–527.

11. British Library, Harleian MS 3785, fol. 35v, as cited in Slack, *Impact of Plague*, 17.

12. Ambrose Parey, *A Treatise of the Plague, Contayning the Causes, Signes, Symptomes, Prognosticks and Cure Thereof . . .* (London, 1630), 2.

13. Ibid., 27–28.

14. Ibid.

15. Ibid., 26.

16. Mark Wheelis, *Principles of Modern Microbiology* (Boston: Jones and Bartlett, 2007), 410.

17. Parey, *Plague*, 29–30.

18. Margaret Healy, "Discourses of the Plague in Early Modern London," in *Epidemic Disease in London*, ed. J. A. I. Champion, Center for Metropolitan History Working Papers Series, no. 1 (1993), 19–34.

19. Paolo Rossi, *Francis Bacon: From Magic to Science*, trans. Sacha Rabovinovitch (London: Routledge, 1968), x.

20. Thomas Thayre, *A Treatise of the Pestilence: Werein Is Shewed All the Causes Thereof, with Most Assured Preservations against All Infection* (London, 1603), 2. Thayre cites Numbers 11, 12, and 14, Deuteronomy 28:1–4, and Leviticus 26:3 as scriptural evidence of the plague's divine origins. Other writers cite 2 Samuel 24, Psalm 106, 1 Chronicles 21, and Psalm 91.

21. Ronald B. Bond, ed., *"Certain Sermons or Homilies" (1547) and "A Homily against Disobedience and Wilful Rebellion" (1570)* (Toronto: University of Toronto Press, 1987), 210.

22. Thayre, *Treatise*, 3.

23. S. P., *A Letter full of Sweete Comforts for Such as Are Visited by the Pestilence* (London, 1625).

24. Healy, *Discourses of the Plague*, 19–22.

25. S. P., *Letter Full of Sweete Comforts*, 4, 6.

26. Ibid., 4.

27. Cited in Raymond A. Anselment, *The Realms of Apollo: Literature and Healing in Seventeenth-Century England* (Newark: University of Delaware Press, 1995), 120.

28. Democritus Junior [Robert Burton], *The Anatomy of Melancholy* (New York: A. C. Armstrong and Son, 1880), 373.

29. William Wager, A *Comedy or Enterlude Intituled, Inough Is as Good as a Feast: Very Fruteful, Godly and Ful of Pleasant Mirth* (London, 1570?), image 5 of 27.

30. Ibid., image 6 of 27.

31. A *New and Mery Enterlude, Called the Triall of Treasure: Newly Set Foorth, and Neuer before This Tyme Imprinted* (London: Thomas Purfoote, 1567), image 13 of 21. For an excellent discussion of how the plague is personified, see Melissa Smith, "Personifications of Plague in Three Tudor Interludes: *Triall of Treasure, The Longer Thou Liuest, the More Foole Thou Art*, and *Inough Is as Good as a Feast*," *Literature and Medicine* 26, no. 2 (2007): 364–385.

32. *Triall of Treasure*, image 14 of 21.

33. "Vrania," from *John Taylor's Works* (London, 1630), l. 233.

34. [Burton], *Anatomy of Melancholy*, 373.

35. Thomas Adams, *Diseases of the Soule; a Discourse Diuine, Morall, and Physicall* (London, 1616).

36. Ibid., 40.

37. Ibid., 42.

38. Anthony Anderson, *An Approved Medicine against the Deserued Plague* (London, 1593).

39. Ibid., images 4, 5.

40. William Bridge, *The Righteous Man's Habitation, in the Time of Plague and Pestilence* (London, 1665), 15.

41. Margaret Healy, *Fictions of Disease in Early Modern England* (New York: Palgrave, 2001), 94–95.

42. Ibid., 95.

43. Daniel Defoe, A *Journal of the Plague Year*, in *The Works of Daniel Defoe* (New York: C. T. Brainard, 1904), 294.

44. Thayre, *Treatise*, 5.

45. For a treatise on the role of the planets in disease, see Nicholas Culpeper, *Culpeper's Astrologicall Judgement of Disease from the Decumbiture of the Sick* (London, 1655).

46. Thayre, *Treatise*, 5.

47. Bacon, *Works*, 2:603.

48. As cited by Rebecca Totaro, *Suffering in Paradise: The Bubonic Plague in English Literature from More to Milton* (Pittsburgh: Duquesne University Press, 2005), 31.

49. J. N. Hays, *The Burdens of Disease: Epidemics and Human Response in Western History* (Piscataway, NJ: Rutgers University Press, 2003), 10.

50. Ibid. For a discussion of Galenism in the seventeenth century and its transformation in that century see Lester S. King, "The Transformation of Galenism," in *Medicine in the Seventeenth Century*, ed. Allen G. Debus (Berkeley: University of California Press, 1974), 7–31.

51. For a good discussion of the humors, see Nancy G. Siraisi, *Medieval and Early Renaissance Medicine: An Introduction to Knowledge and Practice* (Chicago: University of Chicago Press, 1990), 104–106.

52. Galen, *On the Natural Faculties,* trans. Arthur John Brock (New York: G. P. Putnam and Sons, 1916), 189.

53. Thayre, *Treatise,* 10 (emphasis added).

54. Ibid.

55. Francis Bacon, "Of Ambition," in Bacon, *Works,* 6:465 (emphasis added).

56. According to Bacon, humoral imbalance can also occur from "stoppage" or the inability for humors to properly vent, as if the human body were a furnace or boiling cauldron, what Bacon calls "diseases of stoppings and suffocations." See Bacon, "Of Friendship," *Works,* 6:437.

57. Bacon, *Sylva Sylvarum.*

58. Ibid., 2:662.

59. The use of mercury, though predicated on a similar theoretical basis, can be traced to Paracelsus. Paracelsus disagreed with humoral theory and attempted to use different poisons, including arsenic and mercury, to counteract the poison of the disease. This may be contrasted with Galen and new Galenism, in which poisons might be used to counteract the poison produced by a humoral imbalance. The plague treatments of the sixteenth and seventeenth centuries do not often make sharp distinctions between these theories and both seem to be appropriately grouped beneath Bacon's general rubric of theories of sympathy and antipathy, or poison counteracting poison. On Paracelsus, see W. B. Delchman et al., "What Is There That Is not Poison? A Study of the Third Defense of Paracelsus," *Archives of Toxicology* 58, no. 4 (1986): 207–213.

60. Lionel Gatford, *[Logos Alexipharmikos; or,] Hyperphysicall Directions in the Time of Plague* (Oxford: H. Hall, 1644), 25.

61. Vivian Nutton, *Ancient Medicine* (New York: Routledge, 2004), 150.

62. Douglass Adair writes of Bacon, Newton, and Locke as "the famed trinity of representative great philosophers for Americans and all educated inhabitants of Western Europe in 1783." Adair, *Fame and Founding Fathers,* 94.

63. Given Bacon's significance to Jefferson and the well-documented fact of Machiavelli's influence on Bacon, we can dismiss claims by some scholars that, with the exception of John Adams, Machiavelli had no influence in America. See C. Bradley Thompson, "John Adams's Machiavellian Moment," *Review of Politics* 57, no. 3 (1995): 389–417. Bradley sights the lack of "tangible evidence" of Machiavelli's influence on the founders, including the fact that in the writings of Jefferson there were virtually no "index citations" to Machiavelli (390). This is, obviously, a flawed approach. Paul Rahe, though not speaking of Bacon's debt to Machiavelli and Jefferson's debt to Bacon, speaks instead of an "intellectual hegemony" of Machiavelli over republican thought. See Paul Rahe, "Thomas Jefferson's Machiavellian Political Science," *Review of Politics* 57, no. 3 (1995): 449–481. It is a provocative thesis, but flawed in that it fails to account for the Machiavellian strain in one of Jefferson's most profound influences, Francis Bacon. That is, to what extent is the Machiavellian influence that Rahe sees in Jefferson due to Machiavelli or to Bacon's interpretation of Machiavelli?

64. Thomas Jefferson, *Political Writings*, ed. Joyce Appleby and Terrence Ball (New York: Cambridge University Press, 1999), 427.

65. Thomas Jefferson, *The Complete Jefferson: Containing His Major Writings, Published and Unpublished, Except His Letters*, ed. Saul K. Padover (New York: Books for Libraries Press, 1969), 924.

66. Adair, *Fame and Founding Fathers*, 94.

67. Hamilton, Madison, and Jay, *Federalist Papers*, 316.

68. For a good discussion of Federalist No. 51 and the "necessary partitions of power," see David F. Epstein, *The Political Theory of the Federalist* (Chicago: University of Chicago Press, 2007), esp. ch. 5; Daniel Walker Howe, "The Political Psychology of The Federalist Author(s)," *William and Mary Quarterly*, 3rd ser., 44 (1987): 485–509; and Garry Wills, *Explaining America: The Federalist* (Garden City, NY: Doubleday, 1981). See also Charles T. Rubin, "Ambition Ancient and Modern," in *Educating the Ambitions: Leadership and Political Rule in Greek Political Thought*, ed. Leslie G. Rubin (Pittsburgh: Duquesne University Press, 1992), 31–58.

69. Hirschman, *Passions and Interests*, 20–26.

70. Spinoza, *Ethics*, trans. W. H. White, rev. A. H. Stirling (Hertfordshire, UK: Wordsworth Classics, 2001), 169.

71. Thomas Manton, "A Sermon upon Eccles. VII. 29," in *A Fourth Volume Containing One Hundred and Fifty Sermons on Several Texts of Scripture in Two Parts* . . . (London, 1693), 1158 (emphasis added).

72. Hirschman, *Passions and Interests*, 21–22. Nearly every account of the origins of countervailing adopt, without challenge, Hirschman's formulation. For a notable exception, see Jack Barbalet, "The Moon before Dawn: A Seventeenth-Century Precursor of Smith's *The Theory of Moral Sentiments*," in *New Perspectives on Adam Smith*, ed. Geoff Cockfield, John Firth, and Ann Laurent (Northampton, MA: Edward Elgar, 2007), 96–98. Barbalet cites Thomas Wright's *Passions of the Minde in Generall* (1601) and a theory of countervailing that Wright adopts as predating Bacon's *Advancement of Learning*. That said, Bacon's relative significance remains undisputed.

73. Francis Bacon, *Advancement of Learning, Book I*, ed. F. G. Selby (New York: MacMillan, 1905), 42.

74. Ibid.

75. Ibid., 123.

76. For an older but useful discussion of the madness and the passions, see Lawrence Babb, *The Elizabethan Malady* (Lansing: Michigan State College Press, 1951), esp. chs. 1, 4, and 8. For Seneca and Burton, see chapter 1 of this book.

77. Bacon, *Advancement*, 123.

78. Jamie C. Kassler, "Restraining the Passions: Hydropneumatics and Hierarchy in the Philosophy of Thomas Willis," in *The Soft Underbelly of Reason: The Passions in the Seventeenth Century*, ed. Stephen Gaukroger (New York: Routledge, 1998), 147.

79. Bacon, *Works*, 2:603.

80. John Kelly, *The Great Mortality: An Intimate History of the Black Death* (New York: Harper Collins, 2005), 169.

81. Bacon, "Advancement of Learning, Book 2," in *Works*, 3:438.

82. Ibid.

83. Ibid. (emphasis added).

84. Francis Bacon, *Advancement of Learning*, ed. Joseph Devey (New York: American Dome Library, 1902), 295 (emphasis added).

85. Hirschman, *Passions and Interests*, 23.

86. Ibid., 21–23. For others who simply accept the single Baconian source of countervailing passions most simply cite Hirschman or the source he cites. See, e.g., Pierre Force, *Self-Interest before Adam Smith: A Genealogy of Economic Science* (New York: Cambridge University Press, 2003), 145; and Bruce B. Suttle, "The Passion of Self-Interest: The Development of the Idea and Its Changing Status," *American Journal of Economics and Sociology* 26, no. 4 (1987): 462n23.

87. All citations to the *Essays* are to Francis Bacon, *The Essayes or Counsels, Civill and Morall* (London, 1625), in Bacon, *Works*, vol. 6.

88. Michel de Montaigne, *Essais de Messire Michel Seigneur de Montaigne* (Bordeaux: S. Millanges, 1580); *Essais* (Paris: Abel L'Angelier, 1588). For a discussion of Montaigne's process of revision and addition in the three published forms of his essays, see George Hoffman, "The Montaigne Monopoly: Revising the *Essais* under the French Privilege System," *PMLA* 108, no. 2 (1993): 308–319.

The influence of Montaigne on Bacon is the subject of some debate. Jacob Zeitlin and Pierre Villey have argued that Montaigne's influence on Bacon was negligible. This premise has been challenged by Kenneth Alan Hovey, who argues that Montaigne's influence was "indirect yet clear." In addition, before Bacon's *Essays*, the word was not used in English to describe short-form nonfiction. See Kenneth Alan Hovey, "Montaigny Saith Prettily: Bacon's French and the Essay," *PMLA* 106, no. 1 (1991): 71–82. For arguments against Montaigne's influence on Bacon, see Jacob Zeitlin, "The Development of Bacon's Essays—with Special Reference to the Question of Montaigne's Influence upon Them," *Journal of English and Germanic Philology* 27 (1928): 496–519; and Pierre Villey, *Montaigne et François Bacon* (Paris, 1913).

89. Francis Bacon, *Essayes; Religious Meditations; Places of Perswasion and Disswasion; Seene and Allowed* (London: Humfrey Hooper, 1597).

90. Francis Bacon, *The Essaies of Sir Francis Bacon Knight . . .* (London: John Beale, 1612).

91. Francis Bacon, *The Essayes or Counsels, Civill and Morall, of Francis Lo. Verulan, Viscount St. Alban* (London: John Haviland for Hanna Barret, 1625).

92. Adair, *Fame and the Founding Fathers*, 38. Robert Faulkner, perhaps drawing from Adair, calls the essays a "self-help book," but then qualifies that in the essays "the reader is directed deep into a novel form of self-help." The efforts to inspire modern interest on Adair and Faulkner's part by likening the *Essays* to self-help books, regardless of qualifications, do a disservice. They likewise ignore that many of

them provide practical advice for statecraft. See Robert Faulkner, "Bacon, Francis," in *The Encyclopedia of the Essay*, ed. Tracy Chevalier (London: Fitzroy Dearborn, 1997), 49.

93. Francis Bacon, "Of Friendship," in Bacon, *Works*, 6:441.

94. Francis Bacon, "Of Regiment of Health," in Bacon, *Works*, 6:454.

95. Francis Bacon, "Of Anger," in Bacon, *Works*, 6:511.

96. His debt to Machiavelli has been noted in the literature, and Bacon, like Machiavelli, sought to attempt something entirely new, a "path still untrodden." Ironically he did this while drawing from the ancients and from Machiavelli. Niccolò Machiavelli, *Discourses on Livy*, trans. Julia Conaway Bondanella and Peter Bondanella (New York: Oxford University Press, 2003), 15. I am indebted to Gopal Balakrishnan for a copy of an unpublished paper on Machiavelli, "Repetition and Renewal in Machiavelli's Concept of History," for the concept of Machiavelli's use of history as potentially one "of new beginnings." That is one which is not only a resurrection of the past but an attempt to "transcend the present." I am convinced that Bacon, in both form and content, was aware of Machiavelli's sense of history. It is tempting to read Jefferson's sense of the history of new beginnings in similar terms.

97. I demonstrate how Bacon's philosophy of statescraft is adopted as official state policy in chapter 4.

98. The essay does not appear in his 1597 edition, and first emerges with his later 1612, reprinted without change in his 1625 edition.

99. Bacon, "Of Ambition," 6:465.

100. Thayre, *Treatise*, 10 (emphasis added).

101. Bacon, "Of Ambition," 6:465.

102. Burton, *Anatomy of Melancholy*, 373.

103. Bacon, "Advancement of Learning," 3:438.

104. Bacon, "Of Ambition," 6:466.

105. Bacon drew from Tacitus, who wrote of Sejanus in his influential history of Roman politics, history, and morality. According to scholar Ronald Mellor, with the ascension of James I, Tacitus became a central feature of English intellectual life. Bacon favored his "moral thinking" over Plato and Aristotle as well as his "plain style." John Donne called Tacitus "the oracle of statesmen." See Mellor, *Tacitus* (New York: Routledge, 1994) esp. "The Impact of Tacitus," 148–152.

106. See Annabel Patterson, *Censorship and Interpretation: The Conditions of Writing and Reading in Early Modern England* (Madison: University of Wisconsin Press, 1984), 50–58; and Sean McEvoy, *Ben Jonson, Renaissance Dramatist* (Edinburgh: Edinburgh University Press, 2008), 32–52.

107. Bacon, "Of Ambition," 6:466.

108. Ibid.

109. Ibid.

110. *Oxford English Dictionary*, s.v. "seel."

111. Francis Bacon, *Essays of Lord Bacon with Critical and Illustrative Notes*, ed. John Hunter (London: Longmans, Green, 1873), 153n4.

112. John Ford, *The Broken Heart*, ed. T. J. B. Spencer (Baltimore: Johns Hopkins University Press, 1980), 2.3.3–5.

113. Bacon, "Of Ambition," 6:465.

114. Ibid.

115. Ibid.

116. This would be another example of a disease of "stoppings and suffocations." As I noted earlier, according to Bacon, humoral imbalance can also occur from "stoppage" or the inability for humors to vent properly. Treatments such as blood-letting, cupping, and purges are largely predicated on similar theories. See Bacon, "Of Friendship," 6:437.

117. Bacon, "Of Ambition," 6:467.

118. Francis Bacon, *Novum Organum*, in Bacon, *Works*, 1:162 (emphasis added).

Chapter 4. Harnessing Ambition in the Age of Exploration

1. The title of Bernard Mandeville's *Fable of the Bees; or, Private Vices, Publick Benefits* indicates its intent: how to turn private vices into public benefits. The theme is present throughout. Mandeville engages both countervailing and harnessing. Most illustrative is the "Moral": "Fools only strive / To make a Great an[d] Honest Hive . . . / Without great Vices, is a vain / EUTOPIA seated in the Brain. / Fraud, Luxury and Pride must live, / While we the Benefits receive . . . / So Vice is beneficial found, / When it's by Justice lopt and bound; / Nay, where the People would be great, / As necessary to the State, / As Hunger is to make 'em eat." Mandeville, *The Fable of the Bees; or, Private Vices, Publick Benefits*, 2 vols. (Indianapolis: Liberty Fund, 1988), 1:36–37. For other representative examples, see 1:125, 129, and 2:111–112, 125–127.

2. Vico speaks more to the capacity of civil society to transform and tame the passions. He wrote: "Out of ferocity, avarice, and ambition, the three vices which lead man astray, [society] makes national defense, commerce and politics, and thereby cause the strength, the wealth and the wisdom of the republics." Giambattista Vico, *New Science* (New York: Penguin, 2001), 78.

3. I refer here to Adam Smith's famous "Invisible Hand," first used in his *The Theory of Moral Sentiments*, 2nd ed. (London, 1761), 273. He also employs the metaphor in *An Inquiry into the Nature and Causes of the Wealth of Nations*, vol. 2 (New York: Penguin, 1999), 32.

4. Herder wrote: "All passions of man's breast are wild drives of a force which does not know itself, yet, but which, in accordance with nature, can only conspire to a better order of things." Johann Gottfried von Herder, "Ideen zur Philosophie der Geschichte der Menschheit," in *Werke*, vol. 14, ed. Bernhard Suphan (Berlin, 1909), 213, as cited in Albert O. Hirschman, *The Passions and the Interests: Political Arguments for Capitalism before Its Triumph* (Princeton, NJ: Princeton University Press, 1977), 20.

5. Hegel suggests that man, driven by his passions, unknowingly serves some

higher societal purpose. Georg Wilhelm Friedrich Hegel, *Lectures on the Philosophy of World History*, trans. J. Sibree (London: George Bell, 1902).

6. Hirschman, *Passions and Interests*, 20.

7. J. H. Elliott, *Empires of the Atlantic World: Britain and Spain in America, 1492–1830* (New Haven: Yale University Press, 2006), 155.

8. William Alexander, *An Encouragement to Colonies*, in *Sir William Alexander and American Colonization*, ed. Carlos Slafter and Edmund Slafter (Boston: Prince Society, 1873), 211.

9. George Chapman, Ben Johnson, and John Marston, *Eastward Hoe* (London: William Aspley, 1605); for a modern edition, see *Eastward Ho*, ed. R. W. Van Fossen (Manchester, UK: Manchester University Press, 1999).

10. Jonathan Haynes, *The Social Relations of Jonson's Theater* (New York: Cambridge University Press, 1992), 32.

11. For a detailed analysis of the comments against the Scots, see Joseph Quincy Adams, "'Eastward Hoe' and Its Satire against the Scots," *Studies in Philology* 28, no. 4 (1931): 689–701.

12. William Crashaw, "A Sermon Preached in London before . . . His Maiesties Counsell for . . . Virginea," Feb. 11, 1609 (London, 1610), sig. H4, cited by Howard Mumford Jones, "The Colonial Impulse: An Analysis of the 'Promotion' Literature of Colonization," *Proceedings of the American Philosophical Society* 90, no. 2 (1946): 131–161.

13. Van Fossen, "Introduction," in *Eastward Ho*, 18.

14. Allan H. Gilbert, "Virginia in *Eastward Ho*," *Modern Language Notes* 33, no. 3 (1918): 183–184. For a comprehensive study of the "New World" in English drama, see Robert R. Cawley, *The Voyagers and Elizabethan Drama* (London: Oxford University Press, 1938); and Cawley, *Unpathed Waters* (Princeton, NJ: Princeton University Press, 1940).

15. Julián Juderías, *La leyenda negra: Estudios acerca del concepto de España en el extranjero*, 16th ed. (Madrid: Editoria Nacional, 1974).

16. Rómulo D. Cabria, *Historia de la leyenda negra Hispano-Americana* (Buenos Aires: Ediciones Orientación Española, 1943).

17. Edward Peters, *Inquisition* (Berkeley: University of California Press, 1989), 131. See also Philip Wayne Powell, *Tree of Hate: Propaganda and Prejudices Affecting United States Relations with the Hispanic World* (New York: Basic Books, 1971).

18. Bartolomé de las Casas, *A Short Account of the Destruction of the Indies*, trans. Nigel Griffin (New York: Penguin, 1992), 12.

19. Bartholomew de las Casas, *The Spanish Colonie, or Briefe Chronicle of the Acts and Gestes of the Spaniards in the West Indes* . . . (London, 1583). This English work was translated from a French translation of Las Casas. See David Read, *Temperate Conquests: Spenser and the Spanish World* (Detroit, MI: Wayne State Press, 2000), 25; and Jonathan Hart, *Representing the New World: The English and French Uses of the Example of Spain* (New York: Palgrave, 2001), 73–74.

20. Richard Hakluyt, *A Discourse Concerning Westerne Planting Written in the*

Year 1584 (Cambridge: J. Wilson and Son, 1877). Many scholars focus on the *Discourse* in discussing English attitudes toward Spain. It is a much more virulent denunciation of Spain than found in Hakluyt's published *Divers Voyages* but, again, was a private document.

21. Ibid., 171.

22. Hart, *Representing the New World*, 136.

23. Lynn Glaser, *America on Paper: The First Hundred Years* (Philadelphia: Associated Antiquaries, 1989), 220. For more on De Bry, see Michèle Duchet, *L'Amérique de Théodore de Bry: Une collection de voyages protestante du XVIe siècle* (Paris: CNRS, 1987).

24. Stephanie Moser, *Ancestral Images: The Iconography of Human Origins* (Ithaca, NY: Cornell University Press, 1988), 78; Bernadette Bucher, *Icon and Conquest: A Structural Analysis of the illustrations of de Bry's Great voyages,* trans. Basia Miller Gulati (Chicago: University of Chicago Press, 1981).

25. Alfred W. Crosby, *The Columbian Exchange: Biological and Cultural Consequences of 1492* (Westport, CT: Greenwood, 1972).

26. "1629 Seal of the Massachusetts Bay Colony," image drawn from Smithsonian Source, "Primary Sources," http://www.smithsoniansource.org/display/primary source/viewdetails.aspx?PrimarySourceId=1200. "Come over and help us" is from Acts 16:9–10.

27. Hart, *Representing the New World*, 103.

28. Scholars often cite Hakluyt's *Discourse Concerning Westerne Planting* as evidence of the origins of the Black Legend. Many fail to note that it was not published until the nineteenth century and, as such, is reflective of an attitude but was far less culturally influential than other accounts of Spain's conquest. See, e.g., Mary C. Fuller, *Voyages in Print: English Travel to America, 1572–1624* (New York: Cambridge University Press, 1995), 27–29.

29. Hart, *Representing the New World*, 216.

30. J. A. Leo Lemay, *The American Dream of Captain John Smith* (Charlottesville: University of Virginia Press, 1991).

31. John Smith, *A Description of New England; or, Observations and Discoveries in the North of America in the Year of Our Lord 1614* (1616; Boston: William Veazie, 1865), 25.

32. John Smith, *The Generall Historie of Virginia, New-England, and the Summer Isles: With the Names of the Adventurers, Planters and Governours from Their First Beginning, Ano. 1584 to This Present, 1624* (London, 1624), 109.

33. Lesley Byrd Simpson, "Introduction," in Francisco Lopez de Gómara, *Cortés: The Life of the Conqueror by His Secretary* (Berkeley: University of California Press, 1964).

34. Glen Carman, *Rhetorical Conquests: Cortés, Gómara, and Renaissance Imperialism* (West Lafayette, IN: Purdue University Press, 2006), 83.

35. Ibid., 6.

36. For other scholarly works on Gómara, see also Robert Lewis, "The Human-

ist Historiography of Francisco Lopez de Gómara (1511–1559)" (PhD diss., University of Texas, Austin, 1983); and Cristián A. Roa-de-la-Carrera, *Histories of Infamy: Francisco López de Gómara and the Ethics of Spanish Imperialism*, trans. Scott Sessions (Boulder: University Press of Colorado, 2005).

37. The Spanish crown banned the publication of Gómara's work in 1553, and after 1555 it was not published again in Spanish until the early eighteenth century. That it was known to be banned in Spain may have aided its popularity as anti-Spanish sentiment grew in England in the late 1570s.

38. An English translation of Las Casas was included in Hakluyt's *Discourse Concerning Westerne Planting*, but this was a private document. In addition, as I mentioned, De Bry creates a visual portrayal of Las Casas's text. Las Casas was not translated again until 1656: Las Casas, *Tears of the Indians: Being an Historical and True Account of the Cruel Massacres and Slaughters of above Twenty Millions of Innocent People; Committed by the Spaniards in the Islands of Hispaniola, Cuba, Jamaica, &c. As also in the Continent of Mexico* (London, 1656).

39. Some scholars have traced even Nicholas's influence on John Dryden. See Dougald MacMillan, "The Sources of Dryden's 'The Indian Emperour,'" *Huntington Library Quarterly* 13, no. 4 (1950): 355–370.

40. Hart, *Representing the New World*, 107.

41. *The Pleasant Historie of the Conquest of the West India, now Called New Spaine, Atchieued by the Most Woorthie Prince Hernando Cortés, Marques of the Valley of Huaxacac, Most Delectable to Reade*, trans. Thomas Nicholas (London: Thomas Creede, 1596).

42. Ibid., a2.

43. Ibid.

44. Ibid.

45. Ibid., b1–2.

46. Ibid., 170–171.

47. Ibid., 233–234.

48. Ibid., 1.

49. Ibid., 2.

50. Ibid., 361–362.

51. The Thomistic texts give us some indication of the view in Spain of ambition, though a more thorough consideration of the view in Spain is required to make any definitive conclusion.

52. Bernal Díaz del Castillo, *Historia verdadera de la conqvista de la Nueva-Espanã; Escrita por el capitan Bernal Díaz del Castillo, vno de sus conquistadores* (Madrid: Impr. del Reyno, 1632).

53. All quotations in English are drawn from Bernal Díaz, *The Conquest of New Spain*, trans. J. M. Cohen (New York: Penguin, 1963), 55.

54. Ibid., 47.

55. Ibid.

56. Ibid., 411 (emphasis added).

57. Agustín de Zárate, *The Strange and Delectable History of the Discoverie and Conquest of the Provinces of Peru, in the South Sea . . .*, trans. T. Nicholas (London, 1581).

58. James Lockhart, *The Men of Cajamarca: A Social and Biographical Study of the First Conquerors of Peru* (Austin: University of Texas Press, 1972), 136.

59. Francisco López de Gómara, *La historia general de las Indias, y todo lo acaescido en ellas dense que se ganaron hasta agora y la conquista de Mexico y la nueva España* (1554), vol. 2, ch. 144, 210.

60. Lockhart, *Men of Cajamarca*, 138.

61. Gómara uses the Spanish word *puerca*. "Era hijo bastardo de Gonzalo Pizarro, capitán en Navarra. Nació en Trujillo, y echáronlo a la puerta de la iglesia. Mamó una puerca ciertos días, no se hallando quien le quisiese dar leche. Reconociólo después el padre, y traído a guardar los puercos, y así no supo leer. Dióles un día mosca a sus puercos, y perdiólos. No osó tornar a casa de miedo, y fuése a Sevilla con unos caminantes, y de allí a las Indias." Gómara, *Historia general*, vol. 2, ch. 144, 210.

62. Raymond A. Mentzer, "Marranos of Southern France in the Early Sixteenth Century," *Jewish Quarterly Review* 72, no. 4 (1982): 303. For Spanish pure blood laws and their relation to *marranos*, see A. A. Sicroff, *Les controverses des statuts de "pureté de sang" en Espagne du XVe au XVIIe siècle* (Paris, 1960), 250–51.

63. The dominant medical treatise on breastfeeding was Antonio de Guevara's *Relox de príncipes* (1529). Guevara advised women to breastfeed their own children, because if they did not, the children would not acquire their personality. He writes, "Children many times take after the one who nursed them, rather than the one who gave them birth." He then cites the example of Caligula, attributing his violent madness to the following: "It happened once that, when ready to nurse Caligula, due to some annoyance she tore off the leg and dismembered a girl and above all, with the girl's blood smeared on the nipple of her breast thus made the child nurse both milk and blood." Cited and translated by Carolyn A. Nadeau, "Blood Mother/Milk Mother: Breastfeeding, the Family, and the State in Antonio de Guevara's *Relox de Príncipes (Dial of Princes)*," *Hispanic Review* 69, no. 2 (2001): 167.

64. D. A. Brading, *The First America: The Spanish Monarchy, Creole Patriots, and the Liberal State, 1492–1867* (New York: Cambridge University Press, 1991), 40.

65. Peter G. Bietenholz, *Historia and Fabula: Myths and Legends in Historical Thought from Antiquity to the Modern Age* (Leiden: E. J. Brill, 1994), 49.

66. Simpson, "Introduction," xxiii. Glen Carman, too, notes Gómara's frequent use of puns: "Mil placeres hacían aquellos señores [tlxacaltecas] y mucha cortesía a Cortés" (93; ch. 54); "Conocía Cortés a casi todos aquellos que venían con Narváez. Hablóles cortésmente" (161; ch. 103); "[Pánfilo de Narváez] no hacía otro que dar quejas de Cortés en corte" (304; ch. 195); "Anduvo Cortés muchos años congojado en la corte" (374; ch. 256); all cited in Carman, *Rhetorical Conquests*, 105. I recount these examples as evidence of double entendre as a rhetorical pattern, suggesting that we not underestimate Gómara's linguistic wit in eviscerating Pizarro.

67. "Arqueólogo sugiere que conquistador Francisco Pizarro fue de origen judío," *Historia de Lima virreynal: Textos y apuntes sobre la historia, arquitectura y urbanismo de Lima durante el virreynato del Perú y mas . . .* 3/22/08, available online at: http://limavirreynal.blogspot.com/2008/01/arquelogo-sugiere-que-conquistador.html.

68. Cawley, *Voyagers*, 292.

69. Stuart B. Schwartz, "New World Nobility: Social Aspirations and Mobility in the Conquest and Colonization of Spanish America," in *Social Groups and Religious Ideas in the Sixteenth Century*, ed. Miriam Usher Chrisman and Otto Gründler (Kalamazoo: Western Michigan University, 1978), 23.

70. Ibid. This proverb is perhaps most widely known because of its use in *Don Quixote*. See Miguel de Cervantes, *Don Quijote de la Mancha*, ed. Francisco Rico (Barcelona: Edición del Instituto Cervantes, 1998), ch. 39. For a discussion of the proverb, especially in *Quixote*, see D. José Coll y Vehi, *Los refranes del Quijote, ordenados por materias y glosados* (Barcelona: Diario de Barcelona, 1874).

71. Interestingly, especially given Bacon's assertion of the potential for noble ambition in science and scientific discovery, this saying changes by the early seventeenth century in Spain to "ciencia, casa real y mar," as reflected in the work of Lope de Vega. The sea and royal house remain constant, as science replaces the church as a means to advancement. Lope de Vega, *La Dorotea*, Edición de José Manuel Blecua, vol. 1 (Madrid: Cátedra, 1996), viii.

72. For a discussion of reconquest ideology, see David A. Wacks, *Framing Iberia: "Maqāmāt" and Frametale Narratives in Medieval Spain* (Boston: Brill, 2007), esp. ch. 4.

73. Christopher Columbus, *The Diario of Christopher Columbus's First Voyage to America, 1492–1493*, abstracted by Fray Bartolomé de las Casas, trans. Oliver Dunn and James E. Kelley (Norman: University of Oklahoma Press, 1989). This is a useful edition as it includes both the original Spanish and the English translation side by side.

74. Stephen Greenblatt, *Marvelous Possessions* (New York: Oxford University Press, 1991), ch. 3. William Merrill Decker, *Epistolary Practices: Letter Writing in America before Telecommunications* (Chapel Hill: University of North Carolina Press, 1988), 61–63.

75. Margarita Zamora, *Reading Columbus* (Berkeley: University of California Press, 1993), 10.

76. Columbus, *Diario*; Nigel Griffin, ed., *Las Casas on Columbus* (Turnhout, Belgium: Brepols, 1999).

77. Columbus, *Diario*, 17.

78. Ibid., 17–19.

79. Ibid., 19.

80. Schwartz, "New World Nobility," 26.

81. See Lewis Hanke, *The Spanish Struggle for Justice in the Conquest of America* (Philadelphia: University of Pennsylvania Press, 1949), 54–70; and more recently Oreste Popescu, *Studies in the History of Latin American Economic Thought* (New York: Routledge, 1997), 87–90.

82. Schwartz, "New World Nobility," 27.

83. Ibid.

84. Lockhart, *Men of Cajamarca*, 44–59.

85. For an excellent article on this fear, see Thomas N. Ingersoll, "'Riches and Honour were Rejected by them as Loathsome Vomit': The Fear of Leveling in New England," in *Inequality in Early America*, ed. Carla Gardina Pestana and Sharon V. Salinger (Hanover, NH: Dartmouth University Press, 1999), 46–66.

86. See David Quinn, *The Elizabethans and the Irish* (Ithaca, NY: Cornell University Press, 1966); Quinn, *Ireland and America: Their Early Associations, 1500–1640* (Liverpool: Liverpool University Press, 1991); K. R. Andrews, N. P. Canny, and P. E. H. Hair, eds., *The Westward Enterprise: English Activities in Ireland, the Atlantic, and America, 1480–1650* (Liverpool: Liverpool University Press, 1978); Canny, *Elizabethan Conquest of Ireland: A Pattern Established, 1565–1576* (Sussex, UK: Harvester, 1976); and Canny, *Kingdom and Colony: Ireland in the Atlantic World, 1560–1800* (Baltimore: Johns Hopkins University Press, 1988).

87. Francis Bacon, "Of Ambition," in Bacon, *Works*, 465.

88. Ibid., 466.

89. Francis Bacon, "Certain Considerations Touching the Plantation in Ireland Presented to His Majesty, 1606," in *Letters and Life*, 4:121.

90. One of the best book-length discussions on the motivations for English colonization remains David Cressy, *Coming Over: Migration and Communication between England and New England in the Seventeenth Century* (New York: Cambridge University Press, 1987).

91. As Sarah Lewis notes, "Much of Bacon's work on colonization remains unexplored." Lewis, "'In a pure soil': Colonial Anxieties in the Work of Francis Bacon," *History of European Ideas* 32, no. 3 (2006): 249–262.

92. Bacon, "Certain Considerations," 120.

93. Ibid., 121.

94. This would be consistent with Robert Faulkner's assertion that Bacon formulates a new understanding of honor as a "new, amoral virtue of advancing oneself. Robert Faulkner, *The Case for Greatness: Honorable Ambition and Its Critics* (New Haven: Yale University Press, 2007), 181.

95. Ibid.

96. Ibid.

97. Ibid.

98. *Calendar of State Papers, Domestic Series, of the Reign of James I. 1611–1618, Preserved in the State Papers of Her Majesty's Public Record Office*, ed. Mary Anne Everett Green (London, 1858), 27.

99. Katherine S. Van Eerde, "The Jacobean Baronets: An Issue between King and Parliament," *Journal of Modern History* 33, no. 2 (1961): 137–147.

100. British Museum, Cotton MSS, Titus B IV and V, and Public Record Office, State Papers, Domestic, 14/59, folios 33–44, and 14/64, folio 61 as cited in Van Eerde, "Jacobean Baronets," 137n1.

101. Van Eerde, "Jacobean Baronets," 138.

102. Cited in Wallace Notestein, *Four Worthies: John Chamberlain, Lady Anne Clifford, John Taylor, Oliver Heywood* (London: Jonathan Cape, 1956).

103. Van Eerde, "Jacobean Baronets," 138–139.

104. Van Eerde, "The Creation of the Baronetage in England," *Huntington Library Quarterly* 22, no. 4 (1959): 313–322.

105. Van Eerde, "Jacobean Baronets," 144.

106. British Museum, Sloan MSS 29034, folios 33–34, as cited in ibid., 144 (emphasis added).

107. Van Eerde, "Jacobean Baronets," 146.

108. Alexander, *Encouragement*, 211.

109. Edmund Slafter, "Memoir," in *Sir William Alexander and American Colonization* (Boston: Prince Society, 1873), 19.

110. Ibid.

111. James I, "Charter in Favor of Sir William Alexander, Knight, of the Lordship and Barony of New Scotland in America, 10 September 1621," in *Alexander and American Colonization*, 128.

112. Ibid.

113. Charles I, "Royal Warrant of King Charles I. to the Nova Scotia Baronets, 1629," reprinted in Ephraim Lockhart, *Statement with Reference to the Knights Baronets of Nova Scotia* (Edinburgh: William Tait, 1823), 22.

114. Alexander, *Encouragement*, 151–216.

115. Ibid., 212.

116. Ibid., 213.

117. For example, see David Brion Davis, *Inhuman Bondage: The Rise and Fall of Slavery in the New World* (New York: Oxford University Press, 2006), 29, 32. One wonders, given the Christian associations between improving the land as tantamount to ownership, if the bestialization of slaves in North America isn't another necessary ideological assumption of the master class in order to invalidate the rights of the enslaved to land that they are improving.

118. Alexander, *Encouragement*, 213.

119. Ibid., 213.

120. Ibid., 206, 210.

121. L. B. Kastner and H. B. Charlton, eds., *The Poetical Works of Sir William Alexander, Earl of Stirling*, 2 vols. (Edinburgh: W. Blackwood, 1921–1929), 2:383.

122. Alexander, *Encouragement*, 211.

123. Ibid.

124. Schwartz, "New World Nobility," 28, 23.

125. Peru statistics from Luis de Izcue, *La nobleza titulada en el Perú colonial* (Lima, 1929), as cited by Schwartz, "New World Nobility," 28. The New Scotland statistics are drawn from the "Roll of the Knight Baronets of Nova Scotia Who Had Territorial Grants from Sir William Alexander, Kt., Earl of Stirling," in *Alexander and American Colonization*, 233–237.

126. Obviously many of the years represented are inapplicable to Nova Scotia. But as the first hundred years of Peru should weight the data toward Peru, not against it, the number of noble titles that England granted in comparison to Spain is striking.

127. William Symonds, "A Sermon Preached at White-Chappel, in the Presence of Many, Honourable and Worshipfull, the Adventurers and Planters of Virginia" (London, 1609). For a discussion of Symonds, see Thomas Scanlan, *Colonial Writing in the New World, 1583–1671* (New York: Cambridge University Press, 1999), 105–111. Although he does not discuss ambition, he does speak about the capacity for virtue in the New World.

128. Cited in Scanlan, *Colonial Writing,* 107.

129. Ibid.

130. Anthony Pagden, "Identity Formation in Spanish America," in *Colonial Identity in the Atlantic World, 1500–1800,* ed. Nicholas Canny and Anthony Pagden (Princeton, NJ: Princeton University Press, 1989), 52.

131. Statement made in 1544, cited by Schwartz, "New World Nobility," 35.

132. Fr. Buenaventura de Salinas, *Memorial de las historias del nuevo mundo* (Lima, 1631), cited by Schwartz, "New World Nobility," 35.

133. Juan Ortiz de Cervantes, *Memorial que presenta a Su Majestad . . . sobre pedir remedio del daño y diminución de los indios y propone ser medio eficaz la perpetuydad de encomiendas* (México City, 1619), folio 15, as cited by Pagden, "Identity Formation," 56.

134. N. F. Martin, *Los vagabundos en la Nueva España, siglo XVI* (Mexico City, 1957), 23–38, as cited by Pagden, "Identity Formation," 57.

135. Edmund Morgan suggests that the colonists' failure might have been due to the composition of the colony (too many noblemen and too many "ne're-do-wells") or because the colonists had adopted a military model in which they were not expected to grow their own food. But he also briefly notes how the Spanish experience informed English colonization, though he fails to explore the implications for the starving time based on that model. See Edmund S. Morgan, "The Labor Problem at Jamestown, 1607–1618," *American Historical Review* 76, no. 3 (1971): 595–611.

136. Columbus, *Diario,* 267.

137. López de Gómara, "Cortés," 57–58.

138. Ibid., 58.

139. J. H. Elliott, "The Mental World of Hernan Cortés," *Transactions of the Royal Historical Society,* no. 17 (1967): 41–58.

140. David Carrasco, *Quetzalcoatl and the Irony of Empire: Myths and Prophecies in the Aztec Empire* (Chicago: University of Chicago Press, 1982).

141. Cortés, *Letters from Mexico,* ed. Anthony Pagden and John Huxtable Elliott (New Haven: Yale University Press, 2001), 85–86; Elliott, "Mental World of Hernan Cortés."

142. Gilbert Michael Joseph and Timothy J. Henderson, eds., *The Mexico Reader: History, Culture, Politics* (Durham, NC: Duke University Press, 2002), 92–96.

143. Stuart B. Schwartz, *Victors and Vanquished* (New York: Bedford/St. Martins, 2000), 29–31.

144. Hernando Cortés, "Dowry Agreement for Montezuma's Daughter, June 27, 1526." Copied, Valladolid, 1750. Jay I. Kislak Collection, Rare Book and Special Collections Division, Library of Congress, available online at: http://www.loc.gov/exhibits/earlyamericas/online/exploration/exploration2.html.

145. For a detailed discussion, see Donald E. Chipman, *Montezuma's Children: Aztec Royalty under Spanish Rule, 1520–1700* (Austin: University of Texas, 2005), 96–118.

146. Pagden, "Identity Formation," 67.

147. Ibid., 55.

148. Ibid.

149. Ibid.

150. Stuart B. Schwartz, *Early Latin America: A History of Colonial Spanish America and Brazil* (New York: Cambridge University Press, 1983), esp. ch. 6.

151. C. R. Boxer, *Race Relations in the Portuguese Colonial Empire, 1415–1825* (Oxford: Clarendon Press, 1963), 98.

152. Philip Barbour, *Pocahontas and Her World*, 162, as cited in Christopher Hodgkins, *Reforming Empire: Protestant Colonialism and Conscience in British Literature* (Columbia: University of Missouri Press, 2002), 115.

153. Pagden, "Identity Formation," 68.

154. Magnus Mörner, *Race Mixture in the History of Latin America* (Boston: Little, Brown, 1967).

155. Pagden, "Identity Formation," 68.

156. Ibid.

157. Anthony Pagden, *European Encounters with the New World* (New Haven: Yale University Press, 1993), 12, as cited in Robert Paine, "Columbus and Anthropology and Unknown," *Journal of the Royal Anthropological Institute* 1 (1995): 3.

158. David Brion Davis, *The Problem of Slavery in Western Culture* (New York: Oxford University Press, 1966), 173.

159. Scanlan, *Colonial Writing and the New World*, 60.

160. Zamora, *Reading Columbus*, 135–136.

161. Ibid., 81–82.

162. Karen Kupperman, *Roanoke, the Abandoned Colony* (Totowa, NJ: Rowman and Allanhed, 1984), 17.

163. Las Casas, *A Short Account of the Destruction of the Indies*, ed. Nigel Griffin (New York: Penguin, 1991), 10.

164. Allan Greer, ed., *The Jesuit Relations: Natives and Missionaries in Seventeenth-Century North America* (New York: Bedford/St. Martin, 2000), 33.

165. Arthur Barlowe, *The First Voyage to Roanoke. 1584. The First Voyage Made to the Coasts of America, with Two Barks, wherein Were Captains M. Philip Amadas and M. Arthur Barlowe, Who Discovered Part of the Country Now Called Virginia,*

anno 1584 . . . , electronic edition available at: http://docsouth.unc.edu/nc/barlowe/
barlowe.html, 8.

166. Virgil, *The Georgics*, trans. James Rhoades (London: Kegan Paul, Trench,
Trubner, 1891), 1.125–129.

167. Ovid's *Metamorphoses* was a popular sixteenth-century text, and the century itself has been described as "the great Ovidian age." See Caroline Jameson,
"Ovid in the Sixteenth Century," in *Ovid*, ed. J. W. Binns (New York: Routledge,
1973), 211. Ovid, *Metamorphoses*, trans. Charles Martin (New York: W. W. Norton,
2004), ll. 126–128, 139–140.

168. Ibid., ll. 141–144.

169. Aphra Behn, "The Golden Age" (1684), cited in Malcolm Hicks, ed., *Selected Poems of Aphra Behn* (New York: Routledge, 2003), 2.

170. Davis, *Problem of Slavery in Western Culture*, 70.

171. Lewis Hanke, *Aristotle and the American Indians: A Study in Race Preju-
dice in the Modern World* (Bloomington: University of Indiana Press, 1970), ch. 5.

172. Ibid., 47.

173. John Winthrop to Sir Nathaniel Rich, May 22, 1634, as cited by David
Brion Davis and Steven Mintz, eds., *The Boisterous Sea of Liberty: A Documentary
History of America from Discovery through the Civil War* (New York: Oxford Univer-
sity Press, 1998), 69.

174. Francis Jennings, *The Invasion of America: Indians, Colonialism, and the
Cant of Conquest* (New York: W. W. Norton, 1975), 20. John Peacock, "Principles
and Effects of Puritan Appropriation of Indian Land and Labor," *Ethnohistory* 31 (1)
(1984), 29–44.

175. John Locke, *Second Treatise of Government*, ed. Mark Goldie (London:
Orion, 1993), 128. For a critical discussion of Locke and property, see Richard Ash-
craft, ed., *John Locke: Critical Assessments*, vol. 1 (New York: Routledge, 1991), esp.
Herman Lebovics, "The Uses of America and Locke's *Second Treatise of Government*,"
252–266; and Gopal Sreenivasan, *The Limits of Lockean Rights in Property* (New
York: Oxford University Press, 1995).

176. See Anthony Pagden and David Armitage, *The Ideological Origins of the
British Empire* (New York: Cambridge University Press, 2000).

177. John Cotton, *God's Promise to His Plantation* (London: William Jones/
John Bellamy, 1630), 5, as cited in Peter Harrison, "'Fill the Earth and Subdue It':
Colonial Warrants for Colonization in Seventeenth Century England," *Journal of
Religious History* 29, no. 1 (2005): 10.

178. John White, *A Commentary upon the First Three Chapters of the Book of
Moses Called Genesis* (London, 1656), bk. 1, 113, as cited in Harrison, "'Fill the
Earth,'" 13.

179. John Winthrop, *Winthrop's Journal "History of New England,"* 1630–1649,
vol. 1, ed. James Kendall Hosmer (New York: Charles Scribner and Sons, 1908), 294,
as cited by Harrison, "'Fill the Earth,'" 13.

180. Robert Gray, *A Good Speed to Virginia* (London, 1609), sig. C4r, as cited by Harrison, "'Fill the Earth,'" 15.

181. Richard Middleton, *Colonial America: History, 1565–1776*, 3rd ed. (Malden, MA: Blackwell, 2002), 376.

Epilogue

1. For a discussion of the religious import the Declaration has assumed, see Pauline Maier, *American Scripture: Making the Declaration of Independence* (New York: Vintage, 1998). For the importance the document has assumed globally, see David Armitage, *The Declaration of Independence: A Global History* (Cambridge, MA: Harvard University Press, 2007).

2. See Alan Dershowitz, *America Declares Independence* (New York: Wiley, 2003), for a discussion of how the document has assumed a quasi-biblical status. Jacques Derrida argues that it is not only later Americans who imbue Jefferson with prophetic status: Jefferson may have seen himself in a similar light. See Derrida, "Declarations of Independence," *New Political Science* 7, no. 1 (Summer 1986): 7–15.

3. The story is now well known by scholars of the Declaration. But among the first and most excellent Declaration detectives is Julian Boyd. See Boyd, "The Declaration of Independence: The Mystery of the Lost Original," *Pennsylvania Magazine of History and Biography* 100, no. 4 (1976): 438–467.

4. Thomas Jefferson to Robert Walsh, December 4, 1818, in *The Writings of Thomas Jefferson*, vol. 10 (New York: Putnam, 1899).

5. John Adams to Samuel Chase, July 9, 1776, in *The Works of John Adams*, vol. 9 (Boston: Little, Brown, 1854), 420. For the performance and awareness of public impact, see Michael Warner, *Letters of the Republic: Publication and the Public Sphere in Eighteenth-Century America* (Cambridge, MA: Harvard University Press, 1990).

6. Jay Fliegelman, *Declaring Independence: Jefferson, Natural Language, and the Culture of Performance* (Stanford, CA: Stanford University Press, 1993), 2.

7. Richard Henry Lee to Thomas Jefferson, July 21, 1776, in *The Letters of Richard Henry Lee*, vol. 1, ed. James Curtis Ballagh (New York: MacMillan, 1911), 211.

8. Dumas Malone, *Jefferson and His Time*, vol. 1 (Boston: Little, Brown, 1948), 222.

9. I am referring here to Jefferson's sexual relationship with Sally Hemings. For years, mainstream historians refuted this suggestion as a near impossibility. DNA evidence later substantiated the claim. See Annette Gordon-Reed, *Thomas Jefferson and Sally Hemings* (Charlottesville: University of Virginia Press, 1998).

10. Wills is fundamentally concerned with comparing earlier drafts of Jefferson's declaration with what would become "political liturgy" in order to better understand Jefferson's intent. See Garry Wills, *Inventing America: Jefferson's Declaration of Independence* (New York: Houghton Mifflin, 1978), 307.

11. Maier, *American Scripture*, 133.

12. Stephen E. Lucas, "Justifying America: The Declaration of Independence as a Rhetorical Document," in *American Rhetoric: Context and Criticism*, ed. Thomas W. Benson (Carbondale: Southern Illinois University Press, 1989), 73–74.

13. For Jefferson's "original Rough draught" see www.loc.gov/exhibits/declara/ruffdrft.html. This represents what scholars agree constitutes the rough draft from the work of Julian Boyd, *The Papers of Thomas Jefferson*, Vol. 1: *1760–1776* (Princeton, NJ: Princeton University Press, 1950), 243–247. One of the seminal works on the different versions of Jefferson's declaration is Carl Becker, *The Making of the Declaration of Independence: A Study in the History of Ideas* (New York: Vintage Books, 1970).

14. Maier, *American Scripture*, 132.

15. Fliegelman, *Declaring Independence*, esp. 4–27.

16. James Engell, *The Committed Word: Literature and Public Values* (State Park: Pennsylvania State University Press, 1999), 164. Literary appreciation of biblical parallelism is most often attributed to Robert Lowth in his story of *De Sacra Poesi Hebraeorem Praelectiones Academicae*, 1753. Samuel Johnson was, of course, among the most proficient and elegant practitioners. For parallelism in Johnson, see William Kurtz Wimsatt, *The Prose Style of Samuel Johnson* (New Haven: Yale University Press, 1948), ch. 1.

17. Chris Baldick, *Oxford Dictionary of Literary Terms* (New York: Oxford University Press, 2008), s.v. "parallelism."

18. Notice that Jefferson in the second "which" clause creates a parallel to the first, but it builds by the addition of a further parallel, "laws of nature & of nature's god." The longer clause assumes a greater weight mirroring the gravity in the assertion of the claim. For Burke, see "A Letter from the Right Honourable Edmund Burke to a Noble Lord, on the Attacks Made upon Him and his Pension, in the House of Lords, by the Duke of Bedford, and the Earl of Lauderdale, Early in the Present Sessions of Parliament" (London, 1796).

19. Thomas Jefferson to Charles Yancey, January 6, 1816, in *The Works of Thomas Jefferson*, Federal Edition, vol. 11, ed. Paul L. Ford (New York: G. P. Putnam's Sons, 1904–1905), 497.

20. On the connection between oratory and poetry, see Irène Simon, "Introduction," *Neo-Classical Criticism, 1600–1800* (London: Edward Arnold, 1971), 15.

21. John E. Sitter, *The Cambridge Companion to Eighteenth-Century Poetry* (New York: Cambridge University Press), 25.

22. Maurice Grammont, *Traité de phonétique* (1965), 39, as cited in Patricia M. Ranum, *The Harmonic Orator: Phrasing and Rhetoric of the Melody in French Baroque Airs* (Hillsdale, NY: Pendragon, 2001), 59–60.

23. Peter Ladefoged, *Elements of Acoustic Phonetics* (Chicago: University of Chicago Press, 1996); Keith Johnson, *Acoustic and Auditory Phonetics* (Malden, MA: Blackwell, 2003). For Robert Hagiwara, PhD, refer to Department of Linguistics University of Manitoba, Winnipeg, MB, Canada, R3T 5V5, http://home.cc.umanitoba.ca/~robh/howto.html#manner.

24. Ronald B. Bond, ed., *"Certain Sermons or Homilies" (1547) and "A Homily against Disobedience and Wilful Rebellion" (1570)* (Toronto: University of Toronto Press, 1987), 236.

25. Ibid., 212.

26. For an excellent discussion of the context of the homilies and Thomas Cranmer's role in their creation, see Diarmaid MacCulloch, *Thomas Cranmer: A Life* (New Haven: Yale University Press, 1996), esp. part 3.

27. Roger Chartier, *The Cultural Uses of Print in Early Modern France*, trans. Lydia G. Cochrane (Princeton, NJ: Princeton University Press, 1987).

28. Bond, *"Homily against Disobedience,"* 12–13.

29. C. H. Van Tyne, "Influence of the Clergy, and of Religious and Sectarian Forces, on the American Revolution," *American Historical Review* 19, no. 1 (1913): 51.

30. C. G. Chamberlayne, ed., *The Vestry Book and Register of St. Peter's Parish, New Kent and James City Counties, Virginia, 1684–1786* (Richmond, VA, 1937), 3, October 1968. As cited by John K. Nelson, *A Blessed Company: Parishes, Parsons, and Parishioners in Anglican Virginia* (Chapel Hill: University of North Carolina Press, 2001), 354n6.

31. Nelson, *Blessed Company*, 57.

32. Ibid.

33. Donald Greene, "Augustinianism and Empiricism," in *Selected Essays of Donald Greene*, ed. John Lawrence Abbot (NJ: Rosemont, 2004), 91n12.

34. Understanding this link in many ways supports the link that has been identified between Protestantism and Republicanism at the time of the Revolution. See Mark A. Noll, "The American Revolution and Protestant Evangelicalism," *Journal of Interdisciplinary History* 23, no. 3 (1993): 615–623; Nathan Hatch, *The Sacred Cause of Liberty: Republican Thought and the Millennium in Revolutionary New England* (New Haven: Yale University Press, 1977); Patricia U. Bonomi, *Under the Cope of Heaven: Religion, Society, and Politics in Colonial America* (New York: Oxford University Press, 2003).

35. John Witte Jr., "A Most Mild and Equitable Establishment of Religion: John Adams and the Massachusetts Experiment, in *Religion and the New Republic: Faith in the Founding of America*, ed. James H. Hutson (Lanham, MD: Rowman and Littlefield, 2000), 20. He writes, "Traditionally the New England Puritans stressed ambition, austerity, frugality and other virtues." Regarding ambition, nothing could be further from the truth. This is simply to illustrate the misunderstanding of ambition in early American religious studies. Obviously, the work on religion in early America is voluminous. But a consideration of seminal works reveal no mention of ambition. For example, Jon Butler, *New World Faiths: Religion in Colonial America* (New York: Oxford University Press, 2007); Patricia Bonomi studies the relationship between religion and politics yet ignores ambition. See *Under the Cope of Heaven*. See also Alan Heimert, *Religion and the American Mind: From the Great Awakening to the Revolution* (Cambridge, MA: Harvard University Press, 1966). It is interesting that Heimert includes quotations on ambition in his study. For example, though he includes a

Calvinist preacher who begins his sermon on the anniversary of the Boston Massacre with a denunciation of the "spirit of lawless ambition," he never interrogates ambition or notes its specific associations with sin.

36. Bond, "*Homily against Disobedience*," 236, emphasis added.

37. Ibid., 236, 210.

38. Ibid., 236–237.

39. Jack Lynch, "Dr. Johnson's Revolution," *New York Times*, July 2, 2005.

40. Samuel Johnson, *The History of Rasselas, Prince of Abissinia*, ch. 30, in *The Enlightenment and English Literature*, ed. John L. Mahoney (Lexington, MA: D. C. Heath, 1980), 309. Scholars have often interpreted Imlac as speaking for Johnson, and in this case, I interpret it as such. For example, Geoffrey Tillotson sees Imlac as the "beau ideal" of poet for Johnson in "Imlac and the Business of a Poet," in *Studies in Criticism and Aesthetics, 1660–1800: Essays in Honor of Samuel Holt Monk*, ed. Howard Anderson and John S. Shea (Minneapolis: University of Minnesota Press, 1967), 298, as cited by Howard Weinbrot, "The Reader, the General, and the Particular: Johnson and Imlac in Chapter Ten of Rasselas," *Eighteenth-Century Studies* 5, no. 1 (1971). Weinbrot's article argues against assuming a complete correlation.

41. A more extensive consideration of Samuel Johnson and ambition is beyond the scope of this project, though it would be a fascinating undertaking. In his *Rambler, Rasselas*, and *Vanity of Human Wishes*, Johnson recognizes the folly of the "hunger of the human imagination." The best work on Johnson remains Walter Jackson Bate, *Samuel Johnson* (New York: Harcourt, Brace, 1979). I remain indebted to the late Professor Bate for his patience during my independent study with him as a visiting undergraduate at Harvard.

42. For another example of the dual perception of ambition in Johnson, see "The Rambler: no. 155," in which Johnson talks about "honest ambition" being unfortunately suppressed by flattery, but then speaks of the "folly of ambition" as a vice of court and office. Samuel Johnson, "The Rambler, no. 155," in Mahoney, *Enlightenment and English Literature*, 225–227.

43. For a discussion of the *Pennsylvania Gazette*, see Charles E. Clark and Charles Wetherell, "The Measure of Maturity: The *Pennsylvania Gazette*, 1728–1765," *William and Mary Quarterly*, 3rd ser., 46, no. 2 (1989): 279–303.

44. *Pennsylvania Gazette*, May 1, 1776.

45. Ibid., March 5, 1777.

46. Catherine Snell Crary, "The Tory and the Spy: The Double Life of James Rivington," *William and Mary Quarterly*, 3rd ser., 16, no. 1 (1959): 61–72.

47. Among the best recent accounts of the battle is David Hackett Fisher, "The Fall of New York: A Cataract of Disaster," *Washington's Crossing* (New York: Oxford University Press, 2004), 81–114.

48. *The Battle of Brooklyn; A Farce in Two Acts* (New York: Rivington, 1776), 25.

49. Thomas Paine, *The American Crisis, by a Citizen of the World; Inscribed to Those Members of the Community, Vulgarly Named Patriots* (London: W. Flexney, 1777); General Charles Lee to General Horatio Gates, December 13, 1776, in *Spirit*

of Seventy-Six: The Story of the American Revolution as Told by Its Participants, ed. Henry Steele Commager and Richard B. Morris (Edison, NJ: Castle Books, 2002), 500; George Washington to John Hancock, September 24, 1776, in Commager and Morris, *Spirit of Seventy-Six*, 480.

50. "Adam's Fall: The Trip to Cambridge," in Commager and Morris, *Spirit of Seventy-Six*, 144.

51. Anne Y. Zimmer, *Loyalist in Exile* (Detroit, MI: Wayne State Press, 1978), 175.

52. Jonathan Boucher, *A View of the Causes and Consequences: in Thirteen Discourse, Preached in North America between the Years 1763 and 1775: With an Historical Preface* (London, 1797), 394.

53. Jonathan Boucher, *Reminiscences of an American Loyalist, 1738–1789: Being the Autobiography of Revd. Jonathan Boucher, Rector of Annapolis in Maryland and Afterwards Vicar of Epsom, Surrey, England*, ed. Jonathan Boucher (New York, 1925), 31, as cited in Nelson, *Blessed Company*, 135.

54. Dr. Jonathan Odell, "Inscription: For a Curious Chamber-Stove, in the Form of an Urn, So Contrived as to Make the Flame Descend, Instead of Rise, from the Fire: Invented by Doctor Franklin," in *The Loyal Verses of Joseph Stansbury and Doctor Jonathen Odell Relating to the American Revolution*, ed. Winthrop Sargent (Albany, NY: J. Munsell, 1860), 5–6.

55. For an excellent discussion of the Faust myth, see Ian Watt, *Myths of Modern Individualism* (New York: Cambridge University Press, 1996), 27–47.

56. The best scholarly work on Odell is still Cynthia Dubin Edelberg, *Jonathan Odell: Loyalist Poet of the American Revolution* (Durham, NC: Duke University Press, 1987).

57. Jonathan Odell, "Ode for the New Year," in Sargent, *Loyal Verses*, 59–60.

58. *Pennsylvania Gazette*, January 18, 1775.

59. See http://avalon.law.yale.edu/18th_century/arms.asp.

60. Winthrop Jordan, "Familial Politics: Thomas Paine and the Killing of the King, 1776," *Journal of American History* 50 (1973): 294.

61. Gordon Wood, *The Radicalism of the American Revolution* (New York: Knopf, 1992).

62. For a discussion of Cincinnatus and other classical models during the American Revolution, see Carl J. Richard, *The Founders and the Classics: Greece, Rome, and the American Enlightenment* (Cambridge, MA: Harvard University Press, 1994). Garry Wills also addresses Washington and Cincinnatus and, in addition, ties Jeffersonian architecture to Republican virtue. See Wills, *Cincinnatus: George Washington and the Enlightenment* (Garden City, NY: Doubleday, 1984).

63. Thomas Paine, "Of Monarchy and Heredity," ll. 14–23, in *Common Sense*, available online at: http://www.bartleby.com.

64. Nathan R. Perl-Rosenthal, "The 'Divine Right of Republics': Hebraic Republicanism and the Debate over Kingless Government in Revolutionary America," *William and Mary Quarterly*, 3rd ser., 66, no. 3 (2009): 535–564.

65. John Adams to Unknown, April 27, 1777, in *Letters to the Delegates of Congress, 1774–1789*, ed. Paul H. Smith et al. (Washington, DC: Library of Congress, 1976).

66. For an excellent recent examination of friendship in early America, see Ivy Schweitzer, *Perfecting Friendship: Politics and Affiliation in Early American Literature* (Chapel Hill: University of North Carolina Press, 2006).

67. John Adams to Abigail Adams, April 14, 1776, available online at: http://www.masshist.org/digitaladams/aea/cfm/doc.cfm?id=L17760414ja.

68. James Rivington as cited in *Publications of the Colonial Society of Massachusetts*, vol. 11 (Boston: Colonial Society of Massachusetts, 1910), 448.

69. Kenneth Silverman, *A Cultural History of the American Revolution* (New York: Crowell, 1976), 321, as cited by Ronald Paulson, "John Trumbull and the Representation of the American Revolution," *Studies in Romanticism* 21, no. 3 (1982): 348.

Acknowledgments

First, I would like to thank the Beinecke Library and Samuel Botwinik family for their generous fellowships. Anything I would have written on ambition would have suffered had it not been for their support, as well as the more general support of Yale University. Of course, I must thank Chris Rogers, Christina Tucker, and Laura Jones Dooley at Yale University Press for their support, encouragement, and editorial acumen.

So many people both at Yale and elsewhere have helped along the way. I have tried to thank them all here but apologize to anyone I might have forgotten on my path to completion. Robert Stepto has been supportive of my endeavors, recognizing the arbitrary nature of the line between the creative and the academic. Stuart Schwartz helped me understand that "early America" isn't restricted to the New England town and challenged me to integrate Latin America into my study of North America. John Demos helped me find history in unexpected places and to appreciate the wonder of the seventeenth century. Paul Gilroy supported my study of ambition and turned me on to Christopher Hill. Jon Butler allowed me to explore the Geneva Bible in a seminar setting. John Stauffer was an unwavering mentor and generous friend at Yale as a graduate student and even later when he began to wear a tie every day. Steve Mintz encouraged me at various steps along my way and invited me to present a paper at a conference in honor of David Brion Davis. He later published my essay among a collection of tenured faculty contributions. Robert Johnston thought that what I did mattered and organized softball games. David Waldstreicher afforded me more time than he had. Jean-Christophe Agnew read drafts of my prospectus and meaningfully critiqued early drafts of an article on ambition. Daniel Walker Howe helped me better understand Federalist No. 51 during his semester at Yale. The late Frank Turner helped me appreciate watersheds in the history of science. Gerald Jaynes advocated on my behalf and soothed me by cell phone when all seemed lost. Stephen Parks helped me love the Beinecke and appreciate its many gifts, including the magnificent Osborne Collection. Walter Jackson Bate agreed to work with me individually while I was an undergraduate. Edward Bellamy Partridge taught me to love drama to 1642, and J. L. Simmons taught me to love Shakespeare. Troy Paddock gave me pep talks and practical advice. Peter Peduzzi and Jim Dziura at the Yale Center for Analytical Sciences believed that it mattered even though it seemed far afield. I also want to thank Chris Killheffer for making me feel that Sterling was still home; Yvette Barnard for her wisdom and love; Janet Giarratano, who is among the most supportive, hardest working departmental administrators I have ever met; John and Geneva for picking me off the ground and dusting me off; Henry Schwab for the quality of being "schwaby"; Robert Stone, who helped me learn to write; Keith Wrightson for making me more fully interrogate regicide; Mike Kane for his friendship, camaraderie and constant reminders that "real artists ship"; Bob Vivona for his thirty years of most excellence; Atticus and Caleb for running *around* the towers of books in my office, and learning to love history and literature and music, and respecting and wondering at things that many children don't even notice; Margaret King for instilling Kipling's *IF* into my fabric; and finally Leslie Poirier King for counseling patience and protecting me from the realities of the quotidian long enough to breathe and think.

INDEX